Improving teaching and learning in the humanities

LOOKING AFRESH AT THE PRIMARY CURRICULUM SERIES

Series Editors: Kate Ashcroft and David James,
                University of West of England, Bristol

Improving teaching and learning in the humanities
Edited by Martin Ashley

Improving teaching and learning in the core curriculum
Edited by Kate Ashcroft and John Lee

Improving teaching and learning in the arts
Edited by Mary Kear and Gloria Callaway

Improving teaching and learning in the humanities

Edited by Martin Ashley

FALMER PRESS
Taylor & Francis Group

First published 1999 by Falmer Press
11 New Fetter Lane, London EC4P 4EE

Simultaneously published in the USA and Canada by
Garland Inc., 19 Union Square West, New York, NY 10003

Falmer Press is an imprint of the Taylor & Francis Group

Typeset in Melior by Graphicraft Limited, Hong Kong
Printed and bound in Great Britain by TJ International Ltd,
Padstow, Cornwall

British Library Cataloguing in Publication Data
A catalogue record for this book is available from the British Library

Library of Congress Cataloging in Publication Data
A catalogue record for this book has been requested

Cover design by Carla Turchini

ISBN 0 7507 0801 8

Contents

List of figures and tables		vii
Series editors' preface		viii
Chapter 1	The continuing value of a humanitarian curriculum *Martin Ashley*	1
Chapter 2	The literacy hour and beyond *Martin Ashley with John Lee, Richard Eke and Helen Butcher*	20
Chapter 3	Looking afresh at history *Penelope Harnett*	41
Chapter 4	Looking afresh at geography *Alison Bailey and Don Kimber*	58
Chapter 5	Using artefacts to support children's learning in religious education *Nick Clough and Liz Newman*	81
Chapter 6	Field work, visits and work outside the classroom *Don Kimber and Maggie Smith*	101
Chapter 7	Spiritual, moral and cultural development *Martin Ashley*	119
Chapter 8	Citizenship: a new word for humanities? *Martin Ashley with Steve Barnes*	139
Chapter 9	ICT and the humanities *Martin Ashley and Gaynor Attwood*	162

CONTENTS

Chapter 10 Sustainability and the humanities   184
    Martin Ashley

Chapter 11 Towards uncertain futures?   204
    Martin Ashley and Malcolm Hughes

Notes on contributors   223
Index   225

List of figures and tables

Figure 2.1   A chronology of the broad and balanced curriculum   22
Figure 2.2   Genres   31
Figure 4.1   Campsite plan   61
Figure 7.1   Definitions of moral development   133
Figure 8.1   The domains of citizenship?   148
Figure 8.2   6W Charter of rights and responsibilities   151
Table 10.1   Operative value of cycling   194
Figure 10.1   Preparation for understanding climate change   200

Series editors' preface
Kate Ashcroft and David James

Improving teaching and learning in the humanities is one of a series of books in the Looking Afresh at the Primary Curriculum Series edited by Kate Ashcroft and David James. Other books in the series include:

Improving teaching and learning in the core curriculum, edited by Kate Ashcroft and John Lee; and

Improving teaching and learning in the arts, edited by Gloria Callaway.

Like the other books in the series, *Improving teaching and learning in the humanities* is written as an essential support for students training for primary teaching in colleges and universities, those undertaking inservice teacher education and teachers in schools wishing to use an accessible text to get in touch with some of the more recent thinking about the primary curriculum. It is a natural 'next step' from the two introductory texts published by Falmer Press, that cover the whole curriculum:

The Primary Teacher's Guide to the New National Curriculum, edited by Kate Ashcroft and David Palacio; and

Implementing the Primary Curriculum, edited by Kate Ashcroft and David Palacio.

The present series is intended to build on and further develop knowledge about the curriculum that was included at an introductory level in the two books on the whole curriculum and, in particular, asks the reader to look in more depth at the link between the humanities and children's learning in schools. It is aimed at supporting students and teachers who are beginning to get to grips with what it means to be a curriculum specialist for one of the National Curriculum subjects in a primary school.

The book could be used in various ways. It will be of use for teachers and student teachers wishing to gain an overview of aspects of teacher education programmes related to the humanities curriculum. It is also designed to be used by student teachers at the stage when they are beginning that part of their course that applies to the role of a humanities' specialist in the primary school. The enquiry-based format provides a starting point for the sort of enquiry, reflection and learning that tutors are trying to encourage within initial teacher education and inservice courses based on the Reflective Teacher Model.

The books in the series are well signposted with headings and subheadings, with lots of practical suggestions of ways of going about curriculum planning, reflection and enquiry. There is some reference to theory, but wherever possible, this is illustrated with practical examples in the form of case studies that highlight implications for the enquiring teacher.

The series does not aim to present outcomes of research to be absorbed by teachers, nor does it focus on their skills as educational researchers *per se*; nor does it attempt to give a list of tips. It is focused on enquiry with a view to improving practice through:

■ accessible content at the reader's level about the main issues;
■ knowledge about a range of teaching methods and curriculum content;
■ knowledge about the way information and communicative technologies can influence teaching, learning and curriculum content;
■ enquiry tasks that encourage the reader to:
  − assess and develop their understandings of the issues
  − assess and develop their subject knowledge
  − try out activities in the classroom and collect data about their effects and effectiveness;
■ an annotated reading list at the end of each chapter.

Although some of the ideas contained in the series are complex and could be seen as demanding, the authors have been careful to keep the style of the books straightforward and the language is accessible rather than 'academic'. Wherever possible, new ideas and concepts are supported by concrete examples. The authors' intention is to communicate clearly some of the complexity and subtlety of effective and reflective teaching.

The chapters within the book are linked by common themes: the principles of the Reflective Practitioner Model are an essential element. These are outlined in some detail in Ashcroft and Palacio (1995 and 1997). These principles include the need to look at issues of equality. Inclusivity and the dilemmas raised for the reflective teacher working within a largely constrained curriculum context are important foci for discussion.

The chapters raise the problematic nature of much of our 'taken for granted' knowledge about the curriculum. They look at intended, as well as unintended, consequences of action and the need for teachers to constantly remain openminded and responsible. Openmindedness implies that the reader neither rejects nor accepts the accepted orthodoxies about teaching and curriculum, but rather seeks to test ideas against the reality of their classroom and the available and emerging research and other evidence. The authors stress that this is not an objective and value-free process. The reader will be confronted with issues of responsibility: the need to consider ethical issues and the long-term as well as the immediate consequences of action. In particular, readers will be asked to look beyond a utilitarian stance, beyond 'what works', in order to look at the role of values in teaching and learning.

The authors present a view of reflective practice as an evaluation-led activity, that requires the collection of evidence about teaching, learning, assessment, values, beliefs and behaviour. This analysis is located within a moral, spiritual, social and cultural context. The meanings and experience of the various parties to the educational process are carefully considered.

The book also deals with the more immediate challenges that confront teachers in today's classrooms, including information and communicative technologies: their use and the issues they raise. In dealing with these issues the stress is on creativity in teaching and learning and the ways that such creativity can illuminate possibilities and problems, such as those of match, progression and differentiation in teaching and learning. Throughout, the focus is on the analysis of effective teaching and learning. Understanding effectiveness requires an exploration of meanings underpinning current debates (for example, notions such as 'basics' and 'standards'). In this discussion, the book also addresses the political agenda in which the teaching of the humanities takes place.

A reflective approach to these issues leads to a focus on dilemmas rather than simple answers. This can be frustrating for new teachers looking for simple prescriptions for the problems that they face. We hope that the use of case study material, describing the ways that real-life teachers have tackled some of these dilemmas, their successes and failures, will help to bring the issues alive. Although there can be few 'tips', the inclusion of knowledge-base for action, together with suggested sources for extending knowledge-base beyond that possible within the scope of the book should leave the reader in a position to make better and more informed decisions within their particular context. Such decisions are always context specific: there are many simple educational questions, but we are increasingly certain that there are no simple answers. For this reason, authors have tried to locate the content and tasks within a theoretical framework. This framework is essential to inform action and decision making in a range of contexts.

References

ASHCROFT, K. and PALACIO, D. (eds) (1995) *The Primary Teacher's Guide to the New National Curriculum*, London: Falmer Press.

ASHCROFT, K. and PALACIO, D. (eds) (1997) *Implementing the Primary Curriculum*, London: Falmer Press.

ASHCROFT, K. and LEE, J. (eds) (1999) *Improving teaching and learning in the core curriculum*, London: Falmer Press.

CALLOWAY, G. and KEAR, M. (eds) (1999) *Improving teaching and learning in the arts*, London: Falmer Press.

Chapter 1

The continuing value of a humanitarian curriculum
Martin Ashley

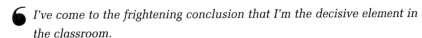 *I've come to the frightening conclusion that I'm the decisive element in the classroom.*
It's my personal approach that creates the climate.
It's my daily mood that makes the weather.
As a teacher I possess a tremendous power to make a child's life miserable or joyous.
I can be a tool of torture, or an instrument of inspiration.
I can humiliate or humour, hurt or heal.
In all situations, it is my response that decides whether a crisis will be escalated or de-escalated . . .
. . . and a child humanised or de-humanised. (Bagnall, Personal View)

Introduction and overview

In this chapter we look at what the humanities are and why there might be a continuing need for something called a humanitarian curriculum. We consider why you, the reader, might want to know these things and we give an overview of the whole book which, hopefully, will encourage your commitment to reading it. Our intention is that you will see how you might come to value an understanding of how to teach the humanities effectively as one of your highest priorities in developing personal excellence in primary school teaching. We assume that you are already confident and proficient in teaching the core subjects of English, maths and science and that you have a commitment to a broad and balanced education which develops children's potential.

The book has been written by a team of authors from varied backgrounds who are committed to this ideal and who are committed to your achieving it. It has been written in a style which will support your own self-directed learning. It draws heavily on the practical classroom experience of the authors, and the students and teachers they themselves have supported in training. It includes a plentiful variety of classroom-based enquiry tasks which, if you are able to carry them out, will bring the text alive with stimulating first hand experience generated with your own children. The enquiry tasks and the associated reflection boxes are designed to enhance your ability to bring about school improvement through the reflective practitioner model. A commitment to the teacher as a reflective practitioner, who is pledged to the constant improvement of his or her teaching through the plan/implement/evaluate/plan cycle, is a fundamental value shared by all the authors.

We have included the word 'value' in the title of this opening chapter because this reflects the commitment of the book to certain values in education. The teacher as a person and as a reflective practitioner is certainly one of these. This is a book which values teachers and values their work. The children as young people, learners and future citizens are equally fundamental and important. This is a book which both values childhood and values children's futures. You may well recognise that the words '. . . at the heart of the education process lies the child' are drawn from the Plowden Report of 1967. You may realise that these words might be associated by some with what is popularly regarded as a discredited, so called 'progressive', or even (to use the most derogatory word in the armoury of the popular press), 'trendy' teaching style. You will probably be familiar with the emergence of a ten subject based National Curriculum in 1988. Depending on your own age and experience of primary education, you may be more or less aware of the significant shift from child-centred toward subject-centred teaching in primary schools that resulted from this.

You are likely to be familiar with the notoriously 'overloaded' nature of Education Secretary Kenneth Baker's original National Curriculum and the subsequent 'slimmed down' version produced by Sir Ron Dearing in 1995. You may well recall the promise of Education Secretary, Gillian Shepherd, that there would be no more changes until the year 2000. If so, you may have been bemused by the changes introduced by Education Secretary, David Blunkett, during 1998. If you have studied the history of education, or are old enough to remember, you may well have noted the way in which David

Blunkett's reforms seem to give a further push to a pendulum swinging towards ideas about schooling fashionable in the 1870s. You may be wondering where it will swing next. The influences to which primary education has been subjected by politicians is a major topic of discussion in the next chapter.

This book is not about 'trendiness' or political fashion in education. The authors are concerned with what they perceive as enduring values which have evolved since classical times and far outlast the limited life span of any particular Education Act. Freedom of thought, rationality, the pursuit of truth and the principle of a broad and liberating education are fundamental. We have already stated that we value teachers and children. We also value our respective subjects. Some of us, for example, are historians because we value history and all that the study of history stands for. We see no conflict between child and 'subject'. We take it as read that the attainment of high standards of literacy and numeracy always were and always will be absolutely fundamental to any child's success. We value literacy and numeracy because of this, and we value literacy and numeracy because no civilised society can function without them.

Literacy and numeracy alone, however, are merely the foundations of a civilised, democratic society. We have to build above the foundations or that society will never become visible. This book is in two parts. The first, after considering the relationship between literacy, numeracy and the rest of the curriculum, discusses each of the humanities subjects in turn. The second broadens the discussion to look at the way in which humanities support the development of the whole child. There is a focus on the child's spiritual, moral, social and cultural development. We consider important emerging issues that are closely related to the humanities, such as citizenship and the application of Information and Communications Technology. We conclude with a consideration of pressing global issues, such as the need to envision and educate for a more sustainable society. In so doing, we reassert the enduring value of the humanities subjects as a prerequisite foundation for a rational response to such matters as threats to our environment, real or imagined. Permeating all of these discussions is the National Statement of Values (Appendix to this chapter). In the remainder of this chapter we shall consider first, in a little more detail, the justification for a 'humanitarian curriculum'. We shall conclude with a consideration of how this relates to some of the values that have been defined in the National Statement.

A humanitarian curriculum

Roberts (1996) has claimed, in the wake of the Dearing Reforms, that the United Kingdom (UK) National Curriculum is the least 'humanitarian' of all European curricula which seek to uphold democratic values. What prompted such a claim?

Enquiry task 1

You are likely to have some understanding of why the subjects of history, geography and perhaps religious education are collectively referred to as 'the humanities'. You may believe that the assumption that schools exist for children is a valid one, even if you are open minded about the degree to which primary education should be 'child centred'.

Discuss with some of your colleagues answers to these questions:
- What is it about history and geography that makes them 'humanities'?
- Are other subjects not humanities? What about science? Why is science not generally included as 'humanities'?
- What connections can you make between the arts and the humanities?

You may consider that a humanitarian curriculum might imply something a little more than a subject-based curriculum which allocates so many hours per week to history, geography and religious education. Behind the desire to teach the humanities there exists the desire for a curriculum which has everything to do with making children fully human. That statement might well be considered to be a value judgment. A crucial idea which underpins all the chapters in this book is that the curriculum cannot be 'value-free'. Great battles took place between Education Secretary Kenneth Clarke and the subject associations representing the humanities during the writing of the National Curriculum. The main subject of contention was Kenneth Clarke's insistence that the school curriculum should be 'value-free'. A 'value-free' curriculum is a difficult curriculum for the humanities, because much of what makes the humanities what they are is about values. Kenneth Clarke's desire for 'value-free' factual knowledge is evident in the quotation below, as is his opposition to the Geographical Association and his desire to suppress values and attitudes not approved of by prime minister Margaret Thatcher:

 The Secretary of State recognises that geography lessons will sometimes deal with conflicting points of view on important geographical issues. However, he considers that the main emphasis in the statutory requirements should be on teaching knowledge and understanding of geography, rather than on the study of people's attitudes and opinions. Some statements of attainment which appeared to concentrate on attitudes and opinions have therefore been removed.
(DES, 1991, Draft Orders for geography in the National Curriculum)

The battles between the government and the Historical Association, incidentally, were largely resolved by the direct intervention of Margaret Thatcher. According to the front page of the *Observer* of the 20th August 1989:

 . . . She has made a dramatic intervention and overridden the wishes of former Education Secretary Kenneth Baker by demanding changes in an interim report on history. The report has already been accepted by Mr Baker and his department. She has told the new Education Secretary, Mr John MacGregor, to take a tougher line than Mr Baker and to insist on more British and less world history, a more chronological approach and greater emphasis on facts rather than on skills and understanding . . .

(Judd, 1989)

Education Secretary John Patten was behind a period of notorious confusion and controversy for science teachers when he attempted to separate the mechanical aspects of sex from the moral aspects of relationships. Behind this unfortunate episode was the view that the biology curriculum could and should be 'value-free'. Possibly Mr Patten's own strongly held and stated religious values may have been a contributory factor too. The lesson for us all should be that the curriculum is not and cannot be 'value-free'. If we value the pursuit of truth and freedom through our educational institutions, we should perhaps be wary of the hidden agenda of government ministers who, wittingly or unwittingly, impose their own values in the name of 'value-free'.

In developing the idea of the reflective practitioner model, we will be guiding you in two essential areas. The first is that of becoming aware of and able to articulate the values which you yourself hold. These, perhaps unconsciously, affect both your teaching and your interpretation of this book. The second is that of being able to read the curriculum critically and to be aware of the values and partisan viewpoints that are embodied within it. That is not to say that we wish to impose our own values upon you the reader and therefore, ultimately, the children you teach. To do so would be contrary to two of our most fundamental values; the value of liberty and democratic freedom of thought and the value of the teacher as an autonomous reflective practitioner. You might, as an autonomous and reflective thinker, consider the following:

 Dear Teacher,

I am a survivor of a concentration camp.
My eyes saw what no man should witness:

Gas chambers built by learned engineers,
Children poisoned by educated physicians,
Infants killed by trained nurses,
Women and children shot and burned by
  high school and college graduates.
So I am suspicious of education.
My request is this:
Help your students become human.
Your efforts must never produce learned
  monsters, skilled psychopaths, educated
  Eichmanns.
Reading, writing and arithmetic are
  important only if they serve to make our
  children more human.

There is much to reflect on in this passage.

Enquiry task 2

Debate with some colleagues or friends:

My request is this: help your students become human. Reading, writing and arithmetic are important only if they serve to make our children more human.
- Are the humanities to do with making children more human?
- What is the fundamental purpose of education? Is it to produce a literate and numerate workforce to serve the needs of society and the economy or is it to equip an individual to participate fully in society and the economy? Is there a difference? Are there other ways of defining the purpose of education?
- Does learning in the humanities detract from the 'basics'? Should teaching the humanities be left until the secondary phase of education, leaving primary schools to concentrate upon a high level of competency in literacy and numeracy?
- Should educational success be quantified by how much knowledge has been acquired? Should it be quantified by the degree to which a thinking person has been developed? Should a thinking, feeling person be the measure of success?
- Would a curriculum of reading, writing and arithmetic make people humane?

Arguably, there was a time when society looked more than it does now to the family and the churches for the kind of moral guidance that is implied by the need to create a humane society. We might well suppose that the authors of the 'value-free' elementary school curriculum of the 3Rs envisaged a role for the family and the church in the development of humanity. It cannot be said, however, that the moral guidance that was to be had from the family and the churches did much to prevent the periodic outbreaks of atrocities that punctuated the twentieth century and which inspired the writing quoted above. On the other hand, of course, without the family and the churches there might have been even more atrocities during the twentieth century.

This is surely an important question for historians, philosophers and other scholars to debate, which serves to underline the value of the humanities disciplines.

This fear of the inhumane society has surfaced in another context which is perhaps closer to our current experience than the Second World War:

> *It is worth noting that the world's environmental problems are not the work of ignorant people. Rather, they result largely from the work of people with BAs, BScs, LLBs, MBAs and PhDs. Elie Wiesel once made the same point, noting that the designators and perpetrators of Auschwitz, Dachau and Buchenwald – the Holocaust – were the heirs of Kant and Goethe, widely thought to be the best educated people on Earth. But their education did not serve as an adequate barrier to barbarity. What was wrong with their education? In Wiesel's (1990) words:*
>
> *'It emphasised theories instead of values, concepts rather than human beings, abstraction rather than consciousness, answers instead of questions, ideology and efficiency rather than conscience'.* (David Orr, 1994)

Can we afford to enter the twenty-first century with a curriculum in which the development of humanity is left to chance? If we were to assert that this book is about values instead of theories, human beings rather than concepts, consciousness rather than abstraction, questions instead of answers and conscience rather than ideology or efficiency, might we be describing an approach to the primary school curriculum which merits your serious consideration? We hope that it has become clear that this book in the first part is about the direct or explicit contribution of the humanities subjects to the development of humanity during the primary phase. In the second, it is about the more implicit role of humanity across the whole curriculum. We now proceed to examine more closely the concept of value, particularly as it is defined in the National Statement of Values. This is rather a new departure for education in the United Kingdom and certainly something of a political U turn from Kenneth Clarke's emphasis upon 'value-free' subjects.

The National Statement of Values

Perhaps we should make it clear at the outset that we are not accusing the government of seeking to eliminate the humanities from the curriculum. There is a clear requirement to continue to provide a 'broad and balanced' curriculum. There can be very little doubt that the humanities will continue to be a significant part of this. Schools which return to a pre-1988 diet of English and maths with copying from an encyclopaedia on Friday afternoon will be unlikely to attract much praise. Paradoxically, it was never the intention in 1988 to eliminate values from the curriculum altogether. You will almost certainly be familiar with the phrase '. . . to promote the spiritual, moral, cultural, physical and mental development of children . . .' This comes from the 1988 Education Act. It is instructive to follow how a concentration upon the 'subjects' (encouraged, perhaps, by Standard Assessment Tasks and league tables) has marginalised the task of promoting those aspects of school life which develop the 'whole child'. It is equally instructive to follow the growth of dissatisfaction with spiritual, moral and cultural development which has been influential, amongst other things, in the process which led to the setting up of the National Forum on Values.

The National Forum on Values was an 150-strong body, convened by the Schools Curriculum and Assessment Authority in 1995 to investigate whether it was possible to arrive at a public consensus of values within a modern, multicultural and pluralistic society. It comprised a diverse list of what might be termed 'moral leaders', ranging from representatives of the various faith communities to the British Humanist Association. It included representatives from education, social services, industry and commerce. Much of the Forum's thinking centred upon the perceived need to restore the moral authority of teachers. It was imagined that schools and teachers were discouraged in their attempts to promote a sense of socially acceptable values amongst the young because of a perceived decline in public morality. The Forum hoped that if a national consensus of values could be identified and defined, teachers would be more supported in their work. The result was the draft National Statement of Values, which is reproduced as Appendix I. The Statement immediately attracted hostile critical writing by moral philosophers (see list for further reading), and you may agree that it contains potentially controversial statements which may yet excite public debate.

It is certainly the case, however, that a broader curriculum than mere literacy and numeracy is needed to address many of the concepts and issues raised by the National Statement of Values. We shall show repeatedly in the chapters of this book that the humanities subjects figure prominently in this role. We have stated more than once that literacy and numeracy are to be valued. In the next chapter, we discuss in more depth the relationship between literacy and numeracy. We wish to reiterate at this stage, however, that the humanities subjects have their own intrinsic value. It is true that

Sitting in my kitchen one Sunday afternoon, I observed my next door neighbour polishing his car. It was an almost brand new and very smart sports coupé. I am not an expert on cars. I couldn't tell you whether or not it was a Porsche, but I could tell you almost certainly that it must have cost a great deal of money.

I can tell you with complete certainty that he spent the best part of Sunday afternoon devoting his attention to it. As I became more and more interested in what he was doing, I recorded the fact that he spent forty minutes polishing the mirrors and lights.

- Would you say that my next door neighbour valued his car?
- If so, how did he value his car?
- Would you have chosen to spend your Sunday afternoon in this way?
- If you would have chosen to spend your Sunday afternoon differently, do you have any feelings that your choice of activity might have been in some way 'better'?

history, geography and religious education give children something worthwhile to read and write about. They are therefore a first class vehicle for the development of literacy in context, but they have to be much more than this. Literacy itself is what we might call a utilitarian value. It is simply the necessary skill for children to access higher areas of learning. *Literature* and literary appreciation (as opposed to literacy) is one such area of higher learning. The humanities are certainly another. These higher levels of learning are of a different order of value to utilitarian values. It may help if we focus a little more on what we actually mean by values.

You may have realised that these are rather difficult questions. I would say that my next door neighbour did value his car, and I would cite two pieces of evidence in support of this observation. My first piece of evidence would be that my next door neighbour allocated a not inconsiderable proportion of his economic power to the acquisition of the car. My second piece of evidence would be that my next door neighbour allocated to his car what for me is the most precious of all resources, that of time. It would be fair to say that my values would have been different. In fact, I can give you some evidence and you can make your own judgment. The first piece of evidence I will give you is that I drive a rather nondescript and not very new car and you might find me travelling by train when it is possible to do so. I can't remember the last time I cleaned my car. The second piece of evidence I will give you is that you might quite frequently observe me allocating time on a Sunday afternoon to walks with my partner in what we both consider to be beautiful and inspiring countryside.

I shan't ask you, however, to arbitrate between my neighbour and myself. It would be most unfair to ask whose values you think the better. You may well be thinking that such a judgment is none of your business. You might be critical of me if you suspected that I thought myself some way 'better' than my neighbour on account of my different values. Were you or I to make any such judgment, we would be making a judgment of another person according to our own particular value system. This is not appropriate in a pluralistic society and you may well consider a judgmental attitude to other people to be an outdated mode of moral thought. It is, nevertheless, a difficult problem in the philosophy of values and it gives rise to the notion that we do not have the authority or moral right to impose our own particular values on someone else. Indeed, a large majority of the student teachers I encounter feel that some of their own values are in conflict with the values they perceive to be held by the children they teach. They would like their children to share these values, yet they feel that it is somehow unprofessional or contrary to the fundamental value of freedom of thought to 'transmit' their own values.

This is clearly problematic for the authors of the National Statement of Values whose objectives, as I have explained, were directed at overcoming this very difficulty. Tate and Talbot (1997), in their defence of the Statement, offer a simple answer to the perennially difficult question of whose values we ought to teach. This is that they should be 'our' values. 'Our' values are defined as '. . . the values to which *every* person of goodwill would subscribe'. These have been determined for us by the 150 'persons of goodwill' who constituted the National Forum. A MORI poll of 1500 adults, 95 per cent of whom were said to have agreed with the Forum's values, has been claimed by the authors of the National Statement as sufficient consensus that their values are indeed *our* values. You may feel uncomfortable, however, with the idea of 'authority of consensus'. You may be thinking that just because thousands or even millions of people believe something to be true or right, that doesn't make it true or right. After all, large numbers of Germans assented to the holocaust, but that didn't make it right. Our discussion of citizenship in Chapter 8 looks briefly at charges of totalitarianism that have arisen precisely because of the conflict between individual freedom and the desire to impose consensual values.

What does make things right? In this question lies a second crucial feature of what constitutes a value. The question centres around whether or not there is any difference between a 'value' and a simple 'desire'. You may have been slightly unhappy with the way I portrayed values in terms of the desire to possess an expensive motor car. Are there not other kinds of value? you might ask. What about the value of a beautiful sunset? What about the value of truth, justice or freedom? What about the value of life or the capacity to flourish? The following enquiry task may help both with these questions, and with the problem of 'authority of consensus'.

Enquiry task 3

Gather a small group of friends or colleagues and discuss the following scenario.

Oldchester is an historic market town situated in attractive rural scenery in southern England. For a number of years, Oldchester and its community has suffered increasing damage from the heavy traffic travelling along the major trunk road which passes through the town centre. Drivers and road hauliers have become increasingly frustrated at the lengthening delays to their journeys caused by the need to pass through Oldchester. After much protracted debate, a route for a bypass has been agreed. However, construction of the bypass has been delayed in order to hold a public enquiry into objections to the fact that the route unavoidably cuts right across an ancient common which itself contains a site of special scientific interest.

The enquiry was attended by a large number of persons of goodwill. Here are the views of two of them:

Mr Goodman:

 This town and its community have suffered for far too long. It isn't safe for children or old people to go down the high street. Jobs are moving away from the area and unemployment is going up. The bypass must be built. We should refuse to support values or actions that may be harmful to individuals or communities.

Mrs Williams:

 A new road will merely generate even more traffic in the long run. The people in this community need a good quality of life. The common has been used for centuries as a haven of calm and solace. People need contact with nature and peaceful open space is an essential part of any community. The bypass must not be built. We should refuse to support values or actions that may be harmful to individuals or communities.

- Are both of these citizens genuinely people of goodwill?
- Can this dispute be settled conclusively by objective scientific evidence?
- Whose values are the better in this instance?
- What difficulties have you encountered in answering these questions?

You may well have realised that the sentence 'We should refuse to support values or actions that may be harmful to individuals or communities' has been taken directly from the National Statement of Values. It is possible that I will be accused of deliberate perversity. Those who accept the assertion that the National Statement of Values represents a genuine consensus which is truly unproblematic may say that the problem in Enquiry task 3 is 'unrealistic' or 'not the sort of example that was intended'. Alternatively, it is possible, of course, that you may not have perceived a problem. You might not have seen any difficulties in answering the second and third questions. This might indicate a certain blindness on your part to the fact that questions which cannot be answered by scientific evidence alone are usually settled by value judgments, which almost certainly involve opposing but valid viewpoints.

It is less uncertain that what we have here is the very flesh of geography. It is in situations such as this that the humanities come into their own. It is *not* our job as primary school teachers to 'tell' children whether or not they should be in favour of the bypass. We should be uncomfortable if we are responsible for the airing of naive prejudices which go unchallenged. It certainly *is* our job to teach children about towns and villages, roads and railway lines, communities, shopping centres, lakes, rivers, areas of scenic beauty. It certainly *is* our job to impart the skills of field work, map reading, photograph analysis, data processing and the writing of factual reports or persuasive arguments. If we are making a good job of this, we will almost certainly encounter value judgments such as the example above. If we have the competency to make children articulate and reflect upon their own values and to see and consider alternative viewpoints, then we are developing children spiritually, morally, socially and culturally. We are indeed doing a good job.

This tells us something else important about values. A value judgment differs from a moral judgment in that it is personal, whilst the latter is public. Groups of people or sectors of society, often large ones, may share the same values. A value is not the same thing as an opinion, however. Values lie somewhere between scientific 'facts' and mere bigotry and prejudice. There are always good reasons for holding a particular value. It may not be possible to establish the 'rightness' of one's position by a conclusive scientific proof. However, one's position can be defended by valid argument. The types of argument used in defending a value judgment will themselves draw upon tendencies or dispositions to value certain things or states of affairs. Thus Mr Goodman, in the above dispute, will defend his position by appealing to the altruism of concern for employment prospects in Oldchester. Observation of his behaviour may well reveal that he 'values' his car in a way similar to my next door neighbour. He also 'values' the comfort and convenience of a speedy journey to work. He may well make the judgment that quiet and peace within an historic town centre is a 'better' state of affairs than quiet and peace in open countryside, given that an ancient town centre can be demonstrated to be scarcer than open countryside.

Reflection 3

Without any pre-judgement upon your part, attempt to list all the valid arguments that might first of all lend validity to Mr Goodman's values and then the ones that would lend validity to Mrs Williams's values.

- *On the basis of this, do you conclude that both value judgments are defensible?*
- *What truly scientific evidence might lend weight to either of the positions?*
- *Look through the National Statement of Values (see Appendix I). Can you find other values in it which support either Mr Goodman or Mrs Williams?*
- *Are there any other statements which appear superficially unproblematic but which might not withstand such scrutiny?*

You may wish to undertake a similar analysis of the history curriculum and the National Statement of Values. The statement says, for example, that on the basis of valuing relationships with others, 'we should respect others, including children'. The Statement is rather unclear about how far in time or space this definition of 'others' is to extend. Is it to extend, for example, to the victims of the slave trade in the eighteenth century, or indeed to the living descendants of that trade? We are told also by the National Statement of Values that 'we should respect religious and cultural diversity'. Is it possible to teach these values effectively without some reference to history? History, as an account of our cultural identity, would seem to have a significant role to play here. Penelope Harnett, in Chapter 3, discusses how views of history teaching have evolved from the telling of 'moral exemplar' stories of the lives of the great and good to the development of a morally critical approach. Scientists are not the only seekers of objectivity or providers of evidence. Historians are also providers of evidence, however, the nature of the process of historical enquiry differs from that of scientific enquiry.

Historians cannot construct experiments to test new theories. We rely on their critical approach to accepted beliefs based upon incomplete evidence. Historians ensure that our society does not become morally complacent or blind to distortion of the 'facts' which justify our cultural norms. The continued existence of not just history, but all the humanities subjects, is one of our chief safeguards against an inhumane society of bigotry. Without the humanities, children will grow up, not to hold values, but simply to air whatever personal prejudice is instrumental to their desire for self-gratification. The relationship between a National Statement of Values which is the cultural product of the age we live in and, perhaps, a more timeless commitment to the search for humane truths is an interesting one. History tells us how we have come to have such a cultural artefact as a National Statement of Values. Geography tells us how realistic that Statement is when compared at the present time with the needs and conditions of society at a global level. Could there indeed have been a National Statement of Values without the insights people have gained through their learning in history, geography and religious education? Is such learning to stop now that we have enshrined our values in a national statement?

Let us summarise our argument so far. We have argued that the humanities are an effective context for the development of literacy and numeracy. We have argued for the humanities as necessary to the continued existence or improvement of a humane society. We have linked the humanities with the teaching of values, particularly those values that are wanted for the humane society we envision. Of values, we have said that a value is a personal belief. We have pointed out that many people may share the same beliefs. There are many links between cultural identity and shared values. We have also said that a value differs from a mere opinion in that it can be justified by a degree of valid argument, often grounded in ethical reasoning. There is one more point we should like to make about values before concluding this chapter.

It is easy to list values that are thought desirable and almost as easy to write endlessly about them. You may have reflected already upon the fact that we do not always live by the values we profess to hold. You may have experienced the fact that children, particularly at the top end of the primary school, are quick to spot hypocrisy. What, you may ask, is to be done if we preach one value yet practise another? Talbot and Tate (1997) claim that if you have such a worry, you have misunderstood what a value is. Their solution to the problem of not living up to values is to claim that values are synonymous with ideals, things we try to, or would like to, live up to. We are not wholly content with this view which seems to us potentially a licence for inaction (or indeed, even hypocrisy). We would like to conclude this chapter by putting an alternative view which we hope you will bear in mind as you refer to other chapters in the book.

According to the National Statement of Values, on the basis of the fact that all 'people of goodwill' value relationships, 'we should . . . show others that they are valued . . . earn loyalty, trust and confidence . . . work cooperatively with others . . . resolve disputes peacefully . . .' These are all laudable aims and I doubt that, as a 'person of goodwill', you would wish seriously to dispute any of them. The problem is that they are all values which take time and, indeed, can even cost money to put into practice.

Enquiry task 4

Copy out each of the bullet points onto a separate piece of paper. They represent the calls on time in a day in a typical Key Stage 2 primary class. They are not listed in any particular order of priority. Your task is to sort them into such an order, starting with the most important, ending with the least important. It is much better if you undertake this task with a small group of colleagues on the understanding that the group must agree on its priorities.

- Perform a science investigation to ascertain how mixtures of materials can be separated out.
- Change the children for PE, spend 10 minutes on fitness and 20 minutes on games skills.
- View a video about The Greeks and Democracy and discuss with the children the importance of democracy in modern society.
- Teach the National Literacy Strategy for one hour.
- A child has been bullied at lunch time. Spend 30–40 minutes circle time with your class resolving the problem.
- Develop a creative maths investigation into Islamic patterns.
- Allocate 40 minutes to a whole class activity in creative art: either music, painting or drama.
- Teach the National Numeracy Strategy for one hour.
- Take your class to an act of collective worship for 20 minutes.
- Tell or read the class a story or poem, developing creative writing skills.
- Set the class an exercise in group cooperation and collaborative working, taking about one hour.
- A child's lunch box has been interfered with. Your investigation reveals an on-going problem. Spend 20–30 minutes helping the children understand the importance of respecting each other's property.
- Spend time planning with the children or performing administrative tasks for a field trip that is to take place later in the term.
- Provide a 20 minute silent reading time and hear five children read to you.
- Relax in the staff room for 40 minutes whilst the children play outside.

If you have experience of working in a primary school, you will know that it would be quite impossible to do all these things in one day. Of course, there are five days in a week, but there again, certain things such as acts of worship or the National Literacy Strategy have to be undertaken daily. You may well have experienced the feeling that, by Friday, you have not been able to do all that you wanted as well as you would wish.

Re-sort your priorities to indicate the following:
1 Things you value so highly that they must be accomplished on the given day.
2 Things you also value highly and hope you will accomplish later in the week.
3 Things you value but probably won't have time to do.
4 Things that you do not value and would happily eliminate from school life.

If you, as the National Statement of Values suggests you ought, genuinely value children and other people, and value loyalty, trust, confidence, cooperation and the peaceful resolution of disputes, you may recognise the problem that is embedded in the above enquiry task. The task describes an actual scenario in a real school. It refers to a real pupil who was actually bullied and the victim of injustice, and a real conflict between the desire to resolve the difficulty and the desire to proceed with an English lesson. The school concerned prided itself upon its anti-bullying policy. In each classroom there was posted a notice which said that 'if you are bullied you *must* tell an adult' and that the adult '*will* listen and take your problem seriously'. Unfortunately, of course, listening to a child, hearing fairly both sides in a dispute, and taking a problem seriously takes a lot of time. Although the school prided itself on displaying the right documentation, it did not, in reality, consistently uphold the values claimed in the documentation. It was not prepared to make the necessary time and resources available.

This is the difficult bit. You will recall, I'm sure, how I described the fact that my next door neighbour valued his car. He spent money and time on it. This is what Derek Wright (1971) has called an *operative* value. An operative value is a value that we note a person holds by observation of the fact that he or she allocates time and resources to an object or, more importantly, a *state of affairs* that is desired. The other kind of value, according to Wright, is the *expressed* value. These are values which are written down or claimed, but have only the status of ideals which are seldom, if ever, realised in practice. The school I am describing sometimes had problems with behaviour over lunch break. Research by the senior management team revealed that over 75 per cent of disruptive incidents occurred during or after lunch break. The pupil concerned had been the victim of harassment over lunch time. He had followed the school's policy and reported the incident to one of the supervisory assistants. The assistant did not follow the policy. She told the child 'not to be silly' and, when he protested, 'stood him against the wall' for the rest of lunch break.

Afternoon school began with the child concerned more than a little distraught. Class acts of worship were scheduled for the day concerned, so the teacher convened a circle meeting to resolve the difficulty. During the meeting, pupils openly expressed anger at the hypocrisy of the school's stance on bullying and harassment. The teacher was beginning to make progress with comforting the distressed pupil and assuring the rest of the class that 'something would be done' when the bell rang for the start of a scheduled English lesson. The teacher was faced with a difficult choice. Should he stop the circle time and give the full allocation of time to English, or should he allow the circle time to continue until the issue was resolved? He chose the latter course and was successful in restoring calm and assuring

Reflection 4

You are in the 'management hot seat'. You have £1000 to spend on inservice. What would your spending priorities be? List them in order:

- Send a teacher on a training day for Information Technology.
- Organise inservice training for supervisory assistants on effective management of children's play.
- Employ a consultant for a pre-OFSTED review of the teaching of literacy.

the distressed pupil that the problem would be resolved. The problem was resolved, because the teacher spoke to bully and victim, involved both sets of parents and set and monitored positive behaviour targets. You might imagine, however, that this desire to make operative the values of trust, loyalty, confidence and the peaceful resolution of disputes took a lot of the teacher's time. What other values could have been made operative with the same amount of time?

The story does not quite end there. Two alternative solutions were proposed for the lunch time behaviour problem. The first was that lunch breaks should be cut from one hour to forty minutes. The second was that the supervisory assistants should be given inservice training and a 'safe haven' be set up in a classroom to promote socialisation skills and the playing of games by pupils for whom lunch breaks were seldom a happy experience. The staff were divided on the issue, and it was not resolved, although members of the management team did express the view that resources were too precious to spend on the inservice training of supervisory assistants.

An exercise such as this should focus your mind on where your true values really lie. It is easy to produce long lists of expressed values or 'ideals', but during the course of this book we maintain what we regard as a healthy scepticism toward such a practice. This book is about only those values that might realistically become operative. Hard decisions have to be made. You should, by now, be forming a picture of what we envisage those values ought to be. The idea that valuing supervisory assistants as colleagues, or valuing playtimes as times where vitally important social learning occurs, is one such value that we feel can and should become operative in the creation of a humanitarian curriculum. Somehow, whilst providing the efficient education in the 'basics' that was envisioned by the authors of the literacy and numeracy hours, we have also to find time to promote the spiritual, moral, social and cultural development of pupils. As the discussion of this topic in Chapter 7 clarifies further, this cannot be accomplished simply by briefly reminding pupils of the theoretical rules which govern how they 'ought' to behave.

It is perhaps the humanities subjects themselves, however, upon which the spotlight most brightly falls. Are they valued enough to receive serious attention in your teaching or in your School Development Plan? Are your *operative* values directed solely towards tests, league tables, literacy and numeracy targets or towards the attainment of a good, humane society? We hope that we have made it clear that we do not see a conflict between these value systems. It is possible to have *both* high standards of literacy and numeracy *and* a humanitarian curriculum. In the coming chapters, we hope to show you how. We hope to show you how the humanities subjects can and do make the children themselves operatively value knowledge and learning. Effective teaching of the humanities provides that rich ingredient in the primary curriculum that makes primary schools places of hope and excitement where children will want to be. Effective teaching of the humanities can take learning outside the classroom and provide children with experiences they will recall for the rest of their lives, as the chapter on field work and first hand experience by Don Kimber and Maggie Smith demonstrates.

The National Statement of Values suggests that, as 'people of goodwill' who 'value ourselves as unique human beings capable of spiritual, moral, intellectual and physical growth and development' we should 'strive throughout life, for knowledge, wisdom and understanding'. Primary schools have, for some years now, played a vital role in persuading children that this is a value worth making operative. We believe that the humanities subjects have been at the heart of some of the most effective and inspirational practice that has promoted this value. Can we make operative the value 'clarify the meaning and purpose in our lives and decide, on the basis of this, how we believe that our lives should be lived' without a humanitarian curriculum?

Appendix 1: The National Statement of Values (1997)

The self

> We value ourselves as unique human beings capable of spiritual, moral, intellectual and physical growth and development.

On the basis of these values, we should:
- develop an understanding of our own characters, strengths and weaknesses;
- develop self-respect and self-discipline;
- clarify the meaning and purpose in our lives and decide, on the basis of this, how we believe our lives should be lived;
- make responsible use of our talents, rights and opportunities;
- strive, throughout life, for knowledge, wisdom and understanding;
- take responsibility, within our capabilities, for our own lives.

Relationships

> We value others for themselves, not only for what they have or what they can do for us. We value relationships as fundamental to the development and fulfilment of ourselves and others, and to the good of the community.

On the basis of these values, we should:
- respect others, including children;
- care for others and exercise goodwill in our dealings with them;

- show others they are valued;
- earn loyalty, trust and confidence;
- work cooperatively with others;
- respect the privacy and property of others;
- resolve disputes peacefully.

Society

> We value truth, freedom, justice, human rights, the rule of law and collective effort for the common good. In particular, we value families as sources of love and support for all their members, and as the basis of a society in which people care for others.

On the basis of these values we should:
- understand and carry out our responsibilities as citizens;
- refuse to support values or actions that may be harmful to individuals or communities;
- support families in raising children and caring for dependants;
- support the institution of marriage;
- recognise that the love and commitment required for a secure and happy childhood can also be found in families of different kinds;
- help people to know about the law and legal processes;
- respect the rule of law and encourage others to do so;
- respect religious and cultural diversity;
- promote opportunities for all;
- support those who cannot, by themselves, sustain a dignified life-style;
- promote participation in the democratic process by all sectors of the community;
- contribute to, as well as benefit fairly from, economic and cultural resources;
- make truth, integrity, honesty and goodwill priorities in public and private life.

The environment

> We value the environment, both natural and shaped by humanity, as the basis of life and a source of wonder and inspiration.

On the basis of these values, we should:
- accept our responsibility to maintain a sustainable environment for future generations;
- understand the place of human beings within nature;
- understand our responsibilities for other species;
- ensure that development can be justified;
- preserve balance and diversity in nature wherever possible;
- preserve areas of beauty and interest for future generations;
- repair, wherever possible, habitats damaged by human development and other means.

References

BAGNALL, B. *Personal View*, written statement given to students at Homerton College, Cambridge.

DES (1991) *Geography in the National Curriculum*, Draft Orders, London: HMSO.

JUDD, JUDITH (1989) 'Thatcher changes course of history', The *Observer*, 20th August.

ORR, D. (1994) *Earth in Mind: One Education, Environment and the Human Prospect*, Washington: Island Press.

PLOWDEN REPORT, THE (1967) *Children and Their Primary Schools*, London: HMSO.

QCA (1997) *The Promotion of Pupils' Spiritual, Moral, Social and Cultural Development, Statement of Values*, Hayes: QCA Publications.

ROBERTS, M. (1996) 'A State of Forgetfulness', *Times Educational Supplement*, 7 June 1996.

TALBOT, M. and TATE, N. (1997) 'Shared values in a pluralist society?', in SMITH, R. and STANDISH, P. (eds) *Teaching Right and Wrong: Moral Education in the Balance*, London: Trentham.

WRIGHT, D. (1971) *The Psychology of Moral Behaviour*, Harmondsworth: Penguin.

Further reading

GRAHAM, D. and TYTLER, D. (1993) *A Lesson for Us All. The Making of the National Curriculum*, London: Routledge.
Co-authored by a former chairman of the National Curriculum Council, the book provides a fascinating insight into the 'value-free' debate and the views of various education ministers to which we have referred in this chapter.

SMITH, R. and STANDISH, P. (eds) (1997) *Teaching Right and Wrong: Moral Education in the Balance*, London: Trentham.
This book contains a useful introductory chapter on the National Statement of Values by Nick Tate (chairman of the QCA) and Marianne Talbot. The chapter sets out clearly the reasoning behind the Statement. It is followed by a collection of critical essays which highlight principal shortcomings of the Statement and some of its main philosophical flaws.

STEPHENSON, J., LING, L., BURMAN, E. and COOPER, M. (eds) (1998) *Values in Education*, London: Routledge.
The introductory chapter of this book will clarify further some of the essential concepts about values which we have introduced. The book reports on research which has grappled with some of the difficulties inherent in values education to which we have alluded.

Chapter 2

The literacy hour and beyond

Martin Ashley with John Lee, Richard Eke and Helen Butcher

Introduction and overview

Most people involved in primary education want to see a broad and balanced curriculum. Most people involved in primary education also want children to be literate and numerate. Are these two desires necessarily incompatible? In the previous chapter, we made out a strong case for the humanities. We did not do so, however, at the expense of the basic literacy and numeracy curriculum. We are as aware as anybody of the fact that the humanities cannot be effectively taught in secondary schools to pupils arriving from primary school deficient in basic literacy. In addition to traditional forms of literacy and numeracy, at the beginning of the twenty-first century we have to contemplate exponentially accelerating demands for literacy in Information and Communications Technology. Going on-line with the National Grid for Learning will hardly be comparable with the 'toe in the water' approach to ICT of the late twentieth century.

The job of the twenty-first century primary school teacher is so much harder and more complex than that of his or her twentieth century predecessor that one can be forgiven for wondering what teachers did with their time 30 years ago. To some extent we shall be offering an answer to that question in this chapter. Our main concern, however, is to demonstrate a 'both/and' approach to the curriculum. We believe that it is possible to have children who are both traditionally and electronically literate *and* humanitarian in the sense we outlined in the previous chapter. The literate and humanitarian citizens we envisage, as the outcome of the type of education we advocate, will be able to participate in cultural activities that are centuries old *and* to communicate electronically across the globe. We see no conflict between what is

Reflection 1

Here are some images of primary schools thirty years ago. Which are factually correct?

- Children worked in groups and seldom, if ever, received whole class teaching.
- Few schools taught science, history or geography.
- Creative writing was very popular, but spelling and grammar were seldom taught.
- Boys and girls were segregated, for lining up, register and for activities such as PE or craft.
- Children spent a lot of time outdoors, on nature study or other practical investigations.
- Maths schemes, based on the need for children to work as individuals and to 'understand' rather than learn by rote, were used in most schools.
- There was a lot of art work, often large scale and cooperative, with emphasis upon the child's creativity.
- The teacher always heard every child read nearly every day, even in older junior classrooms.

traditionally of value and what is of value to the development of an education for the twenty-first century.

The form of this chapter is that of a brief proposition or statement about primary education followed by some responses to that proposition. The proposition is that, in order to achieve high standards in literacy, a 'literacy hour' is *necessary but not sufficient*. The responses come, first from Helen Butcher, an English colleague of ours who is concerned directly with the implementation of the literacy hour, and secondly from a group of teachers from some of our partnership primary schools. Through the provision of reflection boxes and enquiry tasks, you, the reader, will also have the opportunity to contribute your response to the proposition that the literacy hour is *necessary but not sufficient*.

The Literacy Hour: necessary but not sufficient

We begin by elaborating briefly on one of our introductory themes: that of what primary teachers did with their time 20, 30 or 50 years ago. Here, straight away, is an argument for the teaching of history and 'historical literacy'. Are we to answer this question by drawing on and perpetuating some of the popular myths and folklore that abound about primary education, or are we to give a reasoned, justified and as far as possible, factual answer to this question? What image does the primary school of 30 years ago create in your mind? A golden age of child-centred topic work? A narrow curriculum of language and number work, with copying from an encyclopaedia on Friday afternoons?

If you identified any of the statements above as adequate factual records, we suggest some serious study of history. However, amidst all this confusion we might find something which could be proposed as a fact. This is that everybody (almost) throughout the history of primary education has desired a broad curriculum. At the same time, dispute over whether adequate standards in 'the basics' (literacy and numeracy) can coexist with a broad curriculum has worried everybody (almost) throughout the history of primary education. Dissatisfaction with the teaching of *basics* is as old as primary education itself. The chronology outlined in Figure 2.1 shows some of the key historical events which have marked the waxing and waning of the various elements of the debate. You may note that the very concept of primary education (which emerged with the Hadow reports of the 1930s) seems closely associated with a desire for breadth and child centredness which dates from around 1900 and has dominated the twentieth century

FIG 2.1
A chronology of the broad and balanced curriculum

1862 Lowe's Revised Code Introduced to counter the 'meagre accomplishment of the younger scholars in reading, writing and arithmetic'. Six 'Standards' introduced for reading, writing and arithmetic. Two shillings and eight pence fine per subject for each scholar failing to pass the examinations in reading, writing and arithmetic.

1870 Forster Education Act Board Schools make elementary education compulsory and available to all. Narrow curriculum retained, very large classes (up to 100). Military drill added to curriculum in 1871.

1902 Balfour Education Act LEAs (Local Education Authorities) created. Shift of emphasis towards the purpose of elementary education being for the development of the child.

1904–1926 The Public Elementary School Code Sets out expectations of a broad and liberal curriculum with diversity of practice.

> *The only uniformity of practice that the Board of Education desire to see in the teaching of Public Elementary Schools is that each teacher shall think for himself and work out for himself such methods of teaching as may use his powers to the best advantage and be best suited to the particular needs and conditions of the school. Uniformity in details of practice is not desirable even if it were attainable.*

1931 First Hadow Report Establishes separate primary and secondary education.

> *The curriculum is to be thought of in terms of activity and experience rather than of knowledge to be acquired and facts to be stored.*

1933 Second Hadow Report Recognition of a distinctive primary ethos.

> *What the good and wise parent desires for its child the nation should desire for all its children.*

Christian Schiller, the first HMI for junior education advocates a broad curriculum.

1937 Handbook of Suggestions for Teachers in Elementary Schools The government advocates child-centred education rather than the learning of subjects as the principle for the newly emerging 7–11 junior schools:

> *There is every reason why the aim of the Junior School should be set out in terms of the nature of its pupils rather than exclusively in terms of subjects or standards of achievement.*

1944 Education Act (Butler) Major post-war reconstruction. Opportunities for all. New school buildings. Selection for 'tripartite system' (grammar/technical/modern) exerts narrowing influence on primary curriculum through pressure of 11+.

> *Educational research critical of streaming in the primary school (Barker-Lunn et al.) and 11+ examinations which were shown to be unreliable predictors of future performance and came to be regarded as segregating children at too early an age.*

1963 Robbins Report on higher education. Universal access to higher education envisaged. Many new universities planned.

1965 Government commitment to universal comprehensive education and abolition of primary school testing (11+).

1967 The Plowden Report The curriculum is too narrow and insufficiently child-centred. Only 10 per cent of schools were 'good' in offering a broad curriculum. Two thirds were 'adequate, mediocre or bad'.

1970s The Plowden Era LEAs and training colleges advocate progressive, child-centred methods.

1975 The Black Papers Right-wing campaign against progressive education.

> *If the non-competitive ethos of progressive education is allowed to dominate our schools, we shall produce a generation unable to maintain our standard of living...Schools are for schooling, not social engineering...The best way to help children in deprived areas is to help them to be literate and numerate.*

1976 The Ruskin College Speech (James Callaghan) Schools are failing society. Insufficient standards in the basics.

1978 Primary Education in England A Survey by HMI. The curriculum is too narrow. HMI hold out against narrowing of curriculum to focus on 'basics'.

1980s Many LEAs continue to advocate Plowden style 'topic' work. LEA 'patronage' ensures career progression for those committed to child-centred methods. Formal teaching of English grammar discouraged.

1988 Education Act The National Curriculum enshrines by statute a broad and balanced curriculum. Science, history, geography etc. compulsory for first time in primary schools.

> *Educational research critical of multiple focus group work (Galton, Simon, Alexander, Rose, Woodhead).*

1995 The Dearing Report The curriculum is overloaded. Slimmed down version produced, with promise of no further change until 2000.

1997 New Labour government. Labour campaign against progressive education. The basics are not taught properly. Literacy and numeracy hours introduced, history and geography Orders no longer compulsory, ambiguity over breadth of curriculum.

1998 QCA issue *Maintaining Breadth and Balance*, in which the techniques of prioritising, combining and reducing are recommended in order to teach a narrower range of content whilst retaining ten National Curriculum subjects plus RE.

right up until its closing decades. To find similar language to that which has been used by some late twentieth century supporters of a narrower and more basic subject centred curriculum, it would seem necessary to return to the late nineteenth century.

Meanwhile, let us proceed with a key argument. This is that there is no conclusive evidence that standards achieved in basic literacy are directly proportional to the amount of time actually allocated to teaching literacy.

Research focus

In classrooms observed by Robin Alexander (1992) for the Leeds Primary Needs Programme between 1985 and 1991, it was found that the average pupil-time spent on English as a specific area of the curriculum was 31.5 per cent. Mathematics received 20.2 per cent, the humanities a mere 6.2 per cent.

Alexander's findings confirmed an earlier (1984) hypothesis. This was that in many pre-National Curriculum primary schools, the curriculum could be divided in to a Curriculum I and a Curriculum II. Curriculum I consisted of language and number work. Curriculum II consisted of whatever other curriculum areas a school covered. Almost all resources were devoted to Curriculum I. Teachers and schools gave Curriculum II low priority, were ill-prepared for it and lacked the subject knowledge to teach it.

A study by Tizard, Blatchford, Burke, Farquhar and Plewis (1988) of 33 London infant schools showed that the breadth of curriculum coverage varied considerably from school to school. Schools which had a narrow curriculum of language and number work justified their policies by claiming that a broader curriculum was too difficult for children of infant age, or inappropriate for a school with a difficult catchment area. However, attainment in all subjects, but particularly language and number, was found to be higher in the schools with the broader curriculum, even where circumstances of catchment area were difficult. The teachers in these schools had higher expectations of their children, and achieved better results in consequence. The researchers concluded that children need to be exposed to an ample range of challenging and interesting tasks.

A second study by Alexander (the PRINDEP study of 1988) see Alexander (1995), focused upon the management of time in the junior class. This study found that children worked the hardest and were the least distracted when undertaking those activities for which they were given the least time to develop. When a lot of time was allocated to activities such as reading and writing, the highest incidences of off-task behaviour were found. The researchers concluded that simply to give a high-priority activity or curriculum area more and more time will not necessarily deliver the learning outcomes sought.

The above research seems to be suggesting a key role for effective time management in the primary classroom. You should perhaps note that a literacy hour five days a week in a school with a nominal 23 hour week gives a total of 21.7 per cent of time to English, as opposed to the 31.5 per cent of time spent on English in the pre-National Curriculum schools described above. It would seem inappropriate, therefore to claim that the literacy hour is going to push humanities out of the curriculum. If the above research is to be believed, the threat to humanities comes, not from the literacy hour, but from the far older problem of lack of adequate subject knowledge by teachers, poor time management in primary classrooms and a restricted view of the curricular opportunities and challenges that should be presented to primary aged children.

A literacy hour in which a prescriptive structure for time management has featured strongly, has not been universally well received by primary teachers used to the relative freedom of 'topic work' and the integrated day. Yet there are questionable practices in primary education, and one of these concerns time management. In some schools, what has become known as 'finishing off' has almost attained the status of a curriculum subject in its own right. This might alert us to a certain lax attitude towards deadlines which would not pass muster in the majority of secondary schools. The literacy hour, with its sharply focused objectives and clear structure for time management has already alerted many primary teachers to the positive benefits of clear goals and deadlines which are explicit to the children.

The rigid and inflexible bell-governed timetable of the secondary school, on the other hand, has for a long period been the subject of criticism by supporters of the integrated day in the primary school. Where, it is asked, is the opportunity for children to pursue extended enquiries? How can the teacher respond to the variable concentration spans of younger children? You might consider that the present is a good time for a reappraisal in which primary education moves forward, building on the best of the past. Somewhere between the two extremes of a robotic approach to the literacy hour clock extended to all subjects and an undisciplined and unstructured approach with no deadlines for anything might lie the effectively managed primary school day.

Such a day would include literacy and numeracy hours. It might also include ten minutes music every day. You might wish to look at some of the recent research on brain and behaviour (see further reading). You might care to consider also a daily physical education session. A relatively brief period of vigorous physical activity which raises heart rates to recommended levels might not only promote health but might also rejuvenate children's capacities for other kinds of work. The fact that when the literacy hour was first proposed, some schools threatened to cut back on physical education, whilst others threatened to eliminate music teaching is alarming to those of us who value a broad curriculum. It tends to suggest that such activities were never particularly valued by such schools and is quite revealing.

An effectively managed primary school day would probably make much greater use of short, intensive ten-fifteen minute time slots, not only for music or PE, but for activities such as mental arithmetic. Surely the advantage of the primary school's flexibility is that the time period can be *shortened as well as lengthened* in order to optimise learning? The lesson we have to learn from past mistakes is that we must be very clear about our objectives and our expectations when we *lengthen* the basic time period (be it 30, 60 or any other arbitrary number of minutes).

In planning your work in humanities, we would suggest that you give clear attention to the amount of time that is to be spent on each activity. We would suggest that you practise justifying your decision to allocate 10 minutes, two hours or whatever to any given activity. If this achieves nothing else, it is likely to result in a considerable sharpening of your critical focus on the management of the literacy hour.

Some work in humanities, particularly where it involves aspects of research, or elements of composing, designing or redrafting is likely to be quite time consuming. Children have to learn not to expect instant answers to everything. We would question, however, the notion that creative work necessarily requires long periods of time. Most musicians would agree that ten minutes practise per day is much more effective than an hour's practice one day a week. Similarly, creative writing may require extended opportunities for development, but *over a period of time*, not all at once. For example, you might desire your children to engage in an extended piece of writing in history, to which you allocate perhaps four hours in total. Quality work is more likely to result from the children writing in shorter bursts which are followed by critical readings and teaching inputs, than from leaving children to work on their own for protracted periods.

Seen in this way, the literacy hour can soon become an opportunity for better work in the humanities, rather than a threat to the humanities. Two key points would seem crucial to success. First, the literacy and numeracy hours do not by any means take up all the available time at school. Second, humanities continue to require a clear and distinct content of their own. A clear vision of learning objectives for the humanities, to which specific time is allocated, should be the strongest defence against a view which sees the humanities purely as an adjunct to, or vehicle for, the teaching of literacy. Perhaps planning which clearly identifies how time will be spent on developing attitudes and values, and on non-verbal elements of learning, will achieve more than generalised aspirations and noble sentiments in those directions to which time was never actually allocated. Perhaps, too, you might bear in mind that if we tire children out by mismanaging their day, we can expect a higher incidence of disaffection and disruption. We can expect an even more impoverished Curriculum II and a Curriculum I which has failed to achieve any significant gain in the quality of literacy. You might decide to investigate management of the school day for yourself.

Enquiry task I

Do not accept the above claims uncritically. Examine them for yourself using a simple systematic measure such as time on task.

Select four children of differing abilities for close observation.

Take five minute samples of each child's concentration level at various times of the day. (One way of doing this might be to record whether the target child is on or off task once every 30 seconds – or you devise a slightly more sophisticated observation schedule. Alternatively, you could take notes or record and transcribe for later analysis the child's language or actions.)

Construct a table or similar representation which enables you to compare contextual factors such as:
curriculum area
length of session
time of day
time child had been on particular task
method of organisation (Child in group/listening to teacher/working on own/etc.)

- What changes in time management could you introduce to address any shortcomings revealed by this enquiry task?
- How could you ensure that both literacy and numeracy hours *and* other areas of the curriculum receive quality teacher input and quality attention by the children?
- Do your observations reveal a curriculum dominated by cognitive and verbal elements, or are emotional and non-verbal features given some importance too?

To summarise the discussion so far:

- Introducing the literacy hour in primary schools has increased our awareness of time management.
- Research evidence suggests that it is quality of teaching input and not length of time allocated that primarily affects pupil attainment, although children can and should be working on tasks that are time-constrained.
- The most significant factors affecting quality of teaching and learning in humanities are teachers' subject knowledge and teachers' ability to plan. Well-planned work in the humanities enhances literacy.

A broad and balanced curriculum, which offers well-managed changes of activity and a variety of tasks which challenge pupils in different subject areas, is perfectly possible within the existing primary school day and is associated with higher quality outcomes in both 'basic' and extended curriculum.

We have established the vital importance of time management, and have hopefully laid to rest the quite unsubstantiated and dangerous argument that there isn't enough time for a broad curriculum in the primary school. Let us now look in more detail at this notion that the literacy hour is necessary to raising attainment in certain key areas, but not sufficient to achieve a full literacy. In the remainder of this section of the chapter, we draw attention to the key role played by humanities in filling the gaps left by the literacy hour.

How is it that the literacy hour cannot address the whole of literacy development? The uncritical acceptance of Piaget's theories three decades earlier should alert us to the danger of becoming hooked on terminology and procedure rather than what lies beneath (Donaldson, 1978; Pollard, 1987). You should remember that the literacy hour is but *a part* of the National Literacy Strategy. The literacy hour is a pedagogical prescription to meet, in an efficient way, *some* of the targets of the National Literacy Strategy. There is an immediate danger that the terminology 'literacy hour' will become an uncritical substitute for an effective literacy strategy which permeates most areas of the curriculum. Never forget that language and learning penetrates almost everything that is done in a primary school. There are many aspects of literacy which are not and cannot be covered in a literacy hour.

The Schools Curriculum and Assessment Authority drew attention to the importance of *extended writing* in learning about history at Key Stage 3 (ages 11–14). In their discussion document (SCAA 1997) they describe and exemplify standards which are quite demanding in terms of what is expected in such areas as organising material. It is unlikely that a pupil whose experience of primary schooling had been limited to short bursts of teacher-directed writing in the literacy hour would cope well with such demands. It would be unfortunate and a cause for concern if there was a decline in the ability of older and more able pupils to engage in extended writing as a consequence of restricted views of literacy in the primary school. The need for the primary teacher to provide opportunities for sustained writing and for pupils to organise and plan their own writing in areas of the curriculum such as humanities should not be overlooked.

Another question which should not be overlooked is that of audience for children's writing. Much excellent work has been achieved in primary schools where the importance of audience is appreciated. The question is closely linked to genre, which we discuss shortly. The key words are Purpose, Function, Time. A wide range of purposes for writing, such as the composition of literature, the writing of reports or the construction of persuasive arguments is accomplished with greater success if the purpose can be made more than simply 'pleasing the teacher'. Work in the humanities is an effective way of generating real audiences as, for example, when children might write a short drama for performance in a community historical pageant, or write to the local paper about an environmental issue that concerns them. A teacher who places ticks and crosses on drills and exercises does not constitute an audience, and a textbook of drills and exercises certainly does not constitute a purposeful context. The literacy hour should not be allowed to detract from the task of identifying audiences which motivate children to write.

Fortunately, there are many excellent teachers in our primary schools who are highly proficient at devising stimulating contexts and audiences for children's reading and writing. The literacy hour, with its 20 minute writing slot, is not a substitute for this. It can broaden children's knowledge of writing techniques and increase both fluency and technical accuracy of expression. These are empowering features and a means to an end. Alarm bells, however, might ring if ever the literacy hour were to become an end in itself. Children need reasons to read and write which are outside the literacy hour. An appreciation of the value of the humanities subjects might also act as a check or balance to the somewhat 'literary' view of literacy that has arisen with the literacy hour. This is not a tautology. It is apposite to recall the words of Gunter Kress (1994) who has written that '. . . the kind of writing most widely taught and most highly prized in schools – such as essays, narrative, poetry – is engaged in by very few members indeed of any society'.

Priorities in literacy

Primary education has long embraced such devices as the palindrome as a way of increasing children's awareness of language. The inclusion of, for example, the renga, the tanka or the clerihew in a glossary heavily laden with the specialised jargon of the technical study of literature, begs certain questions. Questions of priority begin to arise. The 1988 Education Act requires us to 'prepare pupils for the demands of adult life'. In this context, Kress reminds us that the world's demands are primarily for transactional writing and not imaginative writing. We are not, in quoting Kress here, suggesting that you abandon poetry altogether, but it is necessary to have things in proportion. David Barton (1994) writes about this 'literary' view of literacy. The 'literary' view of literacy focuses not on the transactional writing that underpins communication in a modern society but upon the poetic writing that underpinned the class division in a society of illiterate peasants and an educated élite. To some extent, this social distinction between the transactional and the literary views of literature is preserved today in the hierarchical distinction between English Language and English Literature at GCSE. Whilst a basic qualification in English language at 16+ has always been thought essential, an additional qualification in English Literature has associations with a 'literary élite' in the higher English sets. How do we begin to make sense of this at the level of the primary school?

Perhaps you are beginning to find that the term 'literacy hour' is problematic. We need to be clear about what we mean by 'literacy'. Do we mean *functional competency* or do we mean *cultural development* – defined here as initiation into the high culture of English literature? If it is possible to have both, then perhaps all well and good. But at what cost to other areas of the curriculum such as the humanities and the arts? Why should primary schools succeed in teaching functional competency *and* the high culture of literature when secondary schools have for years found it so difficult to do so as a general rule for all their pupils? The 'literary' flavour of the literacy hour compels us to ask whether the apparent view that the study of literary aspects of literacy is the best way to promote a broad functional competency. Against the literary model we always have the possibility of a transactional model in which functional competency is promoted by reading and writing the subject matter of the humanities. We need a powerful means to help us in our analysis of this problem such as genre analysis. An example of such a model is given in Figure 2.2. Enquiry task 2, which follows, will help you make sense of it.

FIG 2.2
Genres

Genres – social processes that:

Processes

Describe	Explain	Instruct	Argue	Narrate
ordering things into commonsense or technical meaning	sequencing of phenomena in temporal or causal relationships	logically sequencing actions or behaviours	expanding proposition to persuade readers to accept view	sequencing people and events in time and space

commonly used in

Products

Personal descriptions	Explanations of how	Procedures	Essays	Personal recounts
Commonsense explanations	Illustrations	Instructions	Expositions	Historical recounts
Information reports	Accounts	Manuals	Discussions	Fairy tales
Scientific reports	Directions	Recipes	Reviews	Myths
Definitions	Explanation essays	Evaluations	Interpretations	Narratives
			Fables	

(from Cope and Kalantzis, 1993)

Enquiry task 2

If literacy is to be perceived by pupils as a meaningful activity, we might focus on its products.
- Select from the list of 'products' above a range of genres which you consider representative of the types of literacy pupils will use most in adult life.
- Add to this list a small number of products which you feel the culturally developed active citizen ought to use, but which many adults perhaps don't use.

Now carry out the following analyses:
1   Categorise the 'Products' as mainly transactional and mainly literary. Approximately what percentage falls into each category?
2   Write out as column headings:
    History,   Geography,   RE,   Science,   Technology,   Literature

Copy from the 'Products' column headings in Figure 2.2 under each of these new headings. By all means include any product you think merits it in more than one column.
3   Finally write out the following three further column headings:
    Direct Instruction   Indirect Instruction   Pupil Enquiry
    Literacy Hour   Other Subjects   Extended Writing

Add the 'Processes' (Describe, explain, instruct, argue, narrate) to these columns. Each process may well go into more than one column. Try to write them in rank order. For example, if you think 'narrate' is developed most effectively by direct instruction and marginally by extended writing, you might write it near the top in the left hand column and near the bottom in the right hand column.

This enquiry task may have helped you develop your own understanding of language and literacy across the curriculum. (You may find Ted Wragg's (1997) book *The Cubic Curriculum* clarifies this concept further.) You may feel more confident with the idea of the literacy hour being necessary but not sufficient. Apart from the humanitarian considerations described in the previous chapter, you may now also feel that the humanities have considerable value by virtue of the fact that they provide real access to a variety of genres. This last point is particularly important, given the passion with which the reading schemes versus real books debate has been conducted in primary education. We might ask why it is so necessary for the reading curriculum to be made up of 'pretend books' when the humanities subjects present such a wealth of material for real books which engage and sustain children's interests in what are, after all, very important topics.

You may see the relevance of a broader view of time management. You will almost certainly be following the fairly prescriptive guidance on time management given for the literacy hour. You may also see now the value of a broader view of effective time management across the whole school day. Such a view might include clear targets for direct instruction and equally clear targets for pupil enquiry and creative 'right brain' tasks which include both extended writing and communication through other media, including the expressive arts. Enquiry task 1 may have given you a clearer picture of when your children are the most receptive to these various and different modes of learning. Hopefully you will value 'right brain' activities sufficiently highly to ensure that pupils receive systematic and high quality teaching outside the prescriptive literacy and numeracy hours. The practice which Robin Alexander has condemned of using creative activities as mere time fillers to facilitate an imagined concentration on the basics is neither good management of time nor good management of pupils' learning.

Summary

- We need a broad view of literacy.
- Literacy in the primary school is concerned principally with rapid development of the ability to use spoken and written language in order to learn and communicate ideas and concepts across the whole curriculum. The study of literature is an element of the cultural development of pupils.
- Pupils need opportunities for extended writing and autonomous enquiry as well as direct instruction.

- Pupils need to develop as 'authors' at least as much as 'scribes'. Such development has to be grounded in purposeful tasks in which pupil interest is engaged in meaningful enquiry resulting in communication to an interested audience.
- A fully developed literacy includes elements of logical thinking, linear thinking and reasoning, factual recall, as well as intuition, creativity, risk taking and experimentation, response to feelings, and curiosity. All are equally valuable.
- We should optimise the whole school day, not just the literacy hour.
- We need careful and professional time management which includes closely directed tasks in literacy and numeracy hours and clear targets for pupils to achieve positive goals through their own autonomous learning.

Case Study I

Necessary but not sufficient: a response by Helen Butcher

Literacy is a bit like kindness. Everybody agrees it is a good thing and most people would like to see more of it. Disagreements in both cases centre on definition and form. My personal interest in the improvement of standards of literacy is rooted in three overlapping experiences. As a student working in a Benefit Office I was shocked by the number of young people unable to write down their responses to printed questions. This made me want to become a teacher. As a class teacher I encountered the complexity of the task facing children and spent a great deal of time studying the theory and practice of teaching reading. As a tutor of adult learners I listened to men and women whose self-esteem had been eroded because of the difficulty they had with reading. These adults all relied on the sounding out method of tackling print, convinced that it was they who were inadequate and not the method. These experiences made two things very clear to me; failure in learning to read damages lives and reading involves much more than the successful decoding of print. The means and manner in which reading is taught matters. My goal as an infant teacher was not just to teach children to read the next book but to inspire them to continue reading at 8, 28 and 88.

Like those responsible for the design and implementation of the Literacy Strategy I am keen to endorse improvements in the teaching of reading which will reduce the number of restricted lives and attack the 'long tail of under achievement' (Barber, 1997). As a tutor to training teachers I also have a duty to ask questions about the likely efficacy of this huge investment of time and money (£59million + £23million for books, in the first year alone) and its implications for teaching and learning. As Ted Wragg (1998) pointed out, a prescription is something you take when you are ill. Not all pupils or teachers in England and Wales are ill. I would like to outline some important considerations.

1 In 1996, 78 per cent and in 1997, 80 per cent of Key Stage 1 pupils reached or exceeded their expected level of achievement (Level 2).

2   Since 1995 there have been steady improvements in the number of pupils achieving Level 4 in the Standard Assessment Tasks from 48 per cent in 1995 to 63 per cent in 1996 and 72 per cent in 1997 (DfEE, 1998).

These improvements have been made without the Literacy Strategy.

3   The 10 subject National Curriculum, brought in to extend 'breadth and balance' in the primary school is now acknowledged by researchers (Brember and Davies, 1997) and government as partly responsible for reducing the emphasis on the core subjects. In April 1998 the DfEE announced a slimmed down curriculum to enable schools to devote more time to English, mathematics and science.

4   Early indications from the National Foundation for Educational Research suggest that pupils entitled to free school meals made less significant progress than those not entitled. In many cases these are the very pupils in the target group.

These considerations cause me to ask whether a more focused use of the money and energy might yield more valuable results in the long term. An evaluation of Reading Recovery, an intensive intervention programme for pupils experiencing difficulty in reading developed by Marie Clay in Australia, found it was effective but expensive. As a result, government funding ceased, though some local authorities continued to fund it because it worked, typically seventeen months' improvement in reading age following nine months' intervention.

The previous radical overhaul of primary schooling – the introduction of the National Curriculum – required an Act of Parliament (Education Reform Act, 1988). The National Literacy Strategy, with its intensive training programme, A4 binders and massive financial investment, looks very similar to the way the National Curriculum was presented. In fact it is not statutory. Nevertheless schools are expected to be achieving above the target figures (80 per cent of 11 year olds achieving Level 4) before they can decline to implement the Hour. It is worth considering the values implicit in the strategy. The desirability of improved standards of literacy is not in question, although the method may be. It seems to me that the values are contemporary management values; order, uniformity and control. In their desire to act, and be seen to act quickly, politicians short-circuited teachers' professional integrity.

David Reynolds (1998) pointed to research evidence which underlines the importance of 'significant practitioner input' in curriculum initiatives and wonders whether the 'absence of engagement by teachers in the educational process they were to be involved with from Summer 1998 may have damaging consequences on the reliability and implementation of good practice'.

The value of the literacy hour, in conjunction with the slimmed down curriculum, is the opportunity it affords pupils and their teachers to focus on the key skills for all their learning. In an information age, the ability to skim and scan print, process text and make judgments about its personal relevance and value are essential. I welcome the emphasis on the explicit teaching of reading, particularly at Key Stage 2. OFSTED inspections have, over a period of time, drawn attention to the fact that once children could read fluently they received no further instruction or guidance in how to develop their reading skills. There is a great deal of merit in the attention devoted to genre. For too long, many children have been asked to produce recounts, letters, reports and stories without being given insight into the processes involved. Similarly, reducing the emphasis on hearing children read individually is a tremendous step forward in the effective time management of primary classes.

Literacy is for a purpose and that purpose should not always be literary. The consequence of the narrowing curriculum is the damage done to the foundation and core subjects simultaneously – one through neglect, the other from overkill. Remembering my long term literacy objective for children – that they remain active readers throughout their lives – might the impact of a literacy hour for seven years be to switch them off? May some texts have been so analysed that they lose their magic and integrity? As a former infant teacher I know that the humanities have intrinsic value. Geography and history are a great deal more than vehicles or contexts for the practising of information gathering skills. Children need to be reading history-based texts in order to learn to read, not waiting until they can read before they engage with the meanings of culture and heritage. Studying geographical, historical and spiritual texts offers the opportunity for enriching and extending the value of the literacy hour and maintaining a broad curriculum, which is vital if children are to be well motivated, well rounded and well educated.

> *We have to go beyond literacy to critical literacy, which means helping pupils to see through the linguistic, semantic, intellectual and imaginative deceptions which more and more surround us.*   (Hoggart, 1998)

In summary, the literacy hour is probably necessary for some, though not all children. It is certainly not sufficient to achieve high standards in literacy. Pupils experiencing difficulty may still require additional support, very able children may become disaffected. The test of the literacy hour will not be seen until these children are adults.

Case Study 2

Necessary but not sufficient: the response of a group of primary teachers

I spoke to a 'focus group' of primary teachers, all of whom were subject coordinators for the humanities. The occasion was an inservice training day. At the time, some of the schools represented had recently received their literacy hour training, others had yet to receive it. The teachers were asked to read the draft of the first part of this chapter, and then to discuss and formulate their responses to it. They were then asked how they would respond, both as classroom teachers, and as humanities coordinators, to the task of modifying their curriculum plans in response to the Secretary of State's 'more flexible arrangements'.

None of the teachers supported a narrowing of the curriculum. All of the teachers agreed that competency in literacy and numeracy was a priority. Most thought that it was possible to achieve both, although there were some reservations about the on-going implications for planning. Perhaps significantly, the question of planning did more than any other to highlight differences between individual schools. In general, teachers from schools where planning was reported to be a strong feature were more confident in their ability to both develop basic skills and to offer a broad and balanced curriculum.

There was some dismay and even hostility at the prospect of yet more changes to the curriculum and a majority view was that existing curriculum plans for the humanities should continue to be used. They thought that time management was important and that the curriculum should be managed to be broad, not only in terms of subject content but also in terms of a proper balance of logic and reasoning (left-brained activities) with creative and intuitive (right-brained) activities. Every teacher present in the focus group agreed with the proposition that a literacy hour was necessary but not sufficient. None was entirely satisfied with existing standards of literacy, and all were open-minded about the prospect of guidance and a national strategy. At the same time, all felt that the humanities would have to maintain their own distinctive contribution. There was considerable scepticism about notions that the use of historical or geographical texts in the literacy hour would constitute anything like an adequate approach to the humanities.

A discussion arose on this subject, and the view was put forward that, rather than work in history or geography being extended from a text first put forward in the literacy hour, the literacy hour could instead be used to develop a piece of extended writing based upon a topic first introduced through history or geography, and quite possibly through field work or enquiry. The discussion broadened to include the question of text selection. Would pupils work from a few textbooks with a limited range of publishers' choices of subject, or would the better schools and teachers be able to focus on their own choices of text, made to support interests in the areas of history and geography relevant to a particular school? There was agreement that planning and curriculum management skills would be crucial in determining the quality of the links between the literacy hour and the other subjects.

You might like to work through the enquiry task below which we have devised to help you consider this important question more clearly.

The teachers in the group agreed with the view put forward in the chapter that quality of teaching input rather than gross quantity of time allocated is the primary determinant of pupil performance. They acknowledged that teachers' subject knowledge and ability to plan are crucial elements of effective humanities teaching. They agreed too that a broad and balanced curriculum, which offers well managed changes of activity and a variety of tasks which challenge pupils in different subject areas, is perfectly possible within the existing primary school day and is associated with higher quality outcomes in both 'basic' and extended curriculum.

Some elements of the humanities subjects were cited as indispensable to a broad and balanced curriculum. A frequently quoted example was maps and mapping, with the closely associated topic of photograph interpretation. This was considered a vital skill which was not realistically covered elsewhere in the curriculum. The teachers had a positive view of the success of the National Curriculum in bringing about continuity and progression in the teaching and learning of map work. One school was able to display an impressive portfolio of children's developing skills in map making and map reading across the whole age range from Reception to Year 6. This was thought far too valuable to lose in any 'slimming down' of curriculum content.

Other valued topics in geography were a general knowledge of the world with a particular emphasis upon knowledge of different cultures, and the continued study of environmental issues. The teachers felt that children need to develop an attitude of respect and the knowledge that they would need to become responsible for sustaining and improving the environment. Field work techniques were also valued, with a particular emphasis upon rivers, weather, local settlements and matters of environmental quality. Similarly, in history, the sense of chronology that has been developed by children since the introduction of the National Curriculum was highly prized, as was the ability to examine critically the quality of historical evidence. Textual criticism and the critical evaluation of sources, particularly for older children, were considered to be one of the major advances brought about by National Curriculum history, and there was a strong feeling that children would continue to need exposure to a variety of historical sources, a number of which might not be in the form of written text.

Little remained, within this group of teachers, of the old culture of Plowden-style topic work. The following quotation perhaps summarises the degree to which the National Curriculum, in spite of it various shortcomings has, over 10 years, achieved something of the status of an 'old and trusted friend'.

> ❝ *The National Curriculum was really thought out as a good tool for subject management in the classroom (apart from the fact that e.g. number was divided into three attainment targets and other examples such as this). Teachers worked hard to give children a broad and balanced curriculum and now most of this will go with the literacy hour and the reduced curriculum.*

Perhaps the pessimistic assumption that breadth and balance is to be lost through a National Literacy Strategy betrays a reluctance to change and to incorporate new initiatives into an ever evolving repertoire of 'best practice' that might have stood in the way of the National Curriculum itself 10 years previously. As a conclusion to this chapter, you might like to attempt the enquiry task and to reflect upon this for yourself.

Enquiry task 3

Imagine a class of Year 5 children who are to investigate their local river. You plan a field visit to the river, during the course of which the children become concerned at the amount of rubbish dumping in the part of the river that runs close to the local supermarket. You and the children decide to investigate this topic further, and the children are keen to promote a campaign to clear the river of discarded shopping trolleys and the like.

Read the text level work for non-fiction reading, comprehension and writing composition specified for Year 5.

Note all the text skills specified that must be taught in the literacy hour and which would enable the children to carry out their river and environment work more effectively.

Re-read p. 13, *Links with the rest of the curriculum*, in the National Literacy Strategy.

Make a list of objectives:
a) To be worked at as text work during the literacy hour.
b) To be worked at during time specifically allocated to the humanities.
c) To be worked at during time specifically allocated to PSE or SMSC.

References

ALEXANDER, R. (1992) *Policy and Practice in Primary Education*, London: Routledge.

ALEXANDER, R. (1995) *Versions of Primary Education*, London: Routledge.

BARBER, M. (1997) *Literary Task Force: A Reading Revolution. How we can teach every child to read well*, London: RM.

BARTON, D. (1994) *Literacy: An Introduction to the Ecology of Written Language*, Oxford: Blackwell.

BREMBER, I. and DAVIES, J. (1997) 'Monitoring reading standards in Year 6: a seven year cross-sectional study', *British Educational Research Journal*, **23**, 5.

COPE, B. and KALANTZIS, M. (eds) (1993) *The Powers of Literacy: A Genre Approach to Teaching Writing*, Lewes: Falmer Press.

DfEE (1998) *National Literary Framework*, London: DfEE.

DONALDSON, M. (1978) *Children's Minds*, London: Fontana.

HOGGART, R. (1998) The *Guardian*, 3 December 1997.

KRESS, G. (1994) *Learning to Write*, London: Routledge.

POLLARD, A. (ed.) (1987) *Children and Their Primary Schools: A New Perspective*, Lewes: Falmer Press.

REYNOLDS, D. (1998) 'Schooling for Literacy', *Educational Review*, **50**, 2.

SCAA (1997) Discussion Paper No. 8. *Extended Writing in History*, Hayes: Schools Curriculum and Assessment Authority Publications.

TIZARD, B., BLATCHFORD, P., BURKE, J., FARQUHAR, C. and PLEWIS, I. (1988) *Young Children at School in the Inner City*, London: Lawrence Erlbaum.

WRAGG, E. (1998) 'Last word', *Times Educational Supplement*, 15 April 1998.

Further reading

BOURNE, J. (ed.) (1994) *Thinking Through Primary Practice*, Milton Keynes: Open University Press.
This edited collection contains chapters which usefully expand on many of the issues we have covered in the first part of the chapter. The section on managing learning and the curriculum is particularly relevant and contains a useful chapter by Campbell and Neill entitled 'The use of primary teachers' time: some implications for beginning teachers'.

MACGILCHRIST, B., MYERS, K. and REED, J. (1997) *The Intelligent School*, London: Chapman.
The authors of this book draw upon Howard Gardner's notion of multiple intelligence and on recent thinking about the nature of organisations, to take a fresh look at schools. Written in the tradition of the school improvement movement, the book makes the vital point that there can be no blueprint for improving schools and might prove timely reading for teachers developing ways of adapting a highly prescriptive literacy hour to the needs of their own children and school, as well as maximising their own creative potential as teachers.

WHEWAY, D. and THOMSON, S. (1993) *Explore Music Through Science*, Oxford University Press.
Part of a series of short resource books which explore holistic approaches to education. This book explains the reasoning behind our claim that music is justified

and valuable, both intrinsically and for the effect it has on learning and upon development overall. This is an idea that has been around since Plato and Aristotle. The main relevance to the present chapter is, of course, the question of time management in primary classrooms.

WRAGG, E. (1997) *The Cubic Curriculum*, London: Routledge.
Ted Wragg's analysis of the primary curriculum is an imaginative response to the core question of breadth and balance that has preoccupied this chapter. The book offers a visionary alternative to a sterile battle between breadth and basics. It is one influential writer's response to the challenge of a both/and curriculum, for which we have argued consistently.

Chapter 3

Looking afresh at history

Penelope Harnett

Learning about the past

At Cheddar Gorge, there is a famous flight of steps called Jacob's Ladder. If you are feeling energetic you might feel inclined to walk up these 274 steps to the viewpoint above. These 274 steps represent the passage of time since the beginning of the world. As you tread on one step, the guidebook asks you to imagine that one million years has passed by, and at various staging points along the flight, notices explain what is happening in the world all the millions of years ago. As one nears the summit, the guidebook explains that human ancestors are beginning to appear around the tenth step from the top. Half way up the last step, human groups are beginning to arrive in Britain. The width of a sheet of paper placed just beneath the top of the final step marks the arrival of the Romans in Britain.

As you climb these steps you gain a tremendous sense of the magnitude of time and of the insignificance of the human race in respect to the age of the earth. The whole of the history National Curriculum is reduced to just over a width of paper placed before the final step. Yet although this period seems so small in relation to the continuing development of the earth, we cannot possibly study it all. Decisions are going to have to be made about what we will study within that width of paper and also how we shall study it.

The purpose of this chapter is to explore some of the issues involved in such decision making. We will explore different understandings of history and consider its importance within the primary curriculum. The current history

National Curriculum will be discussed and we will examine how the curriculum provides opportunities for learning about the past.

Let us begin with a story.

The story of Guy Fawkes

There was once a man called Guy Fawkes. He was a very bad man. Guy Fawkes was a French man. He was a Catholic. English men wanted him to come over to England to blow up the Houses of Parliament, because King James sent his soldiers to all the Catholics to kill them. Guy Fawkes and the rest of the Catholics met in a secret group each night, at the dead of night. They were going to blow up King James when he was sitting on his throne all comfy like, with lots of cushions, in the Houses of Parliament. They had to save their pocket money for a long time to buy the gunpowder and spades. They started to dig a tunnel. They had to run away from the tunnel when they hit the River Thames and they were nearly drowned. Then Peter White remembered that his cellars went right under the River Thames and right by the Houses of Parliament right by where James sat. They were all angry with him so they walked right under, put all the gunpowder there and walked away feeling very happy with themselves. Guido Fawkes prepared his tent and sleeping bag, lantern and tinderbox. November 4th came quickly, Guy Fawkes said goodbye to his mum and dad skeletons because they had already been killed. He rushed into the cellars and put up his tent. He quickly rushed out to the secret hideout where he and his friend always met. He had forgotten his teddy. He could never sleep without his teddy. One of the men in the group remembered that his brother was an eccentric millionaire and he was going to go to the Houses of Parliament. So the man whose brother was a millionaire was so much of a chicken that his brother would be blown to a thousand pieces, he writ a letter to his brother. His brother received the letter and told the king about it. The king sent his soldiers down in the cellars to try and find any gunpowder. They found Guy Fawkes who was just tucking down in to his tent with his sleeping bag and with his teddy just snuggling up to him. The soldiers took Guy Fawkes up to the king. The king was angry. Guy Fawkes would not tell his name so they put him on the rack and stretched him. Finally he told his name and writ it down. The soldiers couldn't read it – it was so squiggly. They finally found out his name and the rest of the gang. Only three including Guy Fawkes were found. Two had their heads chopped off. Guy Fawkes was put on the rack, hung, beheaded and burnt.

The story of Guy Fawkes is familiar to many children and one which Peter has interpreted and amended as he wrote his historical account. Peter has

Reflection 1

- How familiar are you with this story?
- Can you identify any differences in the version above with your own understanding of the events?

Photocopy the story. Underline parts of the story which you consider accurate with a coloured pencil. Select another coloured pencil to underline parts which you consider inaccurate and another pencil for parts which you are not sure about.

- How much of the story do you consider is accurate?
- What other information would you need to verify the parts which you are not sure about?

introduced a fair amount of historical information, for example, the outline of the plot and also historical details such as the tinderbox and lantern. He also drew on knowledge of Guy Fawkes' signature; there remains a very shaky signature, *Guido Fawkes* with which Guy signed his confession.

Peter has used his imagination to suggest a possible sequence of events, and embellished his story with particular details to add further interest. We can recognise where Peter has introduced his own ideas since he has drawn extensively on his own personal experience and knowledge and we recognise that some of his descriptions are unlikely to be true and are anachronistic. As he constructed this narrative, Peter was working in a similar way to many historians. Historians also tell the story of the past and draw on particular details to enliven their accounts. However, their details will be different since they will draw on a depth of historical knowledge. To identify where historians have added their own interpretations, we as readers, also need a similar breadth of historical knowledge.

The story emphasises some of the challenges which we are faced with in teaching history. History is not a straightforward story about what happened in the past. It is an interpretation, whether by an eminent historian, a teacher or a child, of what is likely to have occurred in the past and which draws on different sources of information. Inevitably, as we develop our interpretations we are affected by our own values and beliefs which will influence what we consider is important and significant about different events and features of past ways of life. The identification of values is one of the recurring themes throughout this book and in this chapter we will be questioning how this might influence what counts as history and how history is constructed.

Constructing the history curriculum

We want to begin to explore this theme by discussing how the history curriculum has developed within primary schools during this century. Different views on the importance of the history curriculum can be traced through examining various curriculum documents emanating from the government, HMI and other official sources. Advice was offered to teachers at periodic intervals from the beginning of the century by the Board of Education through the Handbooks of Suggestions.

In 1905, the Handbook cited the purpose of education was to 'provide education in the full sense of the word'. Amongst other things this included preparing children to be good citizens with an awareness of their rights and responsibilities. History provided opportunities for children, '. . . to trace how these rights and duties arise'. Education was also important for character training, inculcating children with such values as, '. . . loyalty to institutions, unselfishness and orderly and disciplined habit of mind'. History contributed towards character training by providing examples of worthy behaviour through a range of stories.

> *The lives of great men and women, carefully selected from all stations in life, will furnish the most impressive examples of obedience, loyalty, courage, strenuous effort and serviceableness, indeed of all the qualities which make for good citizenship.* (Board of Education, 1905, p. 6)

Parallels can be drawn between history and religious education in the nineteenth century. Both subjects had an essentially moral function to provide examples of exemplary behaviour and role models which children were encouraged to emulate. As the dominance of the churches within the education system was reduced in the early years of the twentieth century, historical stories were an alternative to traditional Bible stories.

Stories of the great and good continued to dominate history teaching and are still features in many schools' history curricula. However, increasing knowledge of child development and emerging theories about how children learn, were reflected in government advice to schools by the 1930s. The Hadow Report (Board of Education, 1931) emphasised the importance of activity and children developing their own understanding of their world. In terms of learning in history, there is a noticeable shift in emphasis in the Handbooks following the publication of the Hadow Report. For example, in 1927, the Board of Education concluded, 'From its (history's) study the mature reader may gain a wider intellectual outlook and a saner judgment, but for children it is pre-eminently an instrument of moral training' (Board of Education, 1927, p. 139). Ten years later the emphasis in the Handbook had changed considerably,

> *From its study the mature reader may gain a wider intellectual outlook and a saner judgment, and these benefits in their degree may also accrue to older children. For all children however, history is pre-eminently of value as a stimulus to their imagination and as an appeal to their enthusiasms.*

The Board of Education recognised that content was less important, 'than the spirit behind the teaching' (Board of Education, 1937, pp. 402–403).

The importance of children's active involvement in their learning was reiterated in advice issued after World War Two. The Ministry of Education (1959) advocated beginning from children's own interests, and learning about local and family histories. These ways of learning history were also later endorsed within the Plowden Report (DES, 1967). Stories continued to be told and were valued for captivating children's imaginations and extending their experiences. However, the value of history for moral training was becoming less acceptable. Fresh interpretations of individuals' lives based on systematic research, questioned the straightforward certainties of traditional biographies and also the responsibility of individuals for their actions (Ministry of Education, 1959, pp. 278–81).

The Plowden Report (DES, 1967) emphasised teaching from children's existing understanding and experiences. However, this did create particular difficulties for teaching history in primary schools. Many aspects of the past were beyond children's immediate experiences and consequently it could be argued that the history was too difficult for children to grasp, particularly for very young children (Key Stage 1). This was a major criticism of the Plowden philosophy. Plowden's insistence on learning from children's direct involvement and immediate interest could be limiting, particularly if one took the view that education was about extending children's experiences and opening up their knowledge and understanding of the world. Certainly in the years following Plowden, history in primary schools was not well taught. HMI commented in the *Primary Survey* that there was too much copying out from books and that history was not well planned or taught in a systematic way. The identification of skills and processes involved in teaching history and an outline of progression was needed (DES, 1978).

Work within these areas was already being developed within the secondary history curriculum, through initiatives such as the Schools' Council History Project. This project provided a distinct philosophy for history teaching, emphasising that children should be trained to work as historians, developing their own enquiries and working from historical sources.

The influence of these secondary curriculum initiatives began to impact slowly on the primary curriculum in the 1980s, and was also reflected in documents emanating from HMI. HMI described a possible progression in historical skills and concepts, including reference and information – finding skills, skills in chronology, the use and analysis of evidence, empathetic understanding and asking historical questions. Development in language and historical ideas, and the synthesis of information and ways in which it could be communicated, were also identified (DES, 1985). A later document,

The History Working Group outlined a variety of purposes of school history in the Final Report. These were:

1   to help understand the present in the context of the past;

2   to arouse interest in the past;

3   to help to give pupils a sense of identity;

4   to help to give pupils an understanding of their own cultural roots and shared inheritances;

5   to contribute to pupils' knowledge and understanding of other countries and other cultures in the modern world;

6   to train the mind by means of disciplined study;

7   to introduce pupils to the distinctive methodology of historians;

8   to enrich other areas of the curriculum; and

9   to prepare pupils for adult life.
    (DES, 1990, p. 1)

■   Do you agree with these purposes?

■   Can you think of ways in which these purposes might be achieved in the classroom?

■   Do you think some purposes might be more important than others? Can you prioritise the purposes? List them in rank order and explain your reasons for their order. You might like to compare your rankings with those of a colleague. Have you placed them in a similar order?

■   Why might your colleague have placed them differently?

History 5–16 also made suggestions about the selection of possible historical content across the whole school age range (DES, 1988).

From this brief survey, it is possible to identify several ways in which history's inclusion within the curriculum has been justified. History has been valued for inculcating moral values and developing children's understanding of their place in society, together with their rights and duties as citizens. It has also been taught to stimulate children's imagination and to develop their interest and enthusiasm for the past. More recently, history's contribution towards the development of children's thinking and abilities to retrieve, organise and communicate information has been recognised. In the rationale for teaching history prepared by the History Working Group, which advised on the creation of the history National Curriculum, we can see the influence of these different views (DES, 1990). We have included the History Working Group's rationale in the adjacent reflection, to help you to consider the contribution which history can make to children's learning within the current curriculum.

A rationale for the history National Curriculum

As you do this activity you will need to reach some understanding about how these aims might be achieved in practice. For example, how can history enrich other areas of the curriculum? In what ways is it possible to teach history so that children can develop a sense of their identity? Identifying activities and specific historical knowledge will help you to prioritise these different purposes. As you discuss your priorities with colleagues, you will probably also become aware of the different values that can be placed on education and children's learning.

Research focus

In a recent research study, primary school teachers acknowledged the importance of the above purposes, but were generally unwilling to prioritise them since they saw them all as of equal importance. In subsequent interviews however, teachers recognised the importance of introducing children to history in fun and exciting ways which would arouse their interest in the past. Children's active involvement in historical enquiries was emphasised. Teachers also recognised history's important role in developing personal identities and an awareness of cultural heritages.

(Harnett, 1998)

Constructing the history National Curriculum

Reflection 3

Obtain a copy of the history National Curriculum.
- Can you identify ways in which the curriculum could meet the history Working Group's rationale?
- Why do you think particular History Study Units/Areas of Study have been selected?
- Would you include any other historical content?
- What values does the history National Curriculum reflect in the versions of the past which it presents to children?

The above rationale influenced both the structure and content of the history National Curriculum, which marked a new era in the government's control and organisation of the curriculum. Previously, although HMI (DES, 1988) had suggested possible knowledge to include within a course of history, this was not prescriptive. Until the creation of the National Curriculum, the content of the history curriculum had, by and large, remained very much the concern of individual teachers and schools.

The content of the history National Curriculum has been hotly debated. Indeed, of all the subject working groups, the history Working Group received the most comments from the public on its proposals when they were first drafted. Margaret Thatcher expressed the view that children should know the great landmarks of British history. The difficulty here arises in that we might all have different opinions on defining the great landmarks, as well as different understandings of what constitutes British history.

Several revisions have been made to the history National Curriculum since the original recommendations from the History Working Group. Each revision has considerably reduced the amount of content within the history curriculum. The current slimmed-down version, following the Dearing Report, has been generally welcomed, although many teachers still feel that it is hard to include all aspects of the history curriculum within their teaching (QCA, 1998a).

The National Curriculum prescribes the historical knowledge and understanding to be taught within the Areas of Study (Key Stage 1) and the History Study Units (Key Stage 2). It also emphasises the involvement of children in developing their own interpretations of history and awareness of how historical knowledge is constructed. Ways in which children should learn history are described within the Key Elements. There is therefore, within the curriculum, a dual focus on historical knowledge and also the process by which historical knowledge is constructed.

Learning about history

We have discussed how history has developed as a subject during this century and the different values that have influenced the history curriculum. We turn now to discuss the historical process; how do we learn about history? Let us begin by considering your own experiences.

Reflection 4

Think about the different ways in which you have learned about the past.

- What memories do you have of learning about the past at school?
- What ways do you learn about the past now? Are you interested in any particular aspect of the past?

It is interesting to reflect on your experience of learning about the past at school. Perhaps you remember learning history as deadly dull, with reams of notes to take and dates to learn; long essays to write. Or perhaps you remember the television programmes which you watched which tried to bring history alive to you. Maybe you worked on historical topics and developed investigations into homes through the ages, or transport or costume. Perhaps you can remember a particular vivid period when you drew pictures and made models of people associated with the past. There might be a mixture of all these different ways of learning about the past.

Similarly, as an adult you might learn about the past in a variety of ways. Television costume dramas provide a popular image of the past and television documentaries and reconstructions offer opportunities for everyone to experience the work of historians and archaeologists at first hand. The heritage industry is booming with the growth of theme parks, historical re-enactments, railway preservation societies and so on. Maybe you enjoy reading, not just weighty tomes but also the pulp fiction where the story is set in the past. Or maybe you are interested in your family history and search out relatives, or the locality where you live, browsing in the local record libraries and cutting clippings from local newspapers.

There is a tremendous variety in ways of learning about the past, but can we consider all these ways as good history? The History Working Group made the distinction between history, a critical study of the past, and the past. The past includes everything that has ever happened: a critical study, however, will involve some selection of material from the past. This selection will be dependent on the sort of questions which are raised about the past, and the information which is elicited to create a possible version of events. The following case study will enable you to reflect on this process and show how historical enquiries can be developed in the classroom.

Case Study I

A Year 6 class posed the question of what it was like for children living in Victorian times. They began to think about different aspects of children's life which they would like to find out about and compiled a list. Their list included homes, toys, school, clothes, food and leisure activities. Beside their list the children also noted what sources of information might help them to find out about these different aspects of everyday life. Sources of information such as: pictures and photographs, advertisements, buildings, scenes from TV and films, books, objects in a museum, stories and so on were identified.

Groups of children then began to research the different aspects of Victorian children's lives. As they researched, the class began to discover contrasting information about Victorian children. There was a great deal of difference between the lives of children from poor backgrounds, working in factories or on the streets, and the children of wealthier Victorians in their large houses with servants. A second question was added to the children's initial investigation; did all children enjoy the same way of life? As they returned to their investigations, the class was divided into different groups researching ways of life of either poor or wealthy children.

The investigations resulted in the children acquiring a great deal of information about Victorian times, which they shared with each other as different groups reported back on the various lifestyles which they had researched. The investigation might have stopped there, but the teacher wanted her class to look critically at what they had found out and to draw some conclusions. A final question was included: 'Did Victorian children have a good time?' This question offered the class the opportunity to organise some of the information which they had researched to make their own judgment about Victorian childhood. It also enabled the class to make some personal response to their investigations and make some connections between themselves, living in the twentieth century, and Victorian children. Children wrote down on separate cards, different information which would enable them to answer the question and arranged the cards in order of importance.

The class was then asked to write down their views using the cards to help them. The teacher supported some children to structure their writing, by providing a writing frame which gave them starting points for justifying their points of view.

> *I think children living in Victorian times had a good time because . . .*
> *They also . . .*
> *Finally, they also . . .*
> *However, not all Victorian children had a good time, because . . .*
> *They also . . .*
> *Finally they also . . .*

As you can see there are some good and bad points about Victorian children's lives. I would have liked/not liked to have lived in Victorian times because . . .

In this case study we can see how the teacher has led and supported her children through the process of historical enquiry, through providing an environment where children have been able to become involved in:

    raising questions;
    identifying sources of information;
    acquiring information;
    selecting and organising information;
    making judgments;
    communicating conclusions.

The historical detective

The work of the historian has often been compared to that of a detective. Both are involved in sifting through different sources of information, piecing information together, and trying to reach some conclusions. Like the detective, the historian is very dependent on sources of information, some of which may be incomplete or unreliable. And, like the detective, the historian uses these sources as evidence to create a version of what might have happened. You can explore the historian/detective role further in the following activity.

Enquiry task I

Investigating the contents of a school bag

Imagine that the contents of a child's school bag are tipped onto the floor. Inside the bag you can see a postcard; the green cross code; some tissues; orange peel; a book on sharks; some empty cassettes, music stickers; coloured pencils; a school pencil; 7 marbles; a glue stick; a pair of compasses; 25 pence; 1996 football cards; a burst balloon; a small green rubber band; a red ball; a hairbrush; an ink cartridge: a Kangol cap; salt and vinegar crisps; some A4 lined paper and some playing cards.
- Consider the different objects present in the bag.
- Why do you think they have been kept in the bag?
- What do the objects tell you about the owner of the bag?
- Does the bag provide any information about the values and culture of contemporary society?

Case Study 2

A group of Year 6 children were given the bag described in the enquiry task to look at. They listed the objects in the bag and speculated on their use and reasons for being there. The children were then asked to create a pen portrait of the owner. The portrait written by one of the children follows.

He had a postcard of Spain so he either went there or was given it. (It was not stamped.) Green cross codes are available at cubs, brownies, etc and schools. Tissues don't prove much but he might have had a cold. The orange peel and crisps show he definitely likes food. His hobbies are probably card games, because Squads need money and marbles so that explains the money and marbles. There is a lot of writing equipment, so he is definitely at school or university. An empty cassette case could have anything inside it, but the music stickers might be a favourite band so the cassette would probably be of that band. A burst balloon is probably from a party. A Kangol cap and a hair brush which means he likes his hair and he likes looking good.

The pen portrait outlined in the case study above reveals how Thomas used the objects in the bag to build up a picture of the owner. Firstly, he looked very closely at the items, noting in particular the postcard was not stamped and suggesting alternative views on how the owner might have acquired it. He then drew on different sources to build up his conclusions, for example, the orange peel and the crisps reveal the owner definitely likes food; all the writing equipment suggests he is at school or university. He appreciated how different items might relate to each other to provide a fuller picture of the owner; for example, the cassette case might be linked with the music stickers. Finally, he also demonstrated an awareness of the society and culture in which the owner was living: knowing that the Green Cross Code is available from Cubs, Brownies and schools and that balloons were often used at parties.

As Thomas was constructing his portrait, he was developing many of the skills which historians use as they piece together different sources of information about the past. Our knowledge about what happened in the past and past ways of life is dependent on the sources available. Sometimes there is little information available and historians have to piece together information from a variety of sources, as well as to make some imaginative guesses and fill in the gaps.

Thomas has also recognised the tentative nature of some of his conclusions; he employs words such as, *might*, *probably*, and *could have*, which suggests that he is aware that the items may be interpreted in other ways, or that more information is needed to validate his conclusions. Drawing children's attention to such speculative vocabulary is important, since it provides a useful means for them to generate their own hypotheses and to recognise that historical understanding is often incomplete. Fresh discoveries and sources of information may alter our original understandings.

The objects in the school bag had been selected at random. Many of the items could have been considered as rubbish and thrown away in the waste-paper basket. Yet this rubbish did provide many useful clues about the identity of the owner. Similarly, objects which often have little value at the time they were used can provide historians with very valuable information about past ways of life. For example, at Jorvik, the Viking settlement at York, rubbish tips have provided a great deal of information about different aspects of Viking life. However, the survival of such historical sources is often haphazard and accidental; much of it does not survive. Who for example would consider preserving a twentieth century school bag for historians in the future to analyse?

We have used the school bag as one example of how children can become involved in detective work and some of the key features of such an approach

Reflection 5

Return to your interpretation of the school bag and compare your findings with those of Thomas.
- Are they similar?
- How do you account for any differences which might arise?
- Imagine that you had to select six items from the school bag for an exhibition. Which six would you choose and why? Write a one sentence 'exhibition label', explaining the significance of the item.
- Ask a colleague to complete this activity and compare the different selections and labels which have been made.

have been identified. This investigative approach is not limited to artefacts, but can be developed through a range of historical sources, including pictures and photographs, maps and documents, oral testimony, buildings and sites, music and so on, which are listed within Key Element 4 in the history National Curriculum.

Interpretations of the different sources, however, will vary and we turn now to explore the variety of possible interpretations which are emphasised within Key Element 3 of the history National Curriculum.

Interpreting sources

As you undertake the above activity you will probably become increasingly aware that the selection of items which you have made is dependent on your values and the message you want to present in the exhibition. Your exhibition could illustrate the type of foods eaten by children at the end of the twentieth century, or how children used their leisure time. Alternatively, you might have selected your items to illustrate the technology available in the late twentieth century. Your selection and interpretation of sources will be dependent on the point of view which you want put forward.

In completing this activity, you are mirroring the work of historians whose interpretations from different sources will vary, depending on the viewpoint which they hold. At the beginning of this chapter, Peter described Guy Fawkes as a bad man who met his just desserts in his execution. However, we might question whether Guy Fawkes really was as bad as Peter describes. For the followers of James I and the Protestant settlement, Guy might appear as a criminal, but from the point of view of the Catholics, facing increasing persecution in the country, Guy could also be a hero.

As children develop their own interpretations they can also be encouraged to appreciate how and why others might hold different viewpoints. This can involve discussion of contemporary opinions as well as consideration of views held by people in the past. An important element in trying to understand the past involves the appreciation of other people's opinions and feelings. The story of Guy Fawkes is a powerful reminder that history is about people who actually lived, not fairy tale or imaginary people, but people who had their own points of view and values and who perhaps shared many emotions similar to those of our own. Peter's inclusion of the teddy reveals that he is beginning to recognise other people's emotions and reminds us too, that Guy Fawkes may well have been very scared as he waited in the cellar.

Developing a sense of empathy

Projecting oneself into the past and into other people's feelings and emotions is fraught with difficulties. We would question whether we can fully empathise with people living in the past; inevitably our own values remain with us and we tend to look at the past through spectacles with modern lenses. We can sit on the doorstep of the past, but not go through the open door. However, despite these difficulties, we can still try to experience past ways of life and gain some appreciation of people's feelings through imaginative and creative activities linked with drama and role play and from reading historical fiction.

Case Study 3

A Victorian laundry

A play area in a Year 1 classroom was adapted into a Victorian laundry. The teacher created a fireplace, with a mantlepiece and burning coals in the grate. She collected various washing equipment such as a scrubbing board, wash tub, dolly stick, washing tongs and flat iron and several items of clothing. There was discussion on how the items could be used and the children began to explore the laundry in their play. The laundry provided the children with the opportunity to experience at first hand an aspect of Victorian life, which would deepen their understanding of how the past is different from the present. One child commented, 'It's hard work doing this', as he scrubbed away on the scrubbing board. Another child became absorbed in the monotony of the ironing routine, moving the iron backwards and forwards from the hearth to the pile of clothes waiting to be ironed. As they scrubbed, swished the water in the wash tub and did the ironing, the children were given some insight into the laborious nature of the washing cycle, which could only be achieved by actually doing it themselves.

(Beardsley with Harnett, 1998)

The children involved in the role play were gaining first hand experience of what it would have been like to have lived at that time. There are many opportunities for older children too, to participate in the past through visits to museum reconstructions and historic sites, or creating historic environments in the school or classroom. These opportunities can be extended beyond dressing up, by presenting the children with particular problems and asking them to make some decisions about what course of action to take. In this way, children can be immersed further in the values and opinions of people who lived in the past (Littlefair, 1997; Fines and Nichol, 1997).

Children's awareness of different people's viewpoints can also be developed through historical fiction. A good story provides opportunities for children to identify with the feelings of different characters, to appreciate their motivation and their actions. Stories can also enable children to develop their understanding of complex ideas and situations; to come to terms with some of the 'uncomfortable' events of the past (Little and John, 1986).

Case Study 4

In 'When Hitler Stole Pink Rabbit', the treatment of the Jews in Nazi Germany is recounted through the eyes of a young Jewish girl who escaped with her family first to Switzerland and then to France. Her account provides a vivid picture of the Jewish persecution and how the lives of ordinary people were affected (Kerr, 1971). Year 6 children who were reading this story in class began to question why had this dreadful thing happened. What were the motives of the Nazis in harming this apparently very ordinary family? Several children became quite indignant: **'They (the Nazis) can't do that.' 'That's not fair.' 'Why did they pick on the Jews?' 'How did the Nazis get away with it? Why didn't someone stop them?'**

Such comments reveal the powerful impact a good story can have. They also remind us of the potential which history has in developing our consciousness of humanity and our awareness of our interdependence on each other. In 1905, the Handbook of Suggestions emphasised the importance of children knowing about their rights and responsibilities. As we argue further in Chapter 8, this still remains an important feature of history education.

Conclusion – looking to the future

Curriculum subjects are not set in tablets of stone, but are constantly evolving and changing in response to different ideologies of education. This chapter has sought to describe some of the dominant influences on the history curriculum during this century. Since the introduction of the National Curriculum, teaching and learning in history has considerably improved in primary schools, although there are still some concerns relating to assessment and planning for progression (OFSTED, 1993; OFSTED, 1995; Hamer, 1997). Such observations from HMI in the 1990s are a stark contrast to their criticisms of the history curriculum twenty years previously (DES, 1978). Moreover, there is much evidence which indicates that primary school teachers generally enjoy teaching history, although they have concerns about 'fitting everything in', and would like more flexibility and less prescription (QCA, 1998a; Harnett, 1998).

The National Curriculum, despite its revisions, has always been overloaded. In some respects this was to be expected from the structure of the different subject working groups planning the National Curriculum. There were few organising principles to draw the curriculum together and the establishment of separate subject groups for the curriculum led to a fragmented and piecemeal approach. Although the Dearing review (DFE, 1995) reduced the content of the National Curriculum, there are still difficulties in finding enough time to teach both the core and foundation subjects adequately.

Against this background, many teachers welcomed the statement from David Blunkett in January 1998, which urged teachers to concentrate on literacy and numeracy, together with RE and ICT (DfEE, 1998). However, there are also many legitimate concerns that the drive for standards in literacy and numeracy could have the effect of squeezing other subjects out of the curriculum, leaving children with very impoverished experiences.

Schools still have a statutory duty to provide a broad and balanced curriculum and ways in which this can be maintained have been outlined by the Qualifications and Curriculum Authority (QCA, 1998b). The suggestions for history describe further possible reductions or alterations which could be made to the curriculum, and individual schools will need to make their own decisions on how to manage and implement their history curriculum.

Some might be pessimistic about the future of history in primary schools, and in order to preserve it as a subject seek to emphasise history's close links with other subjects, particularly literacy. Texts to be used in the literacy hour can have an historic focus; for example Anglo-Saxon poems, diary accounts, advertisements, letters and so on. Learning history also does provide wonderful opportunities for developing important skills such as careful reading, comprehension, note-taking and writing analyses and structured accounts.

However, this chapter has also sought to describe the unique contribution which history can make to children's learning and in particular, children's abilities to interpret their world. History has an important role in fostering children's moral awareness and sense of personal identity. It helps children explore human relationships and the interdependence of different groups of people and societies upon each other. History extends children's experiences beyond the familiar, to distant places and far off times, and, through contrasting these different circumstances, can encourage children to reflect on contemporary society and current values.

History is central for children's development and we will need to remember its value and importance as the National Curriculum continues to evolve into the millennium years. If we reflect on how education can shape our future we might begin to question the sort of society which will be created through exposure to a narrow curriculum focusing on the 'basics', and we might find strong justification for the place of history in our primary schools.

References

BEARDSLEY, G. with HARNETT, P. (1998) *Exploring Play in the Primary School*, London: Fulton.

BOARD OF EDUCATION (1905) *Handbook of Suggestions for the Consideration of Teachers and Others Concerned in the Work of Public Elementary Schools*, London: HMSO.

BOARD OF EDUCATION (1927) *Handbook of Suggestions for Teachers*, London: HMSO.

BOARD OF EDUCATION (1931) *Report of the Board of Education Consultative Committee on the Primary School*, London: HMSO (Hadow Report).

BOARD OF EDUCATION (1937) *Handbook of Suggestions for Teachers*, London: HMSO.

DES (1967) *Children and their Primary Schools*, London: HMSO (Plowden Report).

DES (1978) *Primary Education in England. A Survey by HMI*, London: HMSO.

DES (1985) *History in the Primary and Secondary Years. An HMI View*, London: HMSO.

DES (1988) *History from 5–16. Curriculum Matters 11*, London: HMSO.

DES (1990) *National Curriculum History Working Group. Final Report*, London: HMSO.

DFE (1995) *Key Stages 1 and 2 of the National Curriculum*, London: HMSO.

DfEE (1998) *News. Blunkett Strengthens Curriculum Focus on the Basics*, 13.1.98, Press Release.

FINES, J. and NICHOL, J. (1997) *Teaching Primary History*, Oxford: Heinemann.

HAMER, J. (1997) 'History in the primary years', *Primary History*, November, pp. 13–14.

HARNETT, P. (1998) 'Primary school teachers' perceptions of the history curriculum', Paper presented at the *Standing Conference of History Teacher Educators in the United Kingdom*, Swansea University: July 1998.

KERR, J. (1971) *When Hitler Stole Pink Rabbit*, London: Collins.

LITTLE, V. and JOHN, T. (1986) 'Historical fiction in the classroom', *Teaching of History Series, Number 59*, London: Historical Association.

LITTLEFAIR, S. (1997) 'The Young National Trust Theatre', *Primary History*, June 1977, pp. 13–14.

MINISTRY OF EDUCATION (1959) *Primary Education: Suggestions for the Consideration of Teachers and Others concerned with the Work of Primary Schools*, London: HMSO.

OFSTED (1993) *History Key Stages 1, 2 and 3: First Year 1991–92*, London: HMSO.

OFSTED (1995) *History: A review of Inspection Findings 1993/94*, London: HMSO.

QCA (1998a) *Developing the School Curriculum*. Advice to the Secretary of State on the broad nature and scope of the review of the National Curriculum, London: QCA.

QCA (1998b) *Maintaining Breadth and Balance*, London: QCA.

SCHOOLS COUNCIL (1976) *History 13–16 Project, A New Look at History*, Edinburgh: Holmes McDougall.

Further reading

HUSBANDS, C. (1996) *What is History Teaching?* Buckingham: Open University Press.
In this book Husbands explores the ideas behind the teaching of history in school. He analyses different approaches to learning history with classroom examples and reference to research in history education. The book provides plenty of material for you to reflect on and to develop your own ideas about teaching history.

FINES, J. and NICHOL, J. (1997) *Teaching Primary History*, Oxford: Heinemann.
Teaching Primary History describes the work of the Nuffield Primary History Project. Fines and Nichol provide a clear rationale for teaching history in the primary school. They include many practical examples of classroom activities and a very wide range of approaches to teaching history in the classroom.

COOPER, H. (1995) *History in the Early Years*, London: Routledge.
This very useful book for early years teachers explains how young children's views and understanding of the past can be developed. Cooper draws on a range of research relating to children's conceptual development and provides an interesting variety of case study material. The book also provides a useful section on curriculum planning in the early years.

Chapter 4

Looking afresh at geography

Alison Bailey and Don Kimber

Introduction

Case Study 1

A student teacher, Nick Carter, on going in to a Year 3 class for the first time, was asked by the form teacher to work with a group of six children. This in itself was not an unusual request but within seconds it became apparent that these children had been selected for a special reason. These six children (three boys, three girls) all had behavioural and/or educational problems and were all on the Special Educational Needs register. The teacher found them challenging and in her words, 'impossible to teach'. Nick noted that they lacked basic literacy skills and more fundamentally, a belief that they could achieve anything. Nick's task was to teach them geography and he was determined to succeed. The children informed him that they wouldn't work if asked to write anything. Fortunately, Nick valued these children and wanted them to achieve something. He devised a series of lessons centred on the problem of litter in the school grounds. The intentions were to develop the pupils' awareness of the problem of litter and to foster an appreciation of their environment and to encourage them to institute positive change. The children were able to make observations, record by using a camera and through field sketches.

The pupils were asked to select features around the school grounds and to tell Nick why they had chosen them. The pupils in turn took photographs of their features and Nick wrote down the reasons for their choice. For example, a broken fence was recorded because it looked ugly. Once the children realised Nick meant his promise that they could learn geography without having to write, their enthusiasm grew.

They progressed to making field sketches. Pupil B, for example, had chosen a site that he found distasteful, namely the large bins next to the main hall. He was reluctant to record any work on paper, reasoning that, 'I can't draw and my picture will be rubbish'. Nick discussed with him the problem of proving how bad it was to the others in the group, even though, ideally, his word should be proof enough. B created a sketch that illustrated clearly two of the large bins tipped on their sides with the unpleasant contents in full view. His labelling recorded what he observed in the bins but also noted the smell. This pupil demonstrated some useful geographical skills. He could be seen to be developing the ability to record what he saw, without cluttering the picture with unnecessary detail. Each of the items, which concerned him, were clearly annotated to remind him of his impressions and feelings.

By the next lesson, Nick had developed the photographs and had them photocopied. He asked the children how they could sort them. After some discussion, it was agreed that they could have two columns, one headed by a fist with a 'thumbs up' signal, the other headed by a 'thumbs down' signal. Two of the children drew the fists, which were then cut out and stuck onto a large piece of paper. Pictures of features that the children liked or thought looked attractive (for example, a wooded area) were placed in the first column while those which the children thought spoiled the look of the school grounds (for example, the broken fence, litter) were stuck in the second column.

These six children had experienced a variety of social, personal, emotional and behavioural difficulties, which had a direct effect on their learning and on their relationships with other members of their class. Through this environmental study some positive effects on the children's 'sociability' were observed. They worked together as a group, discussing, collaborating, planning and presenting, growing in self-esteem. At this stage Nick persuaded the pupils that the rest of the class would be interested to know what they had been learning in geography and encouraged his six pupils to present their findings to the class. Indeed, the class had been curious as to what this group had been doing and were attentive throughout the presentation. In turn, each of the six pupils in Nick's group stood up and talked about what she/he had noticed, drawn, photographed and recorded. They were able to display their poster and talk through their interpretation of the school environment. Pupil Y in particular, discussed what she liked and what she did not like. She engaged in discussion with several members of the class, asking them what they liked about her pictures and explaining the difficulty she had in deciding what to photograph and how to order her preferences accurately.

Confidence was boosted and further work on environmental geography grew from this. The group asked to meet the head teacher to ask for help in establishing 'Environmental Agents' and decided to talk to each class in the school in order to promote a tidier environment. A plan for a pond and a nature design was presented to the head teacher and submitted to a local firm who have since promised the money to make it possible. These six children have grown in confidence and in self-esteem, as well as moving from a position of ridicule in the class to one of respect. Indeed, there were times during the project when the children chose to write, for example on their plan, on their sketches, and their oral communication skills progressed significantly too. The rise in self-belief which developed, as peers and teachers became involved in the project, was considerable. Nick noted in particular some comments made by pupil B when discussing the project with Year 6. A member of the class asked what was the point of clearing up the litter when the pupils in the senior school next door dropped more rubbish the next day. Pupil B replied, 'If we clean it up perhaps they will see that we like our school and don't like mess'. When asked what happens if more litter gets dropped, B replied, 'It makes you feel good knowing you're doing something good and if we all did it we would all feel good'.

This is just one example of a series of lessons showing that geography provides opportunities for all children. There are many ways into geography without having to rely on basic literacy skills. Through observation, using pictures, artefacts or investigations in the local area, children can be introduced to many of its themes. Indeed, literacy skills can be encouraged and developed through geography but should not form a barrier to a basic entitlement.

We all act as geographers in many ways most days, if not every day. We use geographical concepts and respond in a geographical way even if it is simply glancing out of the window and grabbing an umbrella before leaving the house. Similarly, if you grow tomatoes outside in your garden you will know the value of planting them against a south-facing wall.

Campsite game

Let us take this a stage further. Imagine you are going on a camping holiday abroad. You are asked to choose where you would like to locate your tent, and all you have to go on is a map or plan of the campsite. (See Figure 4.1.)

Where would you place your tent? Choose the field and put a triangle for location.

Campsite

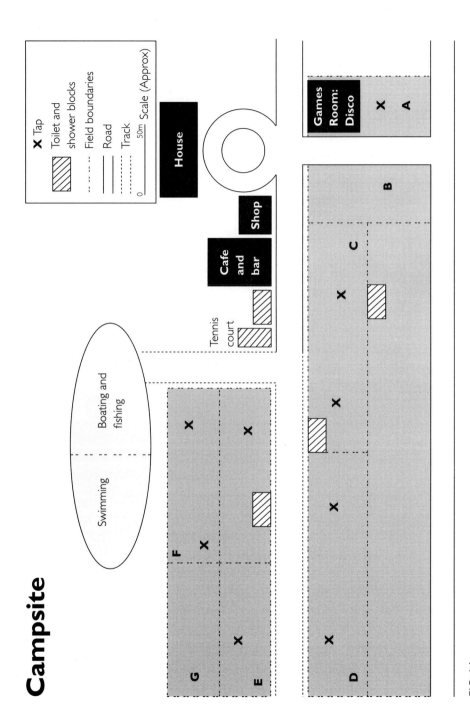

FIG 4.1
Campsite plan

1 What factors influenced your thoughts?
2 What other things would you like to know about this campsite in choosing where to camp?
3 What are other things generally would you like to know about the site?

This activity has been considered by many students. There are typical responses to the three questions from the students. Their suggestions usually can be grouped as follows:

- Locational or spatial factors: 'near to the tennis courts', 'handy to the shop', 'away from the discos or camp site entrance'.
- Physical factors: 'Does the ground slope?' 'Is it stony?' 'What is the weather like?' 'Is there shade from the sun?' 'What direction is the sun?'
- Social or human factors: 'Are children encouraged on site?' 'Are dogs allowed?' 'When does the disco close down?' 'Is food expensive at the shop?' 'How crowded do they allow the site to get?'
- Other more general points might be: 'What is the countryside around like?' 'Is it attractive scenery?' 'Are there shops and other facilities nearby or easy to get to?'

This simple campsite 'game' illustrates how, without being professional geographers, we all readily think about basic geographical questions. Such questions are about:

Location: Where do we put things? How far/near are we from/to particular people or places?

The physical environment: What are characteristics of the weather, or slope of the terrain, and how might they affect our activities?

Human features: People, services, and amenities, which influence our thoughts, feelings, activities and responses.

Places: What gives them their character?

Each of these factors is part of geography. We have tried to establish that as adults we are engaged in thinking about and making decisions which relate to location; to people and place; and to the environment. We can also recognise that there is often some overlap between these elements. This is equally applicable to the child on entry to school. Bale (1987, p. 62) recognises this, stating that 'All children arrive at school with their own little "private geographies" or worlds inside their heads'. Catling (1987a, p. 19) makes the same point when he suggests 'no child in reality comes to school who is not already a geographer'.

Enquiry task 1

Geography on your own doorstep

Take a walk around your 'block' – where you live, or your school grounds and locality. As you go draw a very simple sketch map – it might be a simple line of the route. As you walk, jot down what opportunities there are for raising geographical questions. You may consider including some of the following points.

1 Making a sketch map to show the location of features which interest you: places of work, pubs, busy/quiet points, interesting ornaments. (location and mapping)
2 The style and age of houses: what do these tell you about the area? Are there more pedestrians than cars? Evidence of different types of jobs or work people do – shops, garages, nurseries, recently installed windows? Clues which tell you about the age and affluence of residents? (human geography)
3 Does the ground slope? if so, how much? in what direction? is there any evidence of water movement over the surface? Can you see the underlying rock? What is the vegetation like? (physical geography)
4 What impact do cars have on the environment? Is there any staining on the front of buildings? Have people in your opinion spoiled or improved the environment in any way? (environmental geography)

Use your observations to suggest further ways to support children's learning in geography.

You will be aware that geography, like other subjects, can be broken down into a number of key areas. In the rest of the chapter, we consider in turn each of a number of discrete elements which we consider constitute the subject 'geography'. These are maps and mapwork, a sense of place, the geography of the physical environment, the geography of the human and social environment and environmental geography.

Maps and mapwork

We can all recognise locational patterns on a day to day basis. In an unfamiliar kitchen, for example, you would almost certainly be able to find everyday cutlery, crockery and the kettle close at hand. Larger serving dishes used less frequently, are likely to be stored further away, perhaps on higher shelves or at the back of cupboards. On a larger scale, on entering a supermarket for the first time you would anticipate certain patterns of location: shopping baskets to be located near the entrance; freezer compartments are likely to be located towards the rear of the shop; and packets of sweets at the checkouts.

The reasons for these locations are relatively obvious. Large freezer stores will be sited behind the retailing part of the operation where deliveries are received. You may like to involve children in mapping a supermarket or to develop links with Design Technology in designing an efficiently laid out supermarket.

Similarly, if we look at the layout of a school, or a town, the location and number of facilities and services will relate to the needs of people and the access they have to them. Some locations will be more central while others will be quieter and more peripheral.

How can children use maps?

Enquiry task 2

Make a list of all the maps you have seen or used during the last three days.

You may have included some of the following: 'you are here' type plans for finding your way around a hospital, A–Z map, seating plan (theatre, football stadia), topological maps (bus routes, London Underground) or television weather maps.

If you think back to the maps you have listed above, consider:
- Was a key necessary?
- Was the map to scale and was this important?
- Did the map give you enough information for your purposes? If not, what else should have been included?
- What range of features was provided on the maps? For example, did the plan of the theatre/football stadium only show seating in relation to the stage/field? Would it be useful to show other facilities such as bar, loos etc?

Children might encounter some of those already listed but might be more familiar with 'the village with three corners' map, play mats or models of toy farms or Shepard's picture of Pooh's 'Hundred Acre Wood'. Although as adults we expect maps to have a key, scale and to use symbols, we would not deny that the above are all maps. Indeed you can introduce children to some valuable map concepts through the use of play mats.

It is important to remember that maps have been made for different purposes. The cartographer will have decided what to include or to exclude. We would not choose a 1:25000 Ordnance Survey Explorer map for finding the best bus route within our local city. Ordnance Survey Pathfinder and Explorer maps, for example, are too complex for immediate use by primary children. You as a teacher need to develop skills to select information to simplify maps so that children can interpret and use them more easily.

Mapping skills should be developed progressively throughout the primary school. Some schools keep portfolios of mapwork completed by each year group which illustrates the developing skills. These include, for example, increasing sophistication of using symbols (using own symbols on an imaginary map at Level 1, through to the use of conventional Ordnance Survey symbols by Level 5); progression in location beginning with simple directions such as up and down or left and right through the use of compass points, and letter-number coordinates through to six figure grid references. Examples with respect to distance include beginning with using relative vocabulary such as bigger/smaller, nearer/further, then drawing objects on a table to scale using squared paper. This can be taken through to measuring straight line distance on a plan and then on smaller scale maps. For map use, a beginning can be made by getting children to talk about picture maps which leads to following a route on a plan, for example, round the school grounds, then on to the use of large scale maps of the locality and eventually progressing to the use of small scale Ordnance Survey maps. This progression through the key skills of mapping can be seen more fully in Catling, (1987b) and in Foley and Janikoun, (1996, p. 83).

The following case study illustrates how junior school children can work alongside each other to develop a range of skills in mapping. As you read it consider also how they engage in field work, local history and develop values and social skills.

Case Study 2

This example is from a small village school, Middlezoy in Somerset, in which the 21 7–11 year olds (Key Stage 2 children) are all in one class. The school serves a community predominantly involved in farming but with an increasing number of inhabitants who commute to larger towns. Sue Carter, a final year student teacher, planned a locality study of the village, using it as an opportunity to teach map work and local history involving the children in some fieldwork experience. Sue aimed to retain the 'whole class' ethos which was evident in the school by having similar intentions for each activity for all children, while at the same time catering for the needs of the wide range of abilities present, differentiating tasks in a variety of ways.

The activities were planned to last four weeks and involved looking at a range of maps from tithe maps, through Ordnance Survey maps of 1886, 1902 and 1962, to modern maps, encouraging children to design keys and to use their own methods to show changes. Class discussions about changes in the village over the years took place. The nearby town of Bridgwater was compared to the village. One afternoon, in a planned field work session the children walked round the central area of the village, observing and recording land use and making notes about the ages of the buildings. The lower-attaining children recorded their observations on a pre-planned tally chart with appropriate headings about functions of buildings, others recorded onto a map outline, while a few of the more able pupils were encouraged to draw their own sketch map.

Children concluded this location study working in mixed ability groups dealing with the data they had collected. A village brochure was produced, census data researched (through ICT), results presented, graphs constructed and conclusions drawn. In addition, each child's home was marked on a large-scale map of the locality, allowing them to identify closely with the study area.

Through discussion, children of all ages and abilities were able to contribute, each having first hand knowledge of the village. Children were able to express likes, dislikes and changes they would like to see and were encouraged to respect the opinion of others. During the field work excursion, the teacher was warmed by cooperation shown between pupils. A high-attaining Year 6 boy was particularly thoughtful and patient when helping a Year 3 girl who was having difficulty following the route on her map. The boy suggested turning the map to the direction they were walking after pointing out a landmark which she was able to recognise. Not only does this demonstrate humanity at its best, but also that the boy had clearly mastered the concept of orientation sufficiently well to be able to help another child.

In drawing conclusions, value judgments inevitably emerged in relation to the land use. For example, some children commented that they felt there were too many houses while another did not like a modern extension to an old building.

You may appreciate the opportunities in this sequence of activities for developing the social, moral, spiritual and cultural values central to the humanities. The different groupings for each task clearly made differing demands on individual behaviour. Such a study also provides children with a greater understanding of their own local heritage or traditions.

The pictorial or graphic nature of maps can help younger children to appreciate the topic of study. This can underpin the development of social skills when children of differing ages and abilities are encouraged to work together.

It can be seen then, that with careful planning, and, in this case a stimulus provided by a walk in the local area, that mapping skills can be developed in conjunction with other parts of the geography curriculum. Skills are an integral part of our subject but taught in isolation their purpose can be lost. Having a need to display information in map form can lead to children developing their own symbols and a key, as was the case in Sue's class.

Stories, such as 'Little Red Riding Hood' or 'Katie Morag Delivers the Mail' can be used effectively as a stimulus for mapwork with infants. You will probably be aware of other mapping activities such as using aerial photographs, placing objects in a shoebox, mapping the classroom.

Above all, children enjoy working with maps of their local area. A map which you have drawn, perhaps using a felt tip pen on a large sheet of paper, on which children mark their homes can be of particular interest. Questions about journeys from home to school can be raised, including questions of direction and distance. Questions can also be developed about amenities and facilities for different people in the community. Where are they? Who uses them? Are there other facilities which should be provided to benefit others – a pedestrian crossing, a seat by the park, a nursery? Where would they best be located? Questions like these also give the chance for children to clarify their values.

Such a mapping activity can be developed further and promote learning in other subjects. Literacy is readily involved in many ways in using map information. Literacy is supported by the graphicacy of the map itself which, as a type of picture, is a helpful aid to many children. Science can be fostered by developing investigations about materials; history might involve comparing old and new maps to see examples of change and continuity. There will also be starting points for art and design technology in looking at the local area.

A sense of place

Local and distant places

Enquiry task 3

What sort of place do you live in? How do we learn about people in other places? What do we know and understand about places?

1 Places: if you had the choice of living in, working in, or holidaying in one of the following places, which would you choose? Newcastle, Blackburn, Truro, Margate, Birmingham.
   - Rank them in order of preference.
   - Why have you put them in this order? Is your choice based on first hand knowledge of each place? If not, what was the source of knowledge which influenced your perception of these places? If a friend of yours ranked them in the reverse order to you, suggest reasons which you think might account for this.
2 Select a place you know well – a local main road, a park, a shopping centre.
   - Respond to these questions about place:
     where is this place?
     what is it like?
     why is it like this?
     how is it changing?
     how is it connected to other places?
     how does it feel to be in this place?

We all have some knowledge and understanding of places. This will be highly coloured by our experiences, our likes and dislikes. Children come to school with knowledge and ideas about places. These can be real or imaginary places, those known first hand or those known through stories, television, or pictures. Sue, working with her KS2 class in Middlezoy, observed that children who had lived in the village all their lives had limited knowledge about places in the wider world. On the other hand, these children could name almost every inhabitant of the village and could see the part played by each person as a member of the community. It is important not to under-value this kind of knowledge.

Teaching and learning about place is fundamental in geography. It is essential for children to develop an understanding of the world and of their place in the world. This helps to promote knowledge of self. It also provides a platform for developing understanding and relationships with others in the wider world. Ideas of place underpin key geographical themes, such as mapping and location, and relationships between people and the environment.

Case Study 3

Annette Ball, a fourth year student teacher, worked closely with a Year 3 class as they studied a contrasting locality in the UK. Chepstow, a town with an historical site, was chosen as a contrast to their home locality of Yate, which comprises several large housing estates.

Having located Chepstow on an appropriate map and noting its distance and direction from Yate, the children worked in small groups to look at a range of secondary data in order to answer the key question, 'What is Chepstow like?' Annette noted that one or two pupils found it difficult to share resources and ideas with a partner, but felt that some social skills, as well as geographical skills, were enhanced.

Next the children devised a questionnaire which would be used on the field visit to find out about the people and the town of Chepstow. There was considerable discussion about the suitability of some of the questions for the purpose and about which ones would be the most useful. Questions such as, 'Do you have a dog?' or 'What day is your birthday on?' were thought interesting by the children but not very useful for this study, while questions such as, 'Do you work in the town?', 'What kind of shops are there?' or 'How long are you here for?' were recognised as being more useful for finding out about the place.

As well as developing their geographical skills and thinking about functions of place, the children were clearly developing their English skills. As Foley and Janikoun (1996, p. 24) note, teaching aspects of English and geography together can not only save time but 'provide a more meaningful learning context for children'. The children were not only writing but using and developing their oracy skills through discussion and listening to the points of view of others. In terms of social skills, Annette made sure that everyone's questions were considered and thought worthwhile, even though they could not all be incorporated in the questionnaire.

The field visit to Chepstow followed, allowing the children to observe first hand and to observe with all their senses. They were able to get a feel for the landscape by walking up to the castle which 'made their legs ache', see and touch the sandbags outside the shops and houses on the flat land near the river and to wonder what it would be like when it flooded. They discovered the town's potential for tourism and enjoyed an almost bird's eye view of the River Wye from the castle. The children were asked to sketch the River Wye, to observe carefully and identify key river characteristics. This was to serve as a starting point for learning about rivers later in the term. They played in the park and bought something from the shops, as well as speaking to inhabitants when using the questionnaire.

Follow-up work in the classroom involved handling the questionnaire data, inputting it into a computer program, creating and printing out graphs and charts. (See also Chapter 9.) The children all contributed to making a large three-dimensional map of the town centre of Chepstow, so that they could understand that a real place can be represented by a map. Much geographical discussion about the landscape and the human geography of the town took place during the construction of this map. For example, the children noted where the shopping, industrial and residential areas are, that the town is built on a hill, that the river meanders and that the river water is brown. They discussed why the castle was built by the river on a hill. They also asked questions about Chepstow, which offered the teacher the opportunity to reinforce their learning.

You will note from the case study that the children are learning about place in geography through a range of activities, including enquiry and a field visit. Their understanding of place is enhanced and many cross-curricular skills are developed. In school there are many ways of developing children's understanding of places. The school locality is an obvious starting point. Approaches have been suggested in the examples of work with children here, but you can see others in Chapter 6 on field work. Building up a set of photographs of the school locality is a very useful resource. Very soon you will be using the digital camera as an everyday piece of equipment in the primary school.

It can be especially valuable for a school or class to have direct links with children in another school. This might be within visiting distance or very much further away. In Chapter 8 you will see work on the Avon International Education links. By exchanging pictures, photographs, and

Reflection 1

Listen to a TV news programme.

- List the places named. How many are in Britain? How many in the wider world? Keep a tally by continent.

- How many places are new to you?

- If you had to pay a visit for a week to one of those places, which one would you least like to visit? What are the reasons for this? What do these reasons suggest about our preferences and values?

writing about their own place, children gain a greater appreciation of where they are, and what makes their place tick. Exchanging letters and sending drawings, stories, descriptions of their environment, photographs, accounts of their school day, and cartoons through the post can enrich children's learning in literacy as well as in geography. In some schools, children use e-mail or a modem.

People and place in the wider world

Reflection 1 underlines the importance of knowing about places and of where they are. It is essential that primary children build up a basic knowledge of the world map including continents, oceans, many countries and major cities. This basic knowledge underpins their ability to act as informed and responsible citizens. It is also important that they have a basic grasp of major climatic differences throughout the world, perhaps centering on the rainforests, hot deserts, temperate zones and polar climates. Without being unnecessarily deterministic, climate does indeed place certain constraints upon, and offer advantages to, different types of human activity.

There is a debate about the value to children of learning about places which are accessible and of which they can have first hand experience versus distant places in the wider world. In the early part of the twentieth century there was a strong emphasis in geography on the rote learning of place, the 'Capes and Bays' style of geography. In more recent times there has been more emphasis on using first hand experiences involving field work, often focusing on the immediate locality. We suggest it is important to keep a balance between these two approaches.

You may wish to question what we are wanting children to learn when they study people and distant places. As always it is essential to be clear about the learning intentions for children. Presumably there will be a mix of some *knowledge* (such as factual knowledge of place names, or of where certain countries are located), developing the understanding of selected *concepts* or ideas (for example, this place is very busy because there are many ships being unloaded at the port, or the place has changed recently because of a new airport, or the place is attractive because there is much natural vegetation), taking the chance to enhance *skills* (such as using atlases or research skills), and of clarifying *values and attitudes* (for example, how children feel toward living in a place, or concerns about environmental impacts upon people's ways of life, or responses to people living in the wider world where there are obvious differences, as well as similarities in their daily lives).

Geography and the study of people and places in the wider world has a vital role to play in reducing bias against people of different cultures and backgrounds, and the practice of stereotyping those groups of people we see as 'other' to us. Wiegand (1993, p. 4). argues for the early teaching of distant places for 'international understanding'.

Case Study 4

Jessica Phillips, a fourth year trainee teacher, worked with Year 2 children to investigate their images and perceptions of countries. Initially she asked children to name any countries they could. The table shows their responses:

Name of 'country'	No. of children
Menorca	6
UK holiday destinations	6
Disneyland	5
London	2
Euro Disney	2
Europe	2
Paris	2
Hawaii	1

As her investigation continued through a series of tasks, she concluded that children do have knowledge of distant places through different experiences, through their own travel or that of a friend or relative and through media, mainly books and television. Secondly, their known world beyond England consisted mainly of Australia, France, Africa, America and Spain. Children were unclear about the definition of a country, for example, Disneyland was mentioned as a country. Also children's images of Africa tended to be stereotypical and often negative.

This has serious implications. We hope that by the end of their schooldays children will be well-informed so that they can engage in ideas such as 'justice for developing countries'. There are problems if children have no understanding of what a country is. Primary geography must start to deal with this; it is one of the basic things children need to know.

In the classroom, children can get involved in examining how people and different countries are portrayed in newspapers. They can be helped to develop a critical approach towards the coverage of people, events, and of countries. Sports pages of popular papers unfortunately too often provide examples for children of stereotypes and of racist vocabulary, using words like 'krauts' or 'frogs' to belittle others and to throw up boundaries between 'us' and 'them'. Discussion of adjectives used in writing about people or groups of people, and the way in which they are discussed, can be a useful exercise in literacy, as well as aiming to reduce prejudice. Children with their sense of 'what isn't fair' are able to see through and reject these anti-human tendencies in the media when sensitively supported by their teachers to look at what the paper says, and how it is saying it.

Many schools successfully make use of 'teaching packs' to help children develop knowledge, and indeed an empathy, with people living in a distant locality. These commercial packs are available from a variety of sources, such as the Geographical Association, Action Aid, Christian Aid and Save the Children. The packs commonly focus upon a particular community, and provide background materials to help children sense what it is like to live in a particular place and to be part of the local community.

You might also have the chance on your travels to collect a range of resources which could sustain children in studying people in a locality.

Physical geography

It is important that you have an overview of the school curriculum and have an understanding of how topics such as soil and weather overlap between science and geography. In physical geography there is often the scope for enquiry which in turn can involve the collection, recording and processing of quantitative data. The opportunities for children developing skills in ICT are extensive, and are dealt with in Chapter 9.

Simple weather observations have a long-standing tradition in the infant classrom. Weather conditions around the school provide many opportunities for fruitful investigation. Progression of skills in numeracy and ICT arise from the use of instruments such as thermometers, rain gauges and anemometers. The importance of weather and climate studies in schools is examined in detail in Chapter 10 where the concept of sustainablitiy is explored.

Soil is another of those topics which suffers from the artificial boundaries imposed by the National Curriculum. Whether in science or geography, soil is not just small particles of broken rock. It is a much more valuable and complex asset containing life and being life-giving. It is a vital resource which has taken centuries to develop and it can be blown or washed away in minutes if exposed through greed or mismanagement.

We are focusing on rivers in this section on physical geography. Children enjoy working with water and if streams are not readily accessible to your school then simple activities with running water can be carried out in the playground.

When considering rivers in geography it is helpful to see them as part of the water cycle on the surface of the land. A few basic facts can be established, for example, that most rivers flow into the sea returning the water from the land to the sea and then evaporation, condensation, precipitation continue. This water cycle has obvious links with the science curriculum and with the topic of weather. There are four main agents of erosion: wind erosion (mainly in deserts), ice (glaciers), the sea (in coastal environments), and rivers. Rivers provide the most likely vehicle for developing a knowledge and understanding of erosion, transportation and deposition.

Reflection 2

On a field visit to a stream, a 7 year old child asked his teacher. 'Why is there water in this river, but when I make a river on the beach at the seaside the water all drains away?'

- Consider how you might answer this question.
- Would you need to use specialist vocabulary such as infiltration, water table, surface runoff?
- Could you give a simple answer?
- Would an experiment be an easier way to explain?

Enquiry task 4

Experiment with mixing soil and water in a jar in your classroom. Look at what happens when you allow the mixture to settle.

Experiment out of doors with water soaking away in different locations such as the flower bed, the playing field and the gateway of a field. Does the water 'drain' away (infiltrate) more quickly in some places than in others? If so, why?

Visit a local river.
- What observations can you make which suggest that the processes of erosion, transport and deposition are at work in the river?
- What are the ways in which people's activities are affected by the river?
- What are the ways in which people make use of the river?

The concept of energy in the river and a river's ability to 'carry' a load are introduced through the jar activity. Larger particles will sink to the bottom more quickly than smaller particles, illustrating that the river can more easily transport smaller sediments. Simple infiltration experiments can be valuable in developing understanding of what might happen to rainwater when falling on different surfaces. It is important also to encourage children to view rivers as a resource which need to be looked after. Knowledge of the terminology associated with rivers (for example, source, banks, tributary, meander, mouth) can be introduced through the use of books, maps, sketches and photographs.

Flood events, such as the bursting of the river Severn's banks near Gloucester in April 1998, may give children a sense of wonder and encourage fruitful enquiry. Under such conditions the river's energy and its ability to transport and erode are increased, often with dramatic changes to the landscape.

Human and social geography

As with physical geography, human geography further breaks down into various themes or topics including settlement, economic geography and journeys. Many children will appreciate that they live in a settlement which is a village, town or part of a city. They may also be aware of travelling to bigger towns or centres for major purchases. They will not necessarily have made the leap from this to the geographical concept of the settlement hierarchy. You as the teacher have an important role in developing children's understanding of these patterns.

Settlements can vary in size of population. Larger settlements will usually offer more services and functions. Normally, larger settlements will have more specialised services, will be busier, and serve people (often called consumers these days) who live in smaller settlements. Some settlements have an obvious historical core and function, such as Durham is a cathedral city with a defensive site on a river bend.

The study of settlements provides opportunities for children to think about journeys and social questions, such as the availability of work, and the provision of local amenities (hospitals, schools, playgrounds, shops) within the community. Questions of environmental quality are of great interest to children, and are readily introduced when there is discussion of plans for local developments, such as change of function of major buildings, altering roads, traffic pollution or even noise from local clubs and discos. All these considerations have a strong bearing upon questions of sustainability and the quality of people's lives and upon those values we identify as vital for the community at large. Conflicting messages are conveyed, however, with the growth in out-of-town shopping centres which rely heavily upon car use, whilst the government seeks to reduce our dependency on the motorcar.

Enquiry task 5

Keep a log of your journeys for a week.

What journeys or trips do you make from home – daily? regularly every week or two? occasionally, every now and then? annually? rarely?
- Why do we travel or move?
- Which trips are essential? and which non-essential?

How might we categorise the journeys we make? (Shopping, recreational, economic or work-related, family, social or cultural?

How do these overlap?

How do we travel: by foot, bike, car, bus, train, 'plane?

Our movements or journeys are affected by what we perceive as the fraction of distance between where we are and a possible destination. We can measure distance between places not only in terms of the actual physical distance, but also in terms of the time involved, financial cost, and the comfort or convenience factor. We often unconsciously weigh up the alternative means of travelling influenced by these factors. We might also think of environmental costs as part of the equation.

In addition, studies of trade and how goods are moved from one country to another do not only involve economic questions. Issues and values are raised when linked, for example, to questions of fair trade and problems of exploitation of workers or young children who are involved in the production of goods. Some of these goods we buy as part of our own shopping without being fully aware of the working conditions of those who produce them. Cafod, Oxfam, Christian Aid and Save the Children are among non-governmental organizations that provide teaching materials to promote a fuller understanding of global interdependence.

The responsible management of resources, questions of stewardship and of sustainability are all central to geography and lie within the realm of environmental geography.

Environmental geography

In considering environmental geography you will realise that many aspects of this part of geography have already been touched on. Learning about our environment is a central theme in geography. In doing so, we do not just focus upon problems such as pollution or the mis-management of resources, although these are an important part of this area of geography. One of the strongest arguments for including geography in the primary curriculum is that it provides a natural background for an informed examination of environmental problems. This theme is developed further in Chapters 10 and 11 when it is considered whether an understanding of many environmental issues is beyond children of primary age. At the same time, we make the point that a proper grounding in the 'basics' geography at primary school is the foundation for later work in confronting problems and controversies of an environmental nature.

Decision making needs to have a solid base of factual detail and understanding. Also decision makers need to be appreciative of opposing points of view. This view is reflected by Rawlings (1996) who identifies 'the potential of geography to promote a deep understanding of the state of the environment, to encourage critical reflection about its future and to develop personal commitment and responsibility for its maintenance'. This is only achieved, however, after a number of years of study, and we should not expect too much too soon of primary children with regard to environmental 'problems'.

Environmental geography, as stated above, is broader than questions of environmental disturbance or upset. Like other subjects, such as history and science, the focus can vary. It can be teaching *about* the environment, teaching *through* the environment (field work and visits) and teaching *for* the environment (ecological concern and maintaining 'balance of nature'). The work on Chew Valley Lake and Reservoir which follows, shows children learning *about* features and processes of the environment, for example about rivers, farms and change of land use; it also involves developing concerns *for* the environment. In this instance, it did not involve teaching *through* the environment by going on a visit.

We are all aware of car pollution, rainforest damage, over-fishing, mining scars, exploitation of third world resources and others which you may have identified above. We should not forget, however, that we in the more economically developed countries might learn a great deal from traditional societies and their values. These societies value the Earth as the source of their prosperity and are considered wise enough by some in the West not to take for granted these irreplaceable resources. There are many examples where people have co-existed in harmony with their environment. Rainforest peoples who have practised slash and burn, aboriginal tribes, and the Masai of East Africa before external pressures challenged their nomadic lifestyle are just some such examples. Children need first to know of these peoples and their ways of life before they can reflect meaningfully on our own attitudes in the West to the Earth. In a sense, then, learning about distant places is, for primary children, an important aspect of environmental geography.

It is important to learn how we maintain the resources which our environment provides for us, so that they can be available in similar fashion and sufficient quantity for future generations. This key question of sustainability is discussed more fully in Chapters 10 and 11, where both the moral aspects of the question and the need for children to have the right information are highlighted. Geography topics often can provide questions for children which involve moral education. The questions of right or wrong arise frequently when considering ways in which people relate one to another and have differing values or aims. Also, the ways in which resources are best used, and the environment is best managed, have rich potential for raising issues with children. Very often there is not necessarily a best, or 'right', solution.

The following account of work with 10 year old children illustrates how they can become involved in thinking about people and environment and the issues which arise.

Case Study 5

Emma Bull and Ruth Hale, second year student teachers, working with Angela Hurford their class teacher in Chew Stoke Primary School with Year 5 children, engaged them in a study of Chew Valley Lake and reservoir. The children were involved in role play to help consider this issue of environmental change.

Prior to this they had completed an activity which provided them with an historical background of the damming of the River Chew to form a reservoir. They learned that a village and farms were buried under the lake, along with many trees and hedgegrows. They did not concentrate just on the negative aspects, but also considered the benefits. These included, for example, the reduction of the flooding risk and the provision of water to supply large urban areas such as Bristol and Bath. Children also recognised that the creation of a lake in their area inhibited the development of 'dirty factories' and 'busy roads'.

Newspaper articles had reported the opening of the lake by the Queen, and the children tried to put themselves back in time to imagine what she was wearing, the car she arrived in, and to appreciate the atmosphere of excitement at the time. To help the children to bring it to life, Emma and Ruth involved the class in making a model of the valley.

Next, the students led the children in drama lessons, initially in two separate groups. The children were each given a role and were asked to imagine what their respective views would be. Three were to be builders, four environmentalists, four farmers, four homeowners, the owner of the water works and a local councillor. They had to consider the proposals and decide if they would be for or against and to give their reasons why. They could explore it in their own groups for about ten minutes and then were drawn together.

Ruth initially acted out the role of mayor and Emma the role of police officer 'in case things got out of hand – which they did'. The children had many ideas and some of the children were overzealous. Ruth and Emma saw themselves acting in the role of impartial chairperson.

The following week a girl took over the role of the mayor and the children largely organised the discussion themselves. They wrote their own speeches, made their own posters and many had enlisted the help of their parents. The children gained in terms of empathising with the feelings of people affected by the reservoir development. They started to understand what it must have felt like to lose farms or homes which had been in the family for generations.

Emma and Ruth also recalled some of the questions raised by children. The children differed over whether they would prefer to retain their home or have money as compensation instead. Some children also recognised the importance of memories: 'You can take your memories with you – houses aren't just bricks and mortar'.

Emma and Ruth thought that the success of this role play in stimulating the children's understanding of the issues involved was illustrated by comments such as the following:

 Vanessa said she could appreciate how the people whose houses were going to
  be taken away felt. 'They would be cross.'

 Nicholas felt that it was 'not fair to take people's houses away when they had
  lived there a long time to make someone else's profit'.

 Micah, in the role of an environmentalist, suggested, 'the hedgerows have been
  taken away but the lake has created homes for ducks, other birds and fish'.

We can appreciate in this activity how children were involved in developing and clarifying some of the values listed in the Appendix to Chapter 1.

In discussion with Emma and Ruth, we thought that the following values featured strongly. In relation to 'the self' they were able to develop an understanding of their own characters, strengths and weaknesses, develop self-respect and self-discipline and to clarify the meaning and purpose in their lives and decide how they believe their lives should be lived. In terms of 'relationships' they were able to develop respect for others; the activity involved working cooperatively with others; they learned to resolve disputes peacefully. With respect to 'society', in addition to developing their understanding of responsibilities as citizens, they considered values or actions that may be harmful to individuals or communities and participated in the democratic process offered by the role play. Values in relation to 'the environment' were strongly to the fore. They developed their understanding of the place of human beings within nature and gained experience in considering when development can be justified.

Reflection 3

- Which values from that list do you feel were enhanced in these lessons?

The student teachers, however, recognised the need to question naive or simplistic judgments made by the children. For example, when Nicholas felt that the valley shouldn't be flooded, he could be asked whether his family had a washing machine.

Overall we can see how this work with children helps to develop their knowledge of how society functions socially and politically.

Geography and the whole curriculum

The work with children which has been included in this chapter illustrates the strong case for including studies in geography as part of the primary curriculum. The various elements or themes in geography such as weather, homes, shopping and people in distant localities, provide rich opportunities for investigation and enquiry. In addition, problem solving, practical work and collaboration with peers can each readily be promoted through geography, making it a lively subject.

Geography within the humanities enables the global citizen to become informed about the physical world and many aspects of human relationships. Getting on with people in our own country and other societies is fundamental to humanity. Children should learn how people relate to each other and geography can thus make an invaluable contribution to anti-racist education. Many topics about the environment can be looked at in a measured and balanced way. The contribution of geography to understanding sustainability has already been stressed. Geography also offers a strong vehicle for much cross-curricular work. It has traditionally been described as a 'bridge' subject between the arts and the sciences. It has a similar function today in relation to the subjects currently in the National Curriculum and can readily support, or even enhance, work in literacy and numeracy. Similarly, geography offers fascinating opportunities for developing skills in ICT.

Among the strongest reasons for teaching geography is that it is accessible to all children. Geography can help teachers support children across a range of abilities. It has been noted how children with special educational needs can often be involved in work with others and develop cross-curricular skills and their self-esteem.

In conclusion, we can recall and reflect upon the four aims originally proposed for geography in the interim report for the National Curriculum in 1990. How far do you think these might have got lost in later developments of the curriculum? How valid do you think these aims are today?

 Geographical education should:
  (a) stimulate pupils' interest in their surroundings and in the variety of physical and human conditions on the Earth's surface;
  (b) foster their sense of wonder at the beauty of the world around them;

(c) *help them to develop an informed concern about the quality of the environment and the future of the human habitat;*

(d) *thereby enhance their sense of responsibility for the care of the Earth and its peoples.*

(DES, 1990)

We feel that these are worthy aims for geography in today's society.

References

BALE, J. (1987) *Geography in the Primary School*, London: Routledge.

CATLING, S. (1987a) in MILLS, D. (ed.) *Geographical Work in Primary and Middle Schools*, Sheffield: The Geographical Association.

CATLING, S. (1987b) *The Child is a Geographer.* Sheffield: The Geographical Association.

DEPARTMENT OF EDUCATION AND SCIENCE (1990) *Geography for ages 5 to 16: Proposals of the Secretary of State for Education and Science and the Secretary of State for Wales*, DES and Welsh Office.

FIEN, J. and GERBER, R. (1988) *Teaching Geography for a Better World*, London: Oliver and Boyd.

FOLEY, M. and JANIKOUN, J. (1996) *The Really Practical Guide to Primary Geography*, Cheltenham: Stanley Thornes Ltd.

MARSDEN, W. E. and HUGHES, J. (eds) (1994) *Primary School Geography*, London: David Fulton.

RAWLINGS, E. (1996) 'School geography: some key issues for higher education', *Journal of Geography in HE*, **20**, 3.

SEBBA, J. (1995) *Geography for All*, London: David Fulton.

WIEGAND, P. (1993) *Children and Primary Geography.* London: Cassell.

Further reading

SEBBA, J. (1995) *Geography for All*, London, David Fulton

WIEGAND, P. (1993) *Children and Primary Geography*, London, Cassell
The books by Sebba and Wiegand are particularly recommended. Sebba offers ways into geography for children with learning difficulties with many practical suggestions. Wiegand's book, on the other hand, is more comprehensive, dealing in depth with each of the main themes of geography. The inclusion of a bibliography at the end of each chapter is particularly helpful to student teachers and researchers.

Chapter 5

Using artefacts to support children's learning in religious education

Nick Clough and Liz Newman

Introduction

In this chapter we intend to encourage you to reflect on the way primary school children can express and develop values through the process of religious education. One of the main aims of religious education, as expressed through local agreed syllabuses, is that of developing understanding of what it means to take a religion seriously, even if individual pupils do not themselves belong to a religious community. The case study material presented here has involved children in different schools talking about special and sacred artefacts. Some basic questions emerge which it is important to address before planning and preparing a religious education lesson.

Using artefacts to support children's learning can be as stimulating, instructive and enjoyable in religious education as in other curriculum areas. We argue here that such resources can encourage children to use and develop language in a way that helps them understand their own experiences as well as those of others. The resulting discussion can provide opportunities for teachers to gain insights into children's current understandings about themes which are central to religious education and spiritual development.

You may think that it is an ambitious claim, that an artefact can generate this level of discussion. Much depends on the skill of the teacher in selecting items which can themselves be recognised as symbols of a significant aspect of human experience. The process is more familiar than it might at first appear. There is a human tendency to attach importance to objects of some kind or another at some time in our lives, something which reminds us of

Reflection 1

- How can children of primary school age begin to express what is of value to themselves?
- How can children of this age begin to understand how other people attach value to special and sacred artefacts?
- In what ways can the use of special and sacred artefacts promote such discussion and understanding?

past experience, or reminds us of a sentiment or aspiration in the present, or which represents a hope which we entertain for the future. Such significant objects are visible in so many places, both in shrines in religious buildings and in prominent niches in our homes. It might be a picture or a photograph, a sculpture, a book or a poem, perhaps something made by ourselves or someone close to us. We attempt to illustrate how such objects can be a focus in a special kind of 'show and tell' activity.

Learning about religions and learning from religions

Since the 1988 Act, all authorities have been required to produce new syllabuses for religious education. They vary in how they present their programmes of study, although there is a much commonality about the inclusion of general aims under the related but separate headings of 'learning about religions' and 'learning from religions'. We will be focusing more on learning intentions related to 'learning from religions'. Statements from the agreed syllabuses of two different local authorities help to clarify such intentions:

> *Religious education aims to assist pupils in their own search for meaning and purpose in life by examining those aspects of human experience which give rise to fundamental questions about beliefs and values.*
>
> (*Religious Education in the Basic Curriculum*: Wiltshire County Council, 1994)

> *Religious education enables pupils to explore the spiritual dimension of ex-perience and to develop understanding of various religious and non-religious interpretations of life. These two aspects are sometimes referred to as 'implicit religious education' and 'explicit religious education'. Religious education can*
> - *assist pupils in their own quests for meaning and purpose;*
> - *help them to mature in respect of their own beliefs, attitudes and values; and*
> - *encourage them to appreciate and respect the life stances of others.*
>
> (*Mystery and Meaning: the Agreed Syllabus for Religious Education in South Gloucestershire*, 1998)

The School Curriculum and Assessment Authority (SCAA) model syllabuses published in 1996, provide guidance to the Standing Advisory Council on Religious Education (SACRE) as they prepare the content to be covered in religious education at Key Stages 1, 2 and 3 under both headings, 'learning about' and 'learning from' religions. This resource is invaluable as it has been produced as a result of thorough consultations with representatives from different faith traditions in the UK. It is noticeable, however, that these particular documents do not contain references to child psychology (Cooling, 1996).

At the same time, these materials cause concern for many primary teachers who lack confidence in their own knowledge of the subject, especially with respect to religious traditions of which they do not have any personal experience. This concern is reflected in the new requirements for initial teacher training (DfEE, 1998) which specify that newly qualified teachers (NQTs) should achieve a high level of knowledge and understanding of the content of the SCAA recommendations. The consequence is that advisory staff, curriculum leaders and teacher trainers tend to focus their attention on the content of religious education rather than the learning process itself and the investigation of children's understandings.

It is as important to seek clarification from children about their developing understanding in religious education as in any other subject. We need to use such discussions as opportunities to see what sense they are making of information and concepts in their own terms and with reference to their own experience. This is what is so encouraging about the aims identified above from the local agreed syllabuses. These demonstrate that the process of religious education is less a process of information transfer and more a means for encouraging autonomy and participation.

Such an approach provides a vehicle for challenging prevalent constructivist notions of children's learning in religious education following Goldman's influential research (Goldman, 1965).

> *An exaggerated and misplaced reliance on the research of Piaget and Goldman has encouraged teachers to have low expectations concerning children's abilities. . . We can note that limitations of expression and vocabulary can give the impression of naïveté, just as sophistication in language can hide naïveté in thought. A lively and optimistic search to find hidden depths and insights and questioning within pupils must replace negative attitudes towards children's capacity for thinking.*
>
> (Watson, 1993)

Kay, too, implies that there has been a failure within religious education to match findings from child psychology with curricular and classroom materials (Kay, 1996).

An informal discussion about religious education with children in Key Stage 2 elicited responses which you might anticipate from your own pupils. They had been asked what religious education is and about their involvement in it. Responses included:

What is it? We have done it but I've forgotten.

Some of it is interesting – most of it is a bit boring.

I hate it. I don't know how to be good at it.

When you read about other people's religions it doesn't fit in with me.

In agreement with Hay et al. (1996), we feel that a content based approach focusing on cognitive development at the expense of spiritual development does not adequately meet the demands of the 1988 Act. The requirement of this Act for a broad and balanced curriculum setting religious education within the context of the spiritual, moral, cultural, mental and physical development of pupils and of society demands an approach which goes beyond the merely cognitive.

Building on children's experience

All children possess knowledge and experience on which the teacher of religious education can build. Encouraging children to talk and listen to each other is central to the learning process. Interacting with each other while handling artefacts is one means through which the children are able to share their knowledge and experience in a way that provides you, the teacher, with insights. If you have the knowledge to build on these through intervention, you will be able to progress beyond the cognitive in your teaching.

Research focus

In the discussion below, a group of Year 1 children were talking about figures from a Christmas Crib scene. The figures were wrapped in tissue paper. As they unwrapped them it was clear that they were able to bring their own experience to this learning experience.

Jenny: This one looks like a king or a shepherd. It has got brown and gold sandals.

Oscar: And a lantern . . . to show the way . . . they didn't have lights in those days.

Richard: I know who he is . . . he is Joseph. He has black eyes and golden bracelets.

Teacher: Who was Joseph?

Janet:	Mary's wife . . . no husband.
Marie:	Let's open this one. It's baby Jesus – he's got a white shirt and a crowny thing.
Richard:	That's a halo.
Teacher:	What's a halo?
Richard:	To show that he is good.
Janet:	(arranging the figures) He has got to go in the middle. We can put the others round the outside, so they can look at him.
Teacher:	Why are they looking at him?
Janet:	Because he is very special and they walked a long way to look at him – to worship baby Jesus and be friends with him.
Marie:	All mums look at their babies.
Janet:	But this baby was very special.
Teacher:	There are more parcels here – these crib figures are from a different set.
Marie:	This one is an angel. It's got pink cheeks and a white sash and another crowny thing.
Janet:	It's got wings to help it fly.
Teacher:	What's an angel?
Janet:	It's something of God's when they are dead it's something like stars you see.
Teacher:	Like stars?
Janet:	Yes stars can change into angels . . . like stars they can come down and they are coming to say something to you.
Teacher:	So what is this angel doing here? Does it belong with Mary, Joseph and the baby?
Marie:	Yes, it would come to see the baby.
Teacher:	Why would it come to see the baby?
Marie:	To see if it's all right.
Janet:	And to worship him . . .
Teacher:	What's worship him?
Richard:	Introduce him to the world . . . to the animals . . . to say thank you to God – they did in old days.
Janet:	My Granddad's an angel . . . he had a heart attack and he was very poorly and he died.
Teacher:	Is he an angel?
Janet:	Yes (long pause).
Richard:	The king is carrying gold, the king has brought gold because they haven't much money.
Oscar:	They can get food for the baby.
Teacher:	Can they can spend the gold and get more food for the baby?

Richard:	The king thought he (Jesus) was the greatest king so he brought gold – he gave away his chest of gold, he wanted to give away his favourite thing – he realised Jesus was very poor.
Teacher:	Where would they have got food from?
Richard:	They would have eaten meat and vegetables and they would have drunken water . . . they would have bought them at the outside market.
Oscar:	There were other kings.
Teacher:	And what did they bring?
Richard:	Gold, frankincense and myrrh.
Teacher:	Why did they bring those things?
Richard:	Myrrh makes a nice smell, frankincense I don't know about.
Teacher:	I don't think kings visited me when I was born. Were there any kings around when you were born?
Marie:	Yes kings . . . and queens.
Oscar:	No.
Teacher:	So why did this king come do you think?
Marie:	He came to worship the baby.
Teacher:	Were there any other people when Jesus was born?
Marie:	Shepherds . . . sheep.
Teacher:	What's wrapped up in here, do you think it could be another king?
Oscar:	It might be Santa.

In this transcript you will have noticed the highly personal and idiosyncratic way in which individuals make sense of their world. The children demonstrate that they are bringing a range of knowledge and understanding about the Christmas story to the classroom situation. Some utterances show a developing awareness of the historical context, others reveal that they are able to involve themselves in religious discourse, for example ultimate questions related to birth and death. They are revealing that they are capable of thinking for themselves. Inevitably, there are areas of misconception, for example, the expectation that Santa would be present in the nativity scene. The extract also reveals how the teacher's use of questioning to support the development of the argument/narrative can be minimal when the activity is well-structured. In this case the children continue to be motivated because they are intrigued by the process of unwrapping the figures. The teacher's comments support and open up the discussion and at this stage there is little need for intervention with supporting information.

Of course there are interesting outstanding questions, for example about the children's understanding of worship and it is noticeable that it was a child who introduced this specialised term. It is not clear what conceptual understanding the children have of this. The teacher is presented with sufficient data on which to base subsequent lessons/inputs about the Christmas story.

When asked how they knew so much about the baby born at Christmas, these children explained their sources as: 'my mum's a midwife she talks about babies'; 'the Bible'; 'my head'; 'a TV programme'; and 'Sunday school'. These comments remind us that the classroom setting is but one context within which individual children begin to make sense of their world. This particular lesson allowed the children to use their prior experience while developing their knowledge base.

Identifying questions

The activity and analysis in this section relates to one of the implicit themes identified in 'Mystery and Meaning: the Agreed Syllabus for religious education in South Gloucestershire' (1998). At Key Stage 1 and Key Stage 2 this is one of the eight categories identified and has the title Questions and Beliefs: the Special and the Sacred. For Key Stage 1 its first specification is that 'pupils should have the opportunity to reflect upon people, places, objects, events and experiences which are special to them and begin to appreciate some of the things that are special to religious believers'. The activity was designed to allow children to talk about themselves through the medium of identifying something that was of value to them and to come to appreciate that other people had different reasons for valuing objects in the same way.

The discussion was spread over two teaching sessions. In the first of these the children were introduced to five objects which were of value to other individuals whom they did not know. In the second, the children were invited to bring along objects which were valuable to them and to be ready to discuss these. The activity was conducted with children in both Key Stage 1 and Key Stage 2. The activities relate very closely to the reflection at the beginning of the chapter.

The discussion over the two sessions was structured around a series of pre-prepared questions as presented on the following page.

| 1 | **Describe the artefact**
Children could answer questions such as – What does it look like? What does it feel like? What does it feel like if you touch it? Has it got a smell? |
| 2 | **Tell us about anything else you know that is like this**
Children could do a drawing or a short piece of writing. |

At this point, information was provided about the selected artefact. This material was presented in the form of an incomplete big book, 'Things That Are Precious', which has space available for the children's own material to be included.

At this point children were asked to be ready to bring in an object which was important to them and which they could talk about and write about in the big book.

The five artefacts and supporting information that were introduced were as follows:

| 3 | **Tell us why you think this artefact might be important to the person it belongs to** |
| 4 | **What would they feel like if it was lost or damaged?**
What might they want to do if this happened?
Children's responses could be recorded in different ways – e.g. the teacher might keep notes of significant comments, the children could do a drawing or a short piece of writing. |

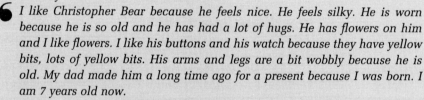

Case Study 1

1   A Teddy Bear

❝ *I like Christopher Bear because he feels nice. He feels silky. He is worn because he is so old and he has had a lot of hugs. He has flowers on him and I like flowers. I like his buttons and his watch because they have yellow bits, lots of yellow bits. His arms and legs are a bit wobbly because he is old. My dad made him a long time ago for a present because I was born. I am 7 years old now.*

I like cuddling him. I talk to him all the time and tell him that I like him, He sometimes tells me what he feels like when I hug him. When I hug him he feels happy and warm. The best thing I like about him is his smile because he looks nice and happy. He is happy because he likes me.

(Robert: 7 years)

| 5 | **Tell us about another object which is important to somebody you know** |
| 6 | **Tell us why you think people have things which are important to them** |

2   An Mbira

❝ *This is an mbira. It is made from wood and metal. It is about the most important thing in my life.*

I can remember having an mbira near me since I was very small. I can remember even playing with an mbira when I was 3 years old. I was trying to make the sounds that the grown up members of my family could make. I can remember starting mbira lessons when I was 6 years old. The instrument felt quite heavy to me then. I still play my mbira every day. Sometimes I play for myself or with friends at home. On other days I play in public. It is how I earn money – playing mbira and singing mbira songs.

It is not just about music. It means more than that to me. For one thing I like the way that mbiras bring people together for music. In my life mbira music has made many friends for me. Something else happens too. When I play I can make links with the spirit world. This is a very important experience for me. When it happens I feel that I am being guided and supported.

My people are the Shona people from Zimbabwe. It was the Shona people who first played mbiras and I hope that one day this music will be enjoyed by many more.   (Chartwell)

3   A wooden box with cuff links

This little box belonged to my father. He made it when he was at school. You can see that he has drawn his initials on the lid of the box. R stands for Ron which was his first name.

Inside the box there are some cuff links which belonged to him. I don't wear cuff links but I still keep them because they remind me a little bit of him. He died when I was a young boy. He had been ill for about a year. I missed him a lot at first, and so did my mum and my sister and my brother. I got used to it after a while but I keep this box and these cuff links in my house. My mum, my sister and my brother all have things that remind them of him too.

Sometimes I like to have small things which remind me of people I love.

4   A Family Bible

When I was little my mum and dad always talked to me about someone called God. They said that God loved everyone. But when I did something wrong they used to say 'You should not do that. God is watching and he won't like you doing that'. It made me think that God was some kind of policeman who looked down to see if people were being good or bad. I thought this was scary because I felt he was waiting to punish me. It did not make sense. How could he love everyone if he did that?

When I got older I had lots of questions that other people could not answer. When my father died I wondered what happened to people after they died. Is there a life after death? That was when I began to want to know more about God too. If God was real, how could I get to know him?

I asked God to show me who he was and what he did! He showed me through other people and through the Bible. I read about Jesus in the Bible and began to learn more about God.

Now I don't think that God is a kind of policeman. He is closer to me now than any other human being. I believe he wants me to know him. Each day as I read the Bible, I learn something new about him. I want to learn more.

5   A photograph of a house in the forest

This is one of my favourite places in the world that I have ever been to. I stayed for two nights in this house. It is built of wood and is kept warm by a wood burning stove. It is in the middle of a very deep forest by the Baltic Sea. There is a dirt track which leads there for about 30 miles. The people who live here do not use cars – except to go to the nearest town which is at the end of the track.

It is so quiet that you can hear only birds and the sea lapping up against the sandy beach about 300 metres from the house. In the morning as you look out of the window you can see deer cropping grass at the edge of the forest.

I love that dog Nears. He is very calm and gentle – but we did not have to lock or even shut the door at night as he thinks that this house belongs to him. He barks at night if he thinks that the deer are coming too close.

Sometimes I wish that I could spend my life in this house.

A ladder for learning

The approach described below was derived in part from an idea presented in Antouris and Wilson (1989) as a ladder for questions. The tasks listed can be seen as a ladder for children to ascend as they develop their understanding about particular concepts and ideas. It might not be appropriate or necessary for all of the children to climb all of the rungs in all of the activities and they will start and finish on different points on the ladder. The purpose of the ladder is to clarify the different thinking and communication processes involved. As such, it can provide a structure for the teacher to use in generating discussion and feedback.

Sixth level	Generalising/drawing conclusions
Fifth level	Demonstration of understanding in terms of own experience
Fourth level	Understanding life stances of others
Third level	Exploring someone else's feelings and responses
Second level	Making comparisons with other similar objects
First level	Describing at a literal level

Working with the children

We told the Year 6 children that we were going to share some precious objects with them and see how well they could talk about them in a group. The aim was not to teach a lesson or impart any particular knowledge, but to elicit the children's responses in order to establish ways of working in the future. The children were not told that the focus was religious education.

For a while the children spent time looking for the 'right' answers from the teacher, rather than engaging in discussion. Having had some experience working with historical artefacts, considering age, material and purpose, they made the assumption that they were to do the same here. Describing the cuff links and the teddy bear (rung 1 on the ladder) they focused on age:

Anna: They look very old, they have got flowery patterns on them.

Elizabeth: It's very worn and soft. It has lots of pretty flowers on it. I think it was made a long time ago with loads of old-fashioned stitching.

After reading the account of why the cuff links were kept, the owner's father was dead, the children began to draw on their own experience:

Elizabeth: I have got some jewellery that was my Nan's, reminds me of her. I wore a necklace once and it broke. It was very delicate. I will keep it though.

Martin: My mum has got a bow tie that belonged to her Dad. I think he wore it for his wedding – she keeps it to remind her of him.

The teddy bear generated talk about relationships:

Michelle: The man that knocked me over sent me a teddy bear – that is my favourite.

He sent it to me to say he was sorry. He sent me a letter as well.

Daniel: I have a monkey that was given to me by the coach of my Dad's football team. I used to stand next to him at the matches. He died and it got given to me.

The picture of the house provoked comments about memories of childhood and the environment:

Elizabeth: Maybe he likes it because he lived there when he was little.

Martin: Maybe he's just a city boy who likes nice quiet places.

Tom: He might like to go there when he is all stressed.

Maybe he wants to buy it for himself and live there forever.

With these children the Bible provoked much interest and comment.

Elizabeth: It is very old and worn. It has lots of foreign writing. It's torn a bit.

One child (who had been almost silent up to that point) said:

Houdah: Why would the person who owned this have written on it in two sorts of pen?

and made a historically orientated guess:

Houdah: She might have been comparing the two sentences to see if they said the same or whether they were different – or whether one added more information . . . perhaps she was trying to find out something.

Following the reading of the owner of the Bible's description, the discussion continued.

Anna: I don't think God is like policemen. I think God is like . . . I don't know.

Houdah: So she was writing out the bits to find out more about Jesus?

Chris: To help her say her prayers.

The children became concerned to find out why the owner of the Bible should mark the pages.

Anna: It could help her with a difficult question like 'Is there life after death?'

These comments were very revealing in a number of ways. The children initially thought it was a history lesson and were searching to give the 'right' answers. This emphasised the importance of learning objectives related to religious education being made explicit at the start of the lesson.

The children knew that adults often kept objects of little monetary value because it reminded them of friends that had moved away or family/friends that had died. This became a powerful theme in the second session. At no point did any child mention something of financial value. They all seemed to understand that objects could be of insignificant value in terms of money, but be of great value to the owner.

One point in the Bible owner's account stimulated controversy. She had indicated that Jesus was her best friend. They were asked to imagine what it might be like to feel that Jesus was even more important than their best friend. They were quite uncomprehending on this point. Daniel was quite offended.

Daniel: She can think that but my best friend is James and he is more important to me.

For the second session we asked the same group of children to bring an object that was precious to them and be prepared to talk about it. One of our aims for this session was to try to see if the children could begin to make the connection between something that is merely special to the owner and something that has a different quality and is sacred to a person or a group – working toward one of the aims identified in the agreed syllabus. To this end we took in a Quran (Houdah who had been very interested in the objects was Moslem) and a crucifix.

Following this we tried to move the discussion and identify whether the children would acknowledge any distinction between their precious things and the crucifix and Quran that had been presented.

The group had a range of views:

Anna: They are a bit more precious because they remind people of Jesus and everything.

Daniel: If that was me I would think my photo was more precious because I couldn't read that book (the Quran), although I might read some pages out of it. But each time I look at the photo or the monkey the coach gave me, it reminds me of him.

Chris: Some people don't believe in Jesus – so it wouldn't be precious to them.

Teacher: How can a tatty not very expensive Bible be precious to the person who reads and owns it?

Tom: It's part of their religion. They think that's why they are here, because God made them. They worship. They have all this stuff and everything, all things and everything, they worship God because he is their maker – he made them – he made us all. That's what the people who come to our assembly tell us.

Teacher: Any other ideas how these objects might be a bit different?

Michelle: Yes, because I've got the doll – because that's like just from the family. That (the crucifix) is like from a shop – you can buy it from anywhere.

Daniel: No you can't. You can't buy it anywhere.

Teacher: Do any of you have a friend that goes to a church or a mosque or belongs to a particular religion?

Martin: Asha is a Moslem.

Teacher: Do you think she would feel that the Quran was different?

Anna: I'm not sure. She don't speak about it.

Daniel: She might read the book at home. She might not read the book at school, but she might be real mad on reading.

Teacher: Why wouldn't she talk at school?

Daniel: I dunno. Because we believe in Jesus. She might think I'd better not say that.

Tyler: She might think we might tease her or something.

The children were asked if they could think of any words that might be used to describe these objects – if they were in a church or a mosque?

Martin: Holy.

Michelle: Religious.

Teacher: What does holy mean?

Michelle: Very religious. They believe in God.

Teacher: I said that these objects were sacred?

Elizabeth: They are special.

Chris: It means they are sort of worshipped.

Elizabeth: Like if you have got a sacred animal, not to kill it or anything. Like people pray to God and things like that.

Anna: Sacred means quite special.

Tom: Important.

Anna: I think these things would be important to the whole of Britain . . . not everybody knows about Michelle's doll or Chris's knife.

Teacher: So is it more special because more people know about it?

All: Yes.

Daniel: Say all of Chris's family know about Jesus and some . . . most of them believe in him.

Anna: There isn't a church for Daniel's picture, but there might be a church with a crucifix.

These last comments indicate that these children were beginning to differentiate between special and sacred objects. At the end of the lesson they were asked to pick a different precious object in the light of the discussion. They all choose objects of a similar nature tied in with relationships with family and friends. Daniel's statement was consistent with his earlier responses.

Daniel: I would have the monkey given to me by our coach.

They were asked if they could think of anything holy or sacred they would choose.

Tom: A necklace with a cross on it, we've got a red Bible in our bookcase. I flick through it sometimes.

Anna: A crucifix on a necklace. I don't wear it.

Elizabeth: A children's Bible. I don't ever read it.

Michelle: A rosary.

Daniel: Nothing except the picture and the monkey.

Their selections show their understanding of what the sacred and holy mean, though it is clear that they themselves have little interest in such concepts. They had little of what Hay and Nye (1998) describe as the traditional language of spirituality, coming as they did from a secularised culture. Their major focus of interest were the human relationships exemplified by the objects they brought to show.

We took a passive, non-judgmental role during these activities, providing a structured context for the children to work in and an appropriately safe atmosphere for discussion in which the children could disclose their personal beliefs openly, discuss spiritual and moral issues and learn from and appreciate one another's thought and insights.

Interestingly, the children also recognised Houdah, who came from an orthodox Moslem family and who seemed to be almost familiar with this type of discussion, as the most informed member of the group and used her as a reference point. Sadly she was absent for the second session.

The responses from a Y2 class in an inner urban primary school showed that the children were enthusiastic about the activity and able to cope with the different demands at different stages of the question ladder in their own ways. The more literal questions, involving the description of the artefacts, was well within their capabilities and this proved to be a useful language extension activity. Their responses to the hypothetical questions were revealing in that they tended to use narrative as a medium for explaining and justifying more complex feelings.

Their responses to questions about the teddy bear are listed below.

Teacher: Why might this teddy bear be precious to someone?

Haiden: Because he looks nice.

Nzinga: A little girl has got a lot of teddy bears and has got some stuff for a picnic and one of the girls can have that teddy bear, all the different girls could have different teddy bears and they are playing picnics.

Zenobia: Because she is old and loved.

Rajanita: Because a little girl was playing with him and you see all these little flowers and the bee came down and she threw the little teddy bear down and it stung her and she said 'Ow' and she throwed the teddy bear because it was his fault and another girl came and she picked it up and said don't kick this teddy bear 'cos it's mine and I am going to take it home because it's a nice teddy bear and it will be very very precious to me.

Cheyenne: I think they find the teddy bear on the floor and they think he is nice and they speak to him and say, you are not going to get away again.

Rajanita's story encompasses themes of loss and recovery within a simple narrative form which was accessible to other children in the group. Having listened to Rajanita, Cheyenne was able to offer another version of the story, emphasising the essence of the question, that the teddy bear was really important and would not 'get away again'. The theme was there for the teacher to develop further with the group.

Teacher: What would they feel like if the teddy bear was lost or damaged?

Zenobia: They would feel angry.

Candice: They would start crying.

Kanika:	They would feel cross and they would be crying.
Rajanita:	They would be looking around in the woods somewhere and they were feeling hungry and he or she went to get an ice cream and the wind blew and it made the teddy bear go up and up and she went back to the place where she left him and she started to cry and she told her mum she was upset.
Nzingha:	They would be upset and everyone would help find the person that had took it.
Zenobia:	Sad.

The group's capacity to respond through the medium of narrative continued to be evident in their subsequent responses, so that the cuff links in the box stimulated a story about gold mines and the mbira a story about a girl in hospital. This tendency of these young pupils resonates with the findings of Wells (1987) and emphasises the responsibility of teachers to provide careful structuring for children's oracy activities. Their fluency with this kind of language use also connects with recent arguments that it is young children's use of narrative in each subject which supports their development of abstract thinking and application of concepts.

The children's response in terms of bringing in objects that were precious to themselves was wholehearted and demonstrated that the modelling provided in the first session was formative. In particular, the introduction of the special relationship between the young boy and teddy bear in the first session would appear to have influenced two of the boys in the group, both of whom brought in teddy bears. One of these children, whose domestic circumstances have been subject to change and who requires support in school with respect to his troubled social responses, talked confidently in front of the whole group about his special friend, Ashley Bear.

Teacher:	What have you brought along?
Child:	A teddy. I have had him from when I was a baby.
Teacher:	What's his name?
Child:	Ashley.
Teacher:	Can you tell me anything about Ashley?
Child:	I sleep with him. I like him. He's cuddly.
Teacher:	Do you talk to him sometimes.
Child:	Yes.
Teacher:	Have you ever lost Ashley or left him somewhere?
Child:	Yes. Downstairs. I went to get him.
Another child:	What about if you left him in someone else's house. What would you do then?
Child:	I would just moan to my mum until she got him.

Perhaps the most significant utterance in this transcript is the unsolicited intervention by another child to support the development of the discussion.

His written recording was extensive by usual standards and was accompanied by a careful drawing to be placed in the big book

> *I like my teddy bear because it is comfy and cheerful and nice. Sometimes it is naughty. It punches me in the face. Sometimes it wakes me up. He always sleeps in my bed.*

When asked at the end of the discussion whether he would take Ashley with him if he went away, he replied

> *Yes (emphatically), but not to school, no way to school.*

It is perhaps ironic that this child did not think of school as a place for sharing stories so close to himself, and this example adds weight to the findings of research into spiritual, moral, social and cultural development by Erriker and Erriker (1997) who understood the importance and power of children's 'stories' and their value in facilitating the development of other children. An important strategy employed was 'taking children's stories to other children'. Perhaps the most poignant response from this group of young children was the child who wrote about her bracelet which she referred to as a bobble.

> *This is the most precious thing to me. I put this by my bed and when I'm tired I look at it. It is a bobble. I've had this for a couple of days. I like this bobble because it is special to me and it makes me happy. It stays still for a long time.*

Conclusion

The classroom interactions described in this chapter have emphasised the power of artefacts to support learning in religious education. The transcripts provide evidence related to the reflection identified at the outset of the chapter. Careful structuring of children's spoken language through the use of artefacts can provide opportunities for personal and social growth so that children can 'begin to express what is of value to themselves'. In particular, the older children had begun to demonstrate 'understanding of how other people attach value to special and sacred artefacts'.

Reflection 2

■ Can such work with children be characterized as spiritual development?

■ How do children in primary schools develop language appropriate to discussions about spirituality?

There is some evidence to suggest that these discussions have provided opportunities for the development of spiritual awareness of the kind referred to by Hay, Nye and Murphy (1996):

The difficulty with almost all research on children's spirituality up to the very recent past is that it focuses on God-talk . . . Given that the religious contexts surrounding children today are typically much less explicit than in the past or even absent, in order to uncover the innate spiritual potential children may possess . . . we suggest the need for researchers to focus on the perceptions, awareness and response of children to those ordinary activities which can act as . . . signals of transcendence.   (Hay, Nye and Murphy, 1996, p. 62)

They refer to ongoing research of transcripts of discussions with children in which

overtly religious language is absent and children are adapting to other cultural idioms to give a framework to their emerging awareness of spiritually signifi-cant experiences.   (Hay, Nye and Murphy, 1996, p. 64)

Hay and Nye (1998) are of the opinion that children growing up in a secularised culture have an innate spirituality which is unable to express itself or to develop because 'God-talk' is no longer seen to be acceptable. They claim to have found empirical evidence of a spirituality possessed by children which educators are seldom in touch with. The research we have reported in this chapter will, we hope, encourage you to develop your awareness of this possibility. You may agree that there was some evidence of an awareness of the sacred developing out of the special. Our work has been undertaken with artefacts. You might like to return to the National Statement of Values (Chapter 1) and consider whether there is any recognition of the spiritual elements that might constitute the values of the self and the values of relationships.

Enquiry task I

Can you capture any of the language children use when describing either themselves or their everyday relationships?

You might like to record discussions such as those that may take place in Circle Time. Ideally, you should obtain the children's permission for this and it might be wise to undertake a few recording sessions to 'habituate' the children to the tape recorder (i.e. wait until they no longer take any notice of it).
■ What sorts of values are evident in the way the children speak about each other? Are they all instrumental values (i.e. the children value each other for what they have or for what they can do) or can you find any evidence of children valuing others for themselves?
■ In what sort of language are such values (if any) expressed by the children?

You may not yet have read Chapter 7 of this volume. In that chapter, we refer to the point made by the Schools Curriculum and Assessment Authority, that spiritual development is for all children, regardless of whether they have any kind of upbringing within a religious tradition. In this chapter, we have demonstrated the power of artefacts to elicit qualities of thought that might be regarded as religious, and values that might be regarded as spiritual. Given our theme of a humanitarian curriculum, you might continue to reflect on the degree to which it might be desirable to promote awareness of the special or even the sacred in the lives of the children you teach.

References

ANTOURIS, G. and WILSON, J. (1989) *Equal Opportunities in Schools: New Dimensions in Topic Work*, London: Cassell.

COOLING, T. (1996) 'Education is the point of RE – not religion. Theological reflections on the SCAA model syllabuses', in ASTLEY, J. and FRANCIS, L. J. (eds), *Christian Theology and Religious Education: Connections and Contradictions*, London: SPCK.

DfEE (1998) *Teaching: High Status, High Standards*, Circular No. 4/98, London: TTA Publications.

ERRIKER, C. and ERRIKER, J. (1997) 'The development of SMSC in the primary school curriculum' in SCAA (1997), *Developing the Primary School Curriculum: The Next Steps*, Hayes: SCAA Publications.

GOLDMAN, R. (1965) *Readiness for Religion*. London: Routledge and Kegan Paul.

HAY, D. (1994) *New Methods in Religious Education*, Edinburgh: Oliver and Boyd.

HAY, D. and NYE, R. (1998) *The Spirit of the Child*. London: HarperCollins.

HAY, D., NYE, R. and MURPHY, R. (1996) 'Thinking about childhood spirituality' in FRANCIS, L. et al. (eds) *Research in Religious Education*, Leominster: Gracewing.

KAY, W. (1996) 'Bringing child psychology to religious curricula: the cautionary tale of Goldman and Piaget', *Educational Review*, **48**, 3.

NORTHUMBERLAND COUNTY COUNCIL (1995) *Spiritual, Moral, Social and Cultural Development: Guidelines for Schools in all Phases*, Morpeth: Northumberland County Council.

SCAA SCHOOL CURRICULUM AND ASSESSMENT AUTHORITY (1996) *Model Syllabuses for Religious Education*, Hayes: SCAA Publications.

SOUTH GLOUCESTERSHIRE COUNTY COUNCIL (1998) *Mystery and Meaning: the Agreed Syllabus for Religious Education in South Gloucestershire*, Thornbury: South Gloucestershire County Council.

WATSON, B. (1993) *The Effective Teaching of Religious Education*, Harlow: Longman.

WELLS, G. (1987) *The Meaning Makers*, London: Hodder and Stoughton.

WILTSHIRE COUNTY COUNCIL (1994) *Religious Education in the Basic Curriculum*, Trowbridge: Wiltshire County Council.

Further reading

BASTIDE, D. (ed.) (1992) *Good Practice in Primary Religious Education 4–11*, London: Falmer.
This book brings together a group of contributors who are all practitioners in the field of primary RE. It contains a useful and practical chapter by Vida Barnett on the use of religious artefacts in the classroom.

BEST, R. (ed.) (1996) *Education, Spirituality and the Whole Child*, London: Cassell.
This edited collection provides a framework of ideas and perspectives on education and spirituality. The book contains both theoretical discussion and practical examples.

Chapter 6

Field work, visits and work outside the classroom
Don Kimber and Maggie Smith

Introduction

The 6 and 7 year old children from Millponds School were working with their class teacher, Carol Budd, on the theme of 'Change'. Millponds is an ethnically diverse primary school in inner city Bristol. For seven Mondays during the summer term they were joined by Sally, Duncan and Andrew, three second year teacher trainees, as part of their classroom based World Studies course.

As part of the general theme on 'Change' they organised a walk from the school and took children in small groups around the school locality. The main intentions for the children were to:

■ enhance key skills from World Studies; including social and cultural development; develop enquiry skills and communication skills; and increase knowledge of our environment.

■ increase children's geographical skills of map work and knowledge of place.

■ develop observation skills by using the senses of smell and hearing, as well as of sight.

■ clarify their values and feelings about certain aspects of their environment.

They spent about an hour walking around a circular route. They passed houses and homes of different types, local shops, the park, crossed over the motorway (M32), and saw other features such as garages and other places of work. There was also access to a digital camera, which was used by some groups. All the children were encouraged to make observations with adults recording or scribing on clipboards.

The children were enthusiastic and greatly enjoyed this activity. They were keen to look at and often pass comment upon the things they saw. Many of these related to environmental concerns, reflecting their values and likes and dislikes. The rubbish in bin liners which had been left uncollected in a doorway was pointed out. Martin felt strongly about a car which was left on its roof. 'I don't like that. It looks messy. If I had my way I would take it away.' They decided to take a picture of the skip parked on the road having first asked what it was. They also discussed the smells 'like gas' as they crossed over the motorway, but did not appear to be aware of pollution.

In the afternoon the follow-up included using information from the digital camera to print out pictures of their choosing. There were perhaps 20 pictures on the monitor. They each chose one picture and it was then 'blown up' and they took it away to work with.

They wrote down what they did and did not like about the picture they had chosen. Many chose a picture they liked, and which also had them or their friends in it. They then recorded their personal thoughts. Leah said of her picture 'I like the river, but I do not like the shopping trolley in it'. Mustapha said 'I liked the green grass – it was a beautiful day'. Maggie said she liked 'the trees and the graffiti house'. (This was a house with a graffiti artist's impression of a dragon.)

Sally, Duncan and Andrew were asked what they thought the children had learnt from this activity. They felt there were a wide range of qualities and insights which the children had gained from this experience. They had developed a greater awareness of themselves. They could observe and describe the key characteristics of what they were observing, and this contributed to their sense of self. They had developed self-confidence and their ability to express opinions on their environment. Although these were mainly by way of likes and dislikes, they had often given reasons to support their suggestions. They had collaborated well in many activities. They were able to share thoughts upon what made them happy or sad, and listen to each other. Overall, these activities helped to build their self-esteem.

Children had also developed other skills, for example using a map. The teacher trainees were greatly impressed by the way that this class of 18 children, from diverse cultural backgrounds, were able to work together with their class teacher and show a huge sense of community of where they were living now. The practical activity and shared experiences of going out of the classroom had made a contribution to this.

Reflection 1

- What do you remember of school trips or going outside the classroom when you were at school?
- What aspects of them do you remember?
- How well do they stay in your mind?

We asked three of our colleagues for their memories of working outside the classroom.

One colleague, looking back over thirty years, recalled a childhood in South Wales when the 11+ scheme was still flourishing and 'where the emphasis was definitely on maths, intelligence and English', and where 'some art was thrown in', said that it was good just to get out of school. The school had a small tarmac playground out of which they were not allowed so they did not see any grass even though there was countryside all around. 'There were no things like nature walks – we were kept penned up really.' He continued, 'We did have one outing after we had done the 11+, as a reward. It was good just to get away from school. We went on a steamer from Barry to Weston-super-Mare. I remember the pier and the steamer well – particularly the engine room. The rest of it (schooldays) I can't really remember – you just sat there and did these things'.

Another colleague, going back forty years to primary school in Exmouth, recalled only one time of going outside the classroom. 'Most of the time we sat in our desks and the teacher taught us parrot fashion – learning our tables and spellings. We didn't move around even from room to room except for PE in the hall where we were stuck in teams to march around or whatever. The only time we went outside school was to walk to school or to walk home.' She went on, 'There were no cars in our day. We did do one trip – we went on the ferry from Exmouth to Starcross. I remember we went to Dawlish Warren to look at the sand washing in and out. We had to write up something about it afterwards'.

Our third colleague recalls primary school in Bath thirty years ago. A very early recollection was in the Infants Department going outside the classroom for a story and then on an other occasion to have the class photograph taken on the school steps. Another time they stood inside the school fence counting the cars going past. There were other visits that came to mind – the trip to the zoo for instance – but she could not remember whether these were with the school or with local groups. The one outstanding school memory was the residential visit to North Wales towards the end of primary school. Clear memories here included seeing a lamb trapped in cold water and dying but not being able to rescue it, and taking home a big pebble from the beach. 'I still have a similar one at home.' Other recollections included a visit to Harlech, walking up Cader Idris, 'a trip on the railway, walking on the beach and visiting a tweed mill'.

Many primary children today will typically enjoy a variety of learning activities outside the classroom. For example maths investigations might use

Reflection 2

- How do your memories compare with these?
- What do these memories mean to you?
- What might all these reflections suggest about the purposes and curricular roles of working outside the classroom in the past?

the school playground, and science investigations involving plants, flowers, mini-beasts, materials in the school grounds are common experiences. Visits reflecting humanities are even more standard. Some Year 5 pupils in a north Bristol school enthusiastically recalled their visit to see the Egyptian exhibition at a museum in Year 3 where they filled in a work sheet in the form of a puzzle. 'I enjoyed looking at the Egyptian exhibition – especially the mummies. The highlight of the day was walking round the shop.' In Year 4 they went to a farm. They followed this up by doing a project on their return to school – 'What would you do if you were a farmer?' They also went on a trip to Roman ruins. They followed a worksheet which guided them to particular areas but they 'had to find out the information for ourselves'. A favourite part was taking pictures of the ruins and they enjoyed shouting to listen to the echoes. There was no major project work on return but they remembered a talk and classroom discussion led by the teacher.

Why do field work and take children on visits?

Working outside the classroom has many attractions for children. Did you find it easy to recall the times when you went outside of the usual classroom setting for lessons which were normally held in the classroom? Some of us can recall quite readily some of the few times when we did go outside, whether for art, science, or other investigations in the school grounds, from our days at school. A physics lesson measuring the speed of sound across the playground is one such memory, a nature walk across the local park is another.

We can readily remember these very occasional field work activities in the grounds, quite apart from more exciting visits such as a trip to a coal mine, to the law courts, or on a geographical field walk. If you can recall field work activities fairly easily, then what might this suggest about the place of field work and visits in children's learning?

Presumably for many of us, such out of doors experiences are more memorable because they had an element of novelty, and of exploring the unknown. In comparison to many classroom based activities – completing worksheets, reading from books, or copying from the board – they often had a real purpose or point, and seemed very relevant. They could be enjoyable, and often there was the chance to interact gainfully with friends. All of these are factors which can enhance the potential for learning: learning not simply in terms of knowledge, understanding and skills, but also in relation to social and personal development and the clarification of values.

What we gained from some field work visits can stay with us for many years. For one of us the visit to a coal mine, and seeing at first hand something of what was involved in winning coal from the bowels of the earth a thousand metres or so below the surface in East Kent, is a memory which is still very vivid after 40 years. In more recent years, it has influenced attitudes towards the rapid rundown and closure of coal mines and the effects upon those who live in mining communities. The claim that the nuclear power industry had been subsidised to the tune of ten pence in the pound on all the electricity bills paid over many years has further affected personal values, and it is unlikely that this effect would have occurred in quite the same way had the learning about coal mines been from textbooks only.

However, it is not realistic to expect that the memories of all field work and of school visits will always stay quite so strongly in our minds. You might consider which of your own experiences of school visits have been most vividly remembered. The following list is of suggested aims for field work and visits. Are there others you might add? Are there any of those suggested in the list below that you would omit from your list of field work aims?

- To provide active learning.
- To develop enquiry skills.
- To extend social skills.
- To increase the relevance of study.
- To enable pursuit of individual interests.
- To add variation to classroom work.

Weldon and Richardson (1995) offer some additional aims and reasons for field work:

- It adds motivation and it can be fun.
- It helps to develop a feeling for the environment.
- It is education for citizenship.
- It helps to develop many key skills of observation, recording and analysis.

Work outside the classroom is also a rich area for promoting spiritual, moral, social and cultural development with children. As always this will depend upon the values which the teacher seeks to promote, and upon how the teacher chooses to organise the field work.

Socially, children working out of the classroom can easily be actively involved in interacting with others in pairs or in a group situation. They can begin to be aware of their own strengths and weaknesses, and learn how to collaborate in any prior planning together in teams. They have to learn how to take on board the views and suggestions of others. Outside the classroom there will often be the sharing and handling of field work equipment. This working together towards a common goal can help them to appreciate the values and qualities involved in developing team work.

Cultural development for pupils can depend very much upon the subject or focus of the field work or visit. Children's own roots can be explored initially for example, by looking closely at the school buildings and grounds. Characteristics can be highlighted when compared to other schools with different features. Those schools which have not been very recently built can give clues as to traditions and customs of former pupils. The layout of classrooms and corridors can be investigated to see if it provides clues as to how children were organised in school in the past. Consideration of the main hall, if there is one, can be fruitful. In some older schools there might be plaques to former pupils on account of their achievements, or more sadly, to commemorate those who died in the wars. Much more likely will be displays of the work of artists and writers from different cultural traditions in the school. Exterior features in some schools show evidence of separate entrances for girls and boys, or of a bell tower.

Such activities in looking at past traditions and practices in the local community can be amplified by examining the school logbook. This will often give insights into former customs and attitudes and values about school and school life to unravel with pupils. Children will have their own views upon curriculum, or the place of sporting activities in school, school uniforms, and school dinners and the myriad of other topics which can arise. Visits to interview local residents and former pupils or staff out of school can also enrich children's appreciation of local traditions and customs, and the values which people hold about them.

Visits to other places, such as museums, art galleries, concerts and places of worship, can also contribute greatly to children's cultural development. More commonly, the visits in relation to the 'Romans' and to 'Ancient Greece' to sites or to museums have helped many children to think more widely about their own and other's cultures. Many museums offer 'experiences' of a Victorian school day. The authoritarian atmosphere makes a strong impression on most children, and they usually have their own opinions about the humanity, or lack if it, in that type of schooling.

Questions of right and wrong can be raised in the practice of how one goes about the work outside classroom. Thus opportunities for **moral development** arise in considering the need for respecting the privacy of other people's property. Keeping to footpaths and shutting gates are simple examples. There will often be stronger questions of a moral nature in relation to some of the subjects or foci of study. Children can identify with questions of how we

Reflection 3

- Are there other ways in which you would like to see SMSC promoted through field work? (You might refer to the National Statement of Values, reproduced in the appendix to Chapter 1.)
- How might the work outside the classroom with young children from Millponds School above have aided their spiritual, moral, social and cultural development?

Consider some work outside the classroom or a field visit in which you have been involved recently.

- What were the aims or intended outcomes for the children? In what ways were there opportunities for developing SMSC?

should treat animals and plant life in habitats outside the classroom. More critical questions can be raised in visits when cruelty and the abuse of other people are involved. However, much will depend upon the values of the teacher and what is considered appropriate for the children concerned. Many would argue that a visit to the Georgian House in Bristol should not ignore consideration of the slave trade, and the exploitation of other humans, upon which the home owner built his fortune.

Similarly, in arranging a visit to the War Museum in London, to what degree should the question of Nazism, racism and the Holocaust be a part of the work and activities with the children? Considerations of controversial issues can arise in all sorts of ways and need to be carefully thought through in advance by the teacher. For example, an ordinary farm visit with young children could trigger questions about factory farming and the treatment of animals and vegetarianism.

We can recognise times when the **spiritual development** of children can be promoted. If we accept that enabling children to develop their 'inner self' and the encouraging of self-esteem are all part of this, field work offers many ways in which the work of children and their thoughts, ideas and suggestions can be valued and accepted. Also there are many times when children can be encouraged to work independently. The Northumberland CC guidelines suggest principles for spiritual development which include 'an understanding of the individual's relationship to other people, animals and the Earth is necessary if we are to determine our identity within the world'. They say 'It is important that the development of an awareness of our world is encouraged through curiosity, reflection and questions concerning why the physical world functions as it does and allows answers that move beyond solely an intellectual understanding'. Experiences outside the classroom provide a very effective means of developing such an awareness.

Approaches to field work

Taking children outside classrooms on visits to specific places such as museums and castles to investigate aspects of their surroundings is a longstanding practice, even if such visits were not commonplace in most schools until recently. A key question for teachers to think about is to what extent the field work enquiry or visit is dominated by the teacher and other adults. Will the activity be strongly structured and directed by the teacher, with the pupils responding only to suggestions from the teacher? Or will pupils be given opportunities to develop their own questions and lines of enquiry which make the investigation more personal to them.

Bland et al. (1996) make the distinction between what they call the 'Cook's tour' approach, the investigative approach and the enquiry approach:

The '**Look and See**' or Cook's tour approach, has the teacher firmly acting in the role of information provider, and perhaps even instructor. The teacher closely supervises the knowledge and skills which children are developing. As Bland et al. (1996) suggest, in this teacher centred process, types of activity might include guided tour, talk and look, and pupils are passive receivers of knowledge.

The **Investigation** process hands much more responsibility to children, as they are encouraged to carry out particular observations, measurements, or other types of recording. Activities have a stronger emphasis upon pupils doing some 'finding out' and they are more active as learners.

In the **Enquiry** approach, children have a much greater say in making suggestions as to how they proceed with the investigation. They can suggest ways of collecting data and will often have been involved in devising the initial questions. There are likely to be stronger elements of discovery, of problem solving, and probably the discussion of issues. Characteristically, there will be greater pupil interaction when working together, and some degree of open-ended study.

Bland et al. (1996) distinguish other typical characteristics of these three approaches in relation to the roles of the pupils and to these types of learning:
- Look and See – likely to be non-participatory and information based.
- Investigative – likely to be participatory and activity based.
- Enquiry – fully participatory and discovery based.

We can take the example of a stream study to illustrate the character of these different approaches. In the 'Look and See' situation children would likely listen to the teacher, take down notes of what is said, and perhaps draw sketches of features of the river or banks which are suggested by the teacher.

With an investigative approach, the teacher would devise activities for the children to engage in e.g. measuring the flow of the water in different pars; measuring depth and cross section; sketching river features, often in discussion with the teacher. A lot of this would involve working in groups.

In a river study with a strong enquiry approach, the teacher would have encouraged children to have identified key questions about the river perhaps before the visit, as well as trying to generate further key questions on the day

Reflection 4

■ What are the factors which you would identify about the extent to which an out of classroom study should be a 'Cook's tour', a structured investigation or a largely pupils' initiated enquiry?

■ Regarding your own memories of field work or visits from your school days, what was the mix or balance of these three approaches? What values were reflected in the teacher's approach?

of the visit. The teacher would often subtly assist in helping children to come up with worthwhile questions e.g. does the water flow at the same speed in all parts of the river? do the river banks have the same slope and height on each side of the river? what animal life is there in the river?

The preferred approach to arranging visits or organising field work will reflect the values of the teacher(s) and maybe school, not least in relation to how pupils are seen as actors in the education process. However, this is not to say that one approach is more appropriate than another; indeed a visit might include a mix of teacher directed observations, with some pupil originated enquiry.

The preferred approaches adopted by the teacher will depend upon a variety of factors. These would include the confidence and experience of the teacher leading the visit or field work enquiry; the experience and abilities of the pupils; the security of the area of investigation or place of visit (e.g. school, place of worship, busy shopping centre); and the resources available, including additional adult help as well as materials.

It can be helpful to consider the approaches to arranging visits and field work, and the ways in which they can provide opportunities for developing values. You might like to refer to the values relating to the self, relationships, society, and the environment (see Chapter 1).

Enquiry task 1

Use the grid below to evaluate the opportunities offered by the 'Cook's tour' approach, the investigation approach and the enquiry approach for engaging children with values from the National Statement (see Chapter 1), for a visit you have organised or might plan.

	A 'Cook's tour'	B Investigation	C Enquiry
Self			
Relationships			
Society			
Environment			

Arguably, we could say that approaches A, B and C might all offer some opportunities for pupils to develop values in environment. What about the other sets of values? Would you rank A, B, or C differently in promoting values in relation to the self, relationships, society and the environment?

We need to remember the different scales of field work or of exploratory activities. Working outside the classroom, children can be involved in activities elsewhere in the school building or in the grounds. Then there are visits on foot beyond the school gates into the local community which will usually require permission from the headteacher, and often from parents.

Trips further afield will involve transport, and may be for a half day or whole day, and will obviously require more detailed planning (see next section). Residential visits are arranged more commonly for older primary children in Years 5 and 6.

Planning

Preparation and administration

Once you have decided where an out-of-school visit will fit into the schemes of work, you can then start planning. Children enjoy the responsibility of being involved in the planning process. First, of course, you will have thought about the scale of the out-of-school visit, as discussed above; will it be local or will it involve some travel? You will also have thought about the balance between teacher and pupil input and responsibilities. There is some information at the end of this chapter that provides ideas of people to contact and the sort of places to go. Some might find it attractive to consider using 'pre-packaged' courses such as those provided by the Field Studies Council, and by commercial organisations such as PGL. Increasingly, major companies, such as the Environment Agency, and companies concerned with tourism and 'heritage', such as Big Pit, a former coal mine in South Wales, are employing an education officer who will set up out-of-classroom activities to suit your requirements. Even for those teachers who are experienced in planning field work activities, organised sessions can provide a valuable source of new ideas, and can provide time during a visit to talk to and help children individually. On the other hand, arranging your own activities allows you to tailor the experiences precisely to suit the pupils, the curriculum work you are doing, and provide appropriate opportunities for independent enquiry by the children.

Enquiry task 2

Visit one or two centres or attractions which advertise organised visits for school groups. You might go on a 'teachers' preview', or you might go incognito. Consider, from an educational point of view, the quality of the guides or organised activities.
- How well would they fit into your specific lesson plans?
- How well do they meet the needs of your pupils?
- Would you have been able to take the children round more effectively yourself?
- What are the advantages and disadvantages of organised visits and of visits that you plan yourself? Create and complete a table like the one below.

	Advantages	Disadvantages
Organised visits		
Visits you plan yourself		

FIG 6.1
School Visit Checklist

1. Feasibility study and preliminary site visit completed.
2. Date booked on school calendar.
    Head/year teams/secretary consulted?
3. Travel arrangements completed.
    Minibus and driver(s) booked?
    Coach hire/party rail?
4. Costings calculated and approved.
5. Staffing agreed.
    Correct ratio?
    Supply cover needed/approved?
    Parent helpers?
6. Bookings confirmed where necessary.
7. Letter to parents.
    Checked by Head?
8. Account set up.
    Checked by financial administrator?
9. Canteen staff and secretary informed.
    Itinerary and name lists?
    Children missing dinners/music lessons etc.?
    Emergency arrangements?

Having completed this preparatory work so that the scale, location and type of visit is decided, there is then a series of steps to follow in order to complete the arrangements. First, you should check the school's guidelines for the conduct of out-of-school visits. Many schools prepare a checklist for use when planning trips, and there are often Local Authority guidelines which you should consult.

If your school does not have such a checklist, you might like to adopt something along the lines of the above. It is very easy to miss out a vital step when you are busy with the other demands of being a teacher.

Risk assessment

For some activities, especially if they are to be held outdoors, it may well be worth considering the risks that are involved and ways of keeping them to acceptable levels. Following the Activity Centres (Young Persons Safety) Act 1995, the DFE issued guidance for safety in outdoor activity centres in 1996. They argued that risk is an essential element of outdoor education and that it should exercise children's sense of adventure. However, this must not be achieved by putting them at unacceptable physical or psychological risk. Many outdoor activities cannot be risk free. The aim must therefore be to minimise the risk to acceptable levels.

Reflection 5

To do this you need to consider:

- the type of activity;
- where it is going to take place;
- the qualifications and experience held by staff;
- the age and temperament of the children;
- the type and suitability of any equipment; and
- seasonal conditions, weather, time of day.

The answer is that you, the teacher, have the final responsibility for the group. If you are not confident that an adult leader (be they parent or qualified instructor) has sufficient control to ensure the safety of the group, you must intervene. You will find this easier if you have undertaken a risk assessment process.

The risk assessment process

To reassure yourself, you may wish to calculate the risk involved in the activity.

Risk = Likelihood × Severity

Likelihood of occurrence is rated on the following scale:

1 Highly unlikely to ever occur.
2 May occur but very rarely.
3 Does occur but only rarely.
4 Occurs from time to time.
5 Likely to occur often.

Severity of outcome is measured according to this scale:

1 Slight inconvenience.
2 Minor injury requiring first aid.
3 Medical attention required.
4 Major injury leading to hospitalisation.
5 Fatality or serious injury leading to disability.

If the likelihood rating multiplied by the severity rating comes to 10, then the risk is unacceptable, a score of 8 means that the risk is high and must be brought to the attention of all. A score of 1 clearly shows a low risk activity.

Example: Visit to a Hindu temple
Likelihood of there being a risk = 1 or 2
Severity of outcome = 1 or 2
Risk = 2 × 2 = 4
Risk is acceptably low

Reflection 6

Think about a trip that you have taken part in.
■ What were the things that caught your attention and interest?
■ What were the things that caused you to lose interest or feel disgruntled?

Planning the session

Planning the field work session involves the same considerations as planning a classroom session. You need to identify the **time** that is available and how the time is going to be broken up. You need to identify what it is that the children are going to **do**. This includes considering how much personal enquiry they will be encouraged to do. Part of the preparation for this could usefully be involving the children in devising and preparing the key questions and tasks so that they feel ownership of the process from the beginning. What **resources** or **equipment** will be needed? How are **differentiation and assessment** going to be achieved? The role and responsibilities of the **teachers and other adults** accompanying the trip need to be made clear and they need to be informed (by meetings or instruction sheets). It is certainly worth discussing how **momentum and interest** will be maintained (by children and adults) throughout the session so that full use is made of the visit. In humanities visits very often there is the chance for children to interview people or to use questionnaires. Very often the questions will have been discussed in the classroom prior to the visit. It can be very rewarding for the teacher to see how some children, who are normally diffident or who lack confidence and motivation, can blossom and really gain so much from having the chance to talk and ask questions of other people. You can see some children display qualities which you did not think they had.

Following up a visit

There are many possibilities for follow-up work. Much depends on how the pupils have recorded their findings while on the visit, also on what the particular values are that you want children to develop and clarify.

Some ideas that could be used are as follows:

Recording the information gathered on the visit

Recording information

1 individually by:

pictures	sketches	written descriptions
poems	maps	taped descriptions
letters	graphs	charts and diagrams

2 group work to present an overview of the visit through:

presentations	creating a topic book
plays	musical performances
displays	

Drawing conclusions from the information

As well as factual conclusions, children will undoubtedly have developed their own values in relation to what was being investigated. They may well have started to appreciate the values of others as, for example, in the visit to the Hindu temple described below. There may be an appreciation of what is 'right' and what is 'wrong' in an investigation of why one building should be pulled down to make way for a road, and a study of traffic clogging up a busy high street might raise issues connected to social values and citizenship.

Communicating the findings

It can be rewarding for pupils and adults to share the findings of the activity or visit with a wider audience. This can be especially effective in promoting confidence, self-esteem, and social skills. Communication could be to

- the rest of the school (e.g. in an assembly);
- displays at parents' evenings or open days;
- a presentation to parents;
- writing accounts for penfriends or exchange schools;
- inviting the local adviser (LEA) to see the results;
- creating a web page or e-mail;
- or even notifying the local press.

Finally you might find feedback from participants useful for planning future visits

Questions that could be asked include

- what did you like most about the visit?
- what did you like least about the visit?
- what parts of the trip would you like to change?
- what did you learn?

Finally, remember that 'thank you' letters are much appreciated by those who helped in the trip and writing and designing them provides opportunities for art and language work for the children.

Case Study 1

The following is an account of a visit to a Hindu temple organised by Kiran Kaur, a second year trainee teacher, working with Jenny Taylor, the class teacher in Hotwells Primary School in Bristol. As you read it, consider ways in which you might have organised it differently, or might have chosen alternative aims for your children's learning.

A field visit to the Hindu Temple

Organizing the visit
The 20 Year 6 children in my class at Hotwells Primary School in Bristol were scheduled to learn about the Hindu temple in my block teaching practice during March/April 1998. The Avon agreed syllabus stresses the importance of visiting places of worship as a vital part of the RE National Curriculum. That is why I decided that a visit to the Hindu temple should be paramount if the learning is to be maximised. I then began the process of finding a person to help me organise a visit. My first enquiry was with a woman who is a friend of the family, who told me the person I needed to locate. I then telephoned this person and arranged a visit for 10am on Monday the 30th of February.

The visit
On arrival the children and the class teacher stayed outside whilst I went inside to find someone to tell us where to go and who to speak to. A man (who must have been a friend of the priest's) told me that we were to take our shoes off and come upstairs. This was done and we all went upstairs to a beautiful room with many statues in it. The priest then told us the purpose of the gods and some of his own personal history (how he became a priest). He explained the basic things about the temple and then the children asked questions. The children asked about what they had seen. In particular they had seen a picture of Mahatma Ghandi (whom they had studied last term) on the wall and asked about it. This was a good observation into how children link things together. The priest said that all of the pictures were gods, but the children felt that Mahatma Ghandi was a person rather than a god, so I explained that Indians respect Ghandi for his role in liberating India and treated him as if he were a god.

The children were given sweets by the priest before we came back to school. On the way back a child decided that he would like to become a Hindu, because he liked what he had seen. I found out later that a lot of this child's enthusiasm was due to his interest in his older sister who was going on a trip to India next year. This visit had then acted as something which helped him to understand the culture of the country that his sister would be visiting.

The follow-up activities
After the visit I planned four lessons on the temple. In the first one the children wrote about what they had seen in the temple and what they had learnt. This activity was done very enthusiastically and in the discussion beforehand the children pointed out many of the things we had learnt and seen. The most memorable fact was the priest saying that there were 36 million Hindu gods and that he could name 3 or 4 thousand of them. This caused a lot of reaction and almost all the children wrote this in their piece of writing. The children were in fact so stunned by the comment that it caused them to talk about it in all the RE lessons.

The second lesson was based on how the temple here differs when compared with the temple in India. The children were very motivated by this topic as they asked many questions about it. Now that they had actually seen a temple they were captivated by its role in life. They were particularly fascinated to know that in India the temples were regularly cleaned with milk, because milk is a symbol of purity in the Hindu religion. I then went on to explain that due to the cow being the sacred animal of India, anything that it gave out was worshipped. The children were then intrigued by the fact that due to the Hindus' strong belief in reincarnation, a cow was thought to be a dead relative who was highly regarded. This would mean a person would be killing this respected relative again and consuming them. This fact was then a stimulus into a discussion about the Hindu belief system concerning reincarnation. The children were questioning what is considered to be a good or bad life and why people are given their next life in accordance with their behaviour in this life. The lesson had encouraged children to discuss an issue which can be hard to understand. This was a good contribution to their spiritual, moral, cultural and social development.

The very same lesson had a very interesting comment from one child who has strong opinions about environmental damage. She claimed that she wanted to become a Hindu because they respected animals and didn't kill them. This is a very significant lesson in this child's life, because she had learned to identify with another culture which had the same values as she did.

The third lesson was about the birth of Lord Krishna. The children loved the story and related it to the story of baby Moses (because he too was sent to drown in water). The children began to discuss the morals of the story. They were clear that selfishness and greed was not a gracious virtue. It is apparent that although the main topic in these RE lessons was the temple, the children were gaining an understanding about the rights and wrongs in life, and what is considered to be the right thing to do.

The final lesson on the temple stimulated a lot of discussion due to the fact that it discussed Hindu ceremonies (religious ones that could be conducted in a temple). We discussed births, deaths and marriages, the first two were facts that the children were interested in and related to ceremonies here in England. In particular they linked the pouring of the water on a baby's head in a Hindu ceremony to the Christian baptism. Again, the children were relating their own lives to those of others. Whilst talking about marriage ceremonies in the Hindu culture, the subject of arranged marriages came up. When I explained what they were, many of the children were against the idea. I personally hold a strong belief against them myself, due to the fact that my family are Sikhs and believe in arranged marriages. I was born and brought up here and have chosen not to follow such a restricting religion. However, my beliefs and values were something that I did not discuss with the children due to my professional conduct as their teacher. Although I agreed with the children's opinions I did not tell them, because as their teacher I am obliged to present them with the facts so that they can make up their own minds. My job is not to impose my opinions within the class, so I simply repeated the fact that this was something that Hindus believed in.

Reflection 7

At least some of the content of the lessons described above could, in theory, have been taught without the time and trouble of visiting a Hindu temple.

- How does the temple visit compare with learning about the Hindu way of life from books or worksheets?
- Can you identify what the children gained from the first hand experience that they would not otherwise have gained?

Conclusion
On the whole the visit to the temple impacted upon the children's learning in so many ways. It mainly stimulated an enormous interest into the Hindu way of life, as well as introducing the children to questioning themselves. The children's attitudes were very positive and the visit has encouraged this, as first hand experiences will result in long-lasting interest and motivation towards the topic.

You may well have answers of your own, but we would certainly include motivation amongst our own answers. We would also venture to suggest that the learning of values took place in a variety of quite subtle ways. Clearly, the children valued the experience itself. They valued the knowledge about the Hindu way of life far more than they would have done had it been given to them in the form of a worksheet or even a book. The children learned to value another culture. The National Statement of Values suggests that, on the basis of valuing society, we 'should respect religious and cultural diversity' (see Chapter 1). You can, of course, *tell* your children that they *ought* to have this value. We doubt very much, however, that they will come to embrace this value as their own unless you are prepared to undertake work of the nature described by Kiran in her case study.

References

BAILEY, P. and FOX, P. (1996) *The Geography Teachers' Handbook*, Sheffield: Geographical Association.

BLAND, K., CHAMBERS, B., DONERT, K. and THOMAS, A. (1996) 'Fieldwork' in BAILEY, P. and FOX, P. (eds) *The Geography Teachers' Handbook*, Sheffield: Geographical Association.

FOLEY, M. and JANIKOUN, J. (1992) *The Really Practical Guide to Primary Geography*, Cheltenham: Stanley Thornes.

MILLS, D. (1988) *Geographical Work in Primary and Middle Schools*, Sheffield: Geographical Association.

WELDON, M. and RICHARDSON, R. (1995) *Planning Geography for the Revised National Curriculum: Key Stages One and Two*, London: John Murray.

Further reading

HALOCHA, J. (1998) *Coordinating geography across the primary school*, Lewes: Falmer Press.

This provides an excellent up-to-date and easy to read guide to planning field work within the geography subject area in primary schools. Written with geography coordinators in mind, it covers how you justify field work to colleagues and write school field work policies. Chapter 7 is particularly useful.

TILBURY, D. and WILLIAMS, M. (eds) (1987) *Teaching and Learning Geography*. London: Routledge.

Chapter 18 of this book, by Nick Foscett, provides 'meaty' substance to thinking about field work. There is useful detail for policy writing. It links theory to practice, uses current 'jargon' and gives a comprehensive coverage of planning. It also contains a useful list of yet further reading!

Chapter 7

Spiritual, moral and cultural development
Martin Ashley

Introduction

Somewhere in a medium-sized market town in the south-west of England, there is a primary school. In the grounds of that primary school, there stands a tree. For those with the time to look, there is a small plaque beneath the tree. The plaque informs the passer-by that the tree is Robert's tree. I was Robert's last teacher. I held Robert's hand as he lay dying in hospital. I heard him speak with bravery and simple nobility about death and what it feels like as it approaches. I spent an hour in his home with his parents on the day after his death. I undertook the poignant tasks of clearing out his redundant work tray, of removing his name from the cloakroom pegs. I faced his former classmates and was part of their coming to terms with a very real death. I played 'Lord of the Dance', his favourite hymn, in the assembly we had after he had gone.

A term later, I played rounders and shared much joy and happiness with his former classmates. But for a period in the previous term, I had faced in reality some of the great 'spiritual' questions: 'Why are we here?' 'What's the purpose of life?' 'Is there life after death?' 'How could a loving God let an innocent 8 year old suffer and die?' I have to admit, recalling the event, that I was no more capable of answering those questions than my 8 year olds. In fact, Robert could well have taught us all a thing or two, for as I have said, he faced death with bravery and nobility, and those are spiritual qualities that Robert, when tested, was found to have in abundance. I think we have to approach the spiritual development of children with a certain degree of humility. We adults may not be the 'experts' we might like to hope to be.

Part of our work in school is not about 'subject knowledge', competency or attainment. It is to do with the children themselves and their growth as unique 'whole people'. As Robert's story illustrates, there is an inevitability about life's ultimate questions which will compel you from time to time to address such matters. You may also feel, out of regard for the children you teach, that you have a humanitarian obligation to promote their development as 'whole people'. You are also (and I mention this last) required by law to do so. There are mandatory OFSTED criteria of inspection for spiritual, moral and cultural development.

I have divided this chapter into three sections to look in turn at spiritual, moral and cultural development. I shall describe the main features of each. I shall also introduce you in each section to a practical or philosophical difficulty which stands between your understanding what you are trying to do in theory and your attaining it in practice. I hope to be able to equip you with means of overcoming the difficulties. I shall also include an element of critical reflection in each of the three sections.

Spiritual development

You may find the term 'spiritual development' a little uncomfortable. If you do, this might well be because of the association that exists in many people's minds between spirituality and religion. It may be that you have rejected religion altogether. If that is the case, your initial feelings might be that the requirement to promote the spiritual development of children borders on the absurd. On the other hand, you might be a deeply religious person to whom spirituality is very important. You might be perplexed at how what you have come to recognise as spirituality is to be promoted in a very secular world. Wherever you come from, you need to be in no doubt that the QCA (Qualifications and Curriculum Authority, previously SCAA and before that NCC) consistently emphasises two fundamental points:

- Spiritual development is for all children, of any religion or none.
- Spiritual development is an expectation for all subjects of the curriculum.

It is important that you are clear about the relationship between religion and spirituality if you are to make sense of these demands. Religion did not create spirituality. Spirituality existed before religion. Religion developed as one possible response to a whole range of deep feelings, an awareness of strong inter-personal and person/nature connections and an awareness of 'other' that seems to be common to human experience. Religions, for some people, have been a way of rationalising, experiencing and sharing these feelings. It has to be said that religions can be a uniquely effective way of exercising the spiritual dimension of our nature. For this reason, religious education, if done well, can perhaps make a special contribution to the growth of children's spiritual understanding. It is equally possible, however, for the outward trappings of religious practice to be largely devoid of any spiritual depth. Religious education, if done badly, can be quite counter-productive to the goal of spiritual development.

You might like to pause for a moment and reflect on what, for you, constitutes this human experience we are calling 'spirituality'. How do your own thoughts compare with the list below?

The spiritual dimensions of life are commonly said to include the following:

The quest for meaning when confronted with life's 'ultimate questions'

I began the chapter with an example of these 'Who am I?' 'Why am I here?' 'What is the purpose of life?' 'Is there life after death?' 'Why do we suffer?' and so on. It should come as no surprise to anyone undertaking a literature search in the area of spirituality that libraries devoted to nurse education seem to throw up far more material than libraries devoted to teacher education. It is nurses, in their daily work, who are confronted with a deep yearning for such questions to be answered. The occasional death of a pupil is one reminder of the inevitability of such questions. Maybe, however, we should be concerned also about the number of young people who seem to lack meaning in their lives and turn perhaps to drugs or crime in consequence. This is an area where the professional competence of primary teachers might contribute much preventative work.

The sense of wonder, awe and reverence

Wonder is the engine of curiosity. Without the curiosity of children, the professional primary teacher is nothing more than a bungling amateur, coercing children to retain pointless pieces of information which they forget as soon as external sanctions are removed. Awe differs from wonder in that it contains an element of proper fear. Without awe, there is not respect for people, no respect for nature and no respect for knowledge. The prospect of scientists who can create nuclear explosions having no sense of awe related to their knowledge is alarming. Reverence is the outcome of an education that has been successful in transforming childish wonder into awe at the mysteries of nature, science and humanity. Reverence for life is a source of values that are strong enough to compel sacrifice. This might be giving one's own life to save another's. It might be simply a preparedness to accept a slightly lower standard of material living in order to promote environmental conservation.

The awareness of self

If you are to be a good primary teacher, it is vital that you remember what an awesome task it is for a new human being to come to terms with all that is involved in self-identity. Children must develop an adequate self-esteem. I cannot begin to discuss that here. There is a huge literature on it with which every primary teacher should have more than a passing acquaintance. Spiritual development perhaps particularly emphasises the 'worth' we have as people, which exists irrespective of our material possessions or accomplishments. If you feel awed by the task of achieving this with children in the face of a multi-billion pound advertising industry which seems to promote contrary values, I would say that you understand the point. Awareness of self also means the development of harmony between mind and body and the ability to reflect deeply. Many adults find this profoundly challenging because it throws up ultimate questions such as 'who am I?' 'what is the meaning of my life?' Music, art, drama, dance, literature can all help with this. I would say that primary teachers need to value these creative activities if they are to be of any help to children in developing the awareness of self.

The awareness of 'other'

The awareness of 'other' begins with the realisation that the 'self' is not the centre of the universe. Psychologists sometimes talk about 'relinquishing the egocentric position'. This is very hard to do at the same time as promoting self-esteem. Children who have no self-worth are notoriously slow to recognise the worth of others. Nevertheless, the promotion of sensitivity towards the feelings of others is part of the daily business of most caring primary teachers. It is paradoxical also that, as we increase in our sense of self and self-worth, we become increasingly aware of our smallness in the cosmos. This is when some people begin to feel the need to subordinate the self to a greater power. For many people, the idea that such a greater power is merely human seems intuitively unsatisfactory. Human beings who have imagined themselves omnipotent and worthy to rule the world are seldom judged kindly by history. Neither, for that matter, have human institutions promising utopia always had a track record inspiring total confidence. You might, then, feel that you have at least a duty to keep open the question of whether there is some kind of ultimate purpose and authority which is not human. It is certainly something about which young children wonder and cynicism in the face of such wonder is not appropriate in primary teaching.

Wisdom

The type of learning that is embodied in the subjects of the National Curriculum is largely to do with 'knowing that . . .' and 'knowing how to . . .' You are less likely to be confronted by questions of 'knowing whether . . .' or 'knowing why . . .' In Chapter 1 I referred to the writing of David Orr (1994), who pointed out that the possession of a BA, BSc or PhD does not necessarily signify the possession of wisdom. His support for this claim, you may recall, was that many of the perpetrators of Auschwitz possessed such qualifications. What is this 'wisdom' element of the curriculum that might be lacking? Can wisdom legitimately be referred to as a spiritual quality?

One possible answer to these questions can be arrived at by means of a thought experiment based upon Orr's criticism of education devoid of wisdom, which he suggests emphasises theories instead of values, concepts rather than human beings, abstraction rather than consciousness, answers instead of questions, ideology and efficiency rather than conscience. If we identify the positive attributes which are the opposites of the negative qualities to which Orr objects, we get a set of qualities or virtues that some would consider descriptive of a 'spiritual wisdom':

- A sense of value;
- Humanity;
- Consciousness and self awareness;
- Questioning and wondering;
- Conscience and a sense of right and wrong.

From my experience of working with children, I would add two more things to this list. The first is *perseverance*. How do you feel about the child who has low self-esteem, anticipates failure or gives up at the first difficulty? How do you feel about the child who storms off the rounders pitch because he or she cannot 'hack' being 'out'? One way of rationalising such behaviour, which you may not have thought of, is to say that such a child is 'spiritually weak'. We think of people or things as being 'spirited' when they give an exciting performance or show some kind of inner strength. People who can keep going when things get bad have a quality which we might describe as a 'strong spirit'. The Christian religion has a prayer which says 'lead us not into temptation'. This is sometimes translated as 'do not bring us to the time of trial' and is really a plea that we will have the strength to go on if things get spiritually tough.

The second is *sensitivity*. I have yet to meet a Year 6 boy with challenging behaviour who does not have a soft, inner self which is very easily hurt and may be protected by a shell of macho behaviour which excludes any form of sensitivity to the feelings of other people or to things of beauty. If we are producing children who are unmoved by things of beauty or unmoved by the feelings of others, then it might be the case that we ourselves are the agents of brutality. Has our education system become brutal? Are its only values efficiency and success in the market place or is there a place for sensitivity to things of beauty? My feelings are that the individual teachers who make up the education system hold the key to this. You might care to reflect. If you have not read the book 'I Am David' by Ann Holm (1963), you might find that reading it helps with your reflections.

You might be beginning to wonder how these things are to be achieved. You can be forgiven for doing so because it is easy to describe the sorts of values schools ought to be teaching. It is harder to specify a set of 'competences' or 'standards' which are meaningful and can be possessed merely by reading a book. It is even harder to develop children spiritually. You cannot simply tell children what values they 'ought' to hold. You may be able to 'tell' them what is right and wrong, but developing within them a conscience and the will to do the right thing is another matter altogether. Didactic methods are not really suited to spiritual, moral and cultural development. Wisdom has to be taught by living and the whole class 'transmissional' model of teaching is not always about living. We are talking here about personal qualities and inspired teaching which has a little bit of magic. The following enquiry task may help:

Enquiry task I

Create a matrix which has the National Curriculum subjects along one axis and the areas of spiritual development described below along the other. To your list of National Curriculum subjects you will almost certainly want to add playtimes, assemblies or acts of collective worship, circle time and any other such times which are a part of the school day. Keep a record of a week in school. Each time you feel that one of the areas of spiritual development is being addressed, add a tally mark to your matrix to show which subject or time of the school day it occurred in. You might want to supplement your observations by notes or a diary.

Areas of spiritual development
Valuation: 'This is good, so I would like it to happen.' 'This matters more than that.' 'Some of the things that matter most cannot be bought with money.'
Humanity: 'I am not the only person. Other people matter too. When others are happy, I am happy with them. When they are sad, I am sad.'
Consciousness and self awareness: 'I am the unique me. I feel good about myself. I have emotions and feelings and I can cope with these.'
Questioning and Wondering: 'I am curious. Finding out is fun. Sometimes I wonder how the world began or what happens to people when they die.'
Conscience: 'Sometimes I do good things, sometimes I do bad things. I want to be sorry when I do bad things because it hurts other people. I feel happy if I make somebody else happy by doing a good thing.'
Perseverance: 'It doesn't matter if I don't win or get it right, people will still love me. I can try again.'
Sensitivity: 'It's OK to feel upset and to show it. I care about how other people feel. Music, drama, pictures or writing can make me feel happy, sad, excited or quiet.'

How did the different curriculum areas and different times of the school day fare? Did you find any particular subjects or times which particularly addressed spiritual development? Did you find any blank areas where spiritual development did not appear to be happening? What sorts of things were going on when you perceived spiritual development to be occurring? What were you or other teachers doing? Could you say with confidence that all children received systematic spiritual development or was it a case of what I call the 'We do that when it happens in the playground' approach?

All subjects, as we have noted, can and should contribute to spiritual development. I would be surprised if you had not come to realise how important the hidden or implicit curriculum is. What sort of balance did you note between children being told what they 'ought' to think, feel or do and children being helped, by sensitive teachers, to reflect upon the meaning of their everyday encounters with their social and physical environment and the subject material of the curriculum? You might care to reflect particularly upon the contributions of science and religious education. If you have read the SCAA (1995) guidance you will have noted that these two subjects are singled out for special mention, and that of the two, it is science that is given the most space.

The SCAA guidance draws attention to a belief in the infallibility of science which is seen to have undermined religious belief. The perception of science, combined with enlightenment humanism as the only way to understand experience, is said by SCAA to have been largely responsible for the demise of the spiritual and moral dimensions of the curriculum. This is a weighty charge against science. The philosophy of science and religion is a very dangerous area, full of traps for the unwary. SCAA are unwise, in my opinion, to meddle at a superficial level. You may well be familiar with the popular and controversial writer on the public understanding of science, Richard Dawkins. In his address to young people at the 1994 Royal Institution Christmas Lecture, Dawkins claimed that '. . . if science has nothing to say, then it's certain that there is nothing to be said at all' (Dawkins, 1994). Presumably this kind of view is the one objected to by SCAA.

Does Dawkins' view represent the consensus of the scientific community? There are plenty of scientists who would dissociate themselves from such a view – Professor John Houghton, chairman of the Royal Commission on Environmental Pollution to name but one (Houghton, 1997). The view Dawkins expressed might be more representative of a nineteenth century dogma known as *scientism*, which is defined as the 'doctrine of the omnicompetence of science'. An unqualified belief in the infallibility of science, or at least the omnicompetence of science, is held by relatively few scientists, and SCAA, by confusing science with scientism do a disservice to both science and religion. They merely promote a popular misconception that science and religion are opposing protagonists in a battle over truth claims. To be fair, SCAA talk of a perception of science, rather than an accepted definition of science. The reflective teacher needs, however, to have thought this issue through if he or she is to avoid promoting the very kinds of belief to which SCAA object.

Modern science has progressed well beyond the seventeenth century concept of *naive realism*, whereby it was believed that any natural phenomenon could be accurately represented by a model. A classic example would be the Niels Bohr model of the atom. You may well be familiar with drawings or even solid models which purport to show atoms as being made of electrons as though these were 'solid' particles orbiting a 'solid' nucleus. You may even hold the misconception that this is what an atom is actually like. Such a *reductionist* approach, however, is wholly inadequate for a modern understanding of atomic structures. The term 'reductionist' derives from a philosophical idea, originally Greek, that matter can be reduced to fundamental particles which cannot be further reduced. Atoms themselves were once thought to be such particles. Modern science has had to abandon this notion in order to progress, and with the abandonment of the reductionist notion of fundamental particles has come the abandonment of naive realism.

Children of primary age, however, are mostly naively realistic in their thinking. Their perceptions are most frequently characterised by *literalism*. They are unable, therefore, to grasp the kinds of concepts that are involved in the difficult area of truth claims, science and religion. This can be a very serious impediment to spiritual development. The reflection below on an 8 year old pupil's understanding may help you develop your thinking about this:

Reflection 1

Eight year old Ben was in a group discussing the rainbow as a sign of the covenant. The teacher had in mind the notion of the covenant as a two way promise and intended to make the point that in return for God's promise never again to create an 'ecocatastrophe' of flooding the Earth man must promise to take good care of the Earth, to be a 'good steward' of creation in other words. Ben's view, however, was that the rainbow was a phenomenon caused by the splitting of white light into its constituent spectral colours by refraction in raindrops and that the matter ended there.

- Was Ben's understanding of the rainbow 'correct'?
- Was Ben's understanding 'adequate'?
- Was Ben's curiosity aroused?
- Did Ben exhibit qualities of wonder or even awe?
- Do you think Ben is capable of understanding the idea of a two way promise?
- Do you think that Ben is capable of understanding the role of symbolism in communicating non-literal beliefs?
- Is the story of Noah and the Flood a suitable topic for 7 and 8 year olds?

It is often assumed that the story of Noah's Ark is a suitable topic for 7 year olds. Perhaps this is because it involves animals, plenty of opportunity for colouring in and moral messages about Noah being rewarded for his 'goodness'. The above example, however, raises fundamental questions about naïve realism, literalism and ultimately reductionism. We need to remember that children of primary age hold naïve views about both science and religion. I would say that a possible outcome for Ben might be the ultimate rejection of religion – on the grounds that 'it tells you stories which aren't true'. The corollary of this might well also be a failure to understand the nature of science and the naïve belief in scientism to which SCAA object. There are two fundamental problems. The first is that few 7 year olds have the capacity to consider the degree to which Old Testament stories should be interpreted literally. This is a failing in religious education. The second is that, to supply a 7 year old with a scientific explanation such as 'the rainbow is caused by refraction' before such a concept can be properly understood and assimilated into a developing conceptual schema leading to further questions is a failing in scientific education. I would like to know whether Ben can explain why rainbows are always curved and never straight. I would like, even more, to know why he didn't ask this question.

These two failings, in religious education and in scientific education, combine to result in a third failing in spiritual development. Spiritual development, you will recall, is kept alive by such features as wonder and awe, or the contemplation of beauty. The word 'mystery' is perhaps a dangerous one, but I shall risk using it in this context, for where there is no mystery there can be no wonder. An approach in education which seeks to eliminate mystery by giving children a simple but naïve diet of 'right answers' that can easily be assessed by crude and simple technologies such as paper and pencil tests is an approach that does not promote spiritual development.

There is thus no modern mystery to the rainbow. It can indeed be explained by stating that it is 'caused by refraction' and the tragedy is that having thus 'rationalised' an intricately complex and beautiful phenomenon, Ben's curiosity is satisfied. Having 'explained away' the mystery, Ben has no need for further wonder and certainly no cause to feel awe. The perplexing difficulty is that this 'profoundly non-spiritual' approach to education has taught Ben (incorrectly) that curiosity ends with the rather limited explanation offered by his school science. This is a paradox because as scientists such as Steven Hawking (1988) argue, the scientific enterprise is driven by wonder and curiosity. Einstein is famously said to have stood 'rapt in awe'. Setting aside the whole question of metaphorical beliefs related to humankind's 'stewardship' of creation, Ben has as yet no inkling of the awesome frontier between mystery and understanding that may be revealed to him by quantum mechanics and such matters as wave/particle probability. Only a relatively small proportion of the population will come to have much understanding of these matters.

Clearly, there are at least two different ways of giving children a scientific education. There is a reductionist approach which destroys mystery and wonder and makes science boring. Alternatively, there is an approach in which curiosity about the wonders and beauties of scientific phenomena develops children spiritually. Similarly, there is an approach to the teaching of religious education which we may also call reductionist because it destroys mystery and wonder by giving children naïve answers to ultimate questions. Unless you yourself hold strongly fundamentalist beliefs, you will probably feel that children are right to reject the claim that there is an old man with a white beard on a cloud in the sky who made the whole world in six days. On the other hand, there is an approach to both scientific and religious education in which a shared sense of mystery and humility in the face of life's ultimate questions develops children spiritually.

Moral development

Case Study 1

Twelve year old Mandy had had a most unfortunate childhood. She came to the urgent attention of the social services when she was found sleeping rough in the streets. She and her 13 year old sister had been living with their father whose drinking problem had resulted in a total loss of control of the children. Mandy's behaviour at school was extremely challenging; spiteful and malicious towards her peers and openly defiant towards her teachers. Social services had extreme difficulty in placing her in care but eventually found a foster family who were able to impose a structure on her life which involved a basic discipline such as regular bedtimes. Mandy's school were amazed at a transformation in her behaviour and contacted the social services for an explanation of the disappearance of much of the malice and defiance.

You will be lucky if you enjoy a career in teaching without meeting children such as Mandy. You may even have had to cope with one or more already, in which case you will readily empathise with Mandy's teachers. You may have tried all sorts of strategies such as assertive discipline or behaviour modification, and you may have had some degree of success. Yet in Mandy's case, the school, which had undoubtedly exhausted its repertoire of strategies for dealing with challenging behaviour, were amazed at a seemingly inexplicable change whereby Mandy became much less unsociable. This is in fact an example of holism. Holism is another form of opposite to reductionism.

A reductionist approach such as behaviour modification aims to reduce a behaviour problem to a simple set of causes and events which can be controlled by the therapist, psychologist or teacher. By manipulating the antecedents of behaviours, we can achieve modifications which can then be reinforced by systems of reward, similar in principle to the methods used in training animals. Such approaches can work in a limited way on specific behaviours occurring in specific situations, but they do not act upon the whole child. They do not, in other words, develop the child spiritually and morally. Mandy's behaviour changed for holistic reasons. The change to a more secure and disciplined home environment with a higher standard of care resulted in unanticipated, unpredictable but positive changes at school. This is an important characteristic of holism. The exact effects are unpredictable but there is a general correlation between positive environments and positive behaviours. This is one reason why it is crucial for the school, home and if necessary social services, to work in partnership. It is why NCC (1993) draw attention to the need for schools to recognise the implications of the fact that moral development begins in the home.

Another important aspect of holism is that it is concerned not just with a child's knowledge, but with a child's feelings and a child's will to act. The National Curriculum Council make it clear that the will to behave morally as a point of principle is an attitude which is fundamental to moral development. The notion of 'weakness of will' is an idea well known in moral philosophy. It refers to the situation whereby a person knows what is considered to be the right thing to do but nevertheless does the wrong thing. This is relevant in Mandy's case because an explanation has to be found for the fact that Mandy knew that many of the things she did were wrong. She had been told many times by her teachers and was quite capable of giving the 'right answers' when asked moral questions. Yet in spite of this knowledge of right and wrong, she continued to do wrong things. We need to understand why Mandy's behaviour was so weak-willed. We need to understand why all children show weakness of will sometimes and why some children are more weak-willed than others.

An important part of the answer lies in the way in which reasoning, emotions and behaviour are all linked closely together. You may be familiar from your science teaching with the so called triangle of burning. In order for burning to take place, there must be a fuel supply, an air supply and heat. The will to behave morally can be thought of in a similar way. Imagine a triangle which has knowledge and reasoning along one side, feeling and emotion along the second and intention to act along the third. As with the fire, take away any one side and the moral development 'goes out'. Thus children first need to have knowledge appropriate to their age of what is considered right and wrong which is combined with the cognitive capacity to reason on the basis of that knowledge. A second and equally important requirement is that they must also have good feelings about themselves and their social and physical environments.

The third and final requirement is that the children must have a mental image of moral actions upon which they can intuitively model their own intention to act. Such an image is likely to be derived from experience of the moral behaviour of people to whom the children are emotionally attached or people to whom they look up. Moral development can proceed when these requirements are met. You will probably have realised, however, that it is much easier to address the first side of the triangle than the second and third sides. If you have reflected upon Mandy's case you will almost certainly have concluded that, although her school undoubtedly tried very hard to teach her 'right' and 'wrong' the second and third sides of the triangle almost certainly received inadequate attention. Mandy had bad feelings brought about by her degraded physical and social environments. She would have had constant negative feedback from hostile peers and a poor self-esteem in consequence. The person to whom she was most emotionally attached was frequently incapacitated by drink.

There is no shortage of guidance on moral development which has a lot to say about the cognitive or intellectual side of the triangle. It is, after all, easy to state that pupils must have knowledge of the codes and conventions of conduct agreed by society. It is similarly easy to write sets of school rules or to agree upon school values which are to be displayed in corridors and the school brochure. To deal with the emotional condition of a child such as Mandy is quite another matter. You may well feel that the emotional condition of children is not your professional concern. If you are an experienced teacher you will be only too well aware of the pressures on your time and the amount of time the 'morally weak' children seem to take up. You may even have emotional feelings of your own towards such children simply because they are so time consuming.

Enquiry task 2

Choose at least two children to observe systematically for at least a week. One should be a child who exhibits a strong moral sense, who is successful at school and seldom in trouble. The other should be a child who is often in trouble and whose moral sense seems to be lacking in certain aspects. Keep a record of the social interactions of these contrasting children by noting which ones appear to be positive in outcome, which appear negative and which appear neutral. (Interactions which are necessary to maintain a game or which are part of talk necessary to perform a classroom task are often neutral.)

- *Are you able to note any differences in the quality of social experience?*
- *Is there any evidence linking moral behaviour to the quality of social experience?*
- *Is it wise to deduce cause and effect in this scenario?*
- *Are any interventions on your part as teacher called for? If so, what?*

The triangle of reason, emotion and intention to act is a model we might well adopt if we are at all concerned about moral development. You can find plenty of ideas for the sorts of intellectual principles of right and wrong you ought to be upholding in the many books published on the subject, not least the guidance from NCC and SCAA, which provides a succinct summary. I shall assume that you will read these and concentrate, therefore, upon a summary of the qualities you might need to attend to the other sides of the triangle and thereby enhance your skills as a teacher who is able to promote the moral development of children.

- A preparedness to value children by giving them time.
- A preparedness to listen to children.
- A willingness to take on the role of children's advocate: to stand up for them and to let them know they are cared about without giving in to them or compromising on right and wrong.
- A preparedness to embrace wholeheartedly the principles of partnership and community education.
- A non-judgmental attitude which does not label children as 'good' or 'bad'.
- A commitment always to hear both sides of a dispute in the interests of fairness and justice.
- The ability to support children emotionally without becoming emotionally involved.
- A knowledge of current affairs as seen from the children's viewpoint and the skill to discuss with children the behaviour of public figures.
- The courage to give higher priority, when appropriate, to children's emotional welfare than to the ability to perform paper and pencil tests and achieve good Standard Assessment Task results.
- The strength to change the things you can change, the serenity to accept the things you cannot change and the wisdom to know the difference.

To summarise the argument so far then, we might say that encouragement of the will to act morally is probably the most important element of the task of developing children morally. We must be quite clear about how the exercise of this autonomous will differs from the performance of apparently moral actions as a result of coercion, fear or persuasion through behaviour modification techniques. The word heteronomy is used to refer to the latter, whilst autonomy refers to the former. Only autonomy can be considered as the product of moral development. As I have explained, we have to promote the cognitive element of moral reasoning, most commonly through confronting children with moral dilemmas appropriate to their age. We have equally to promote the affective element of feeling good through right relationships and self-esteem. Finally, we have to do all this within a climate of moral behaviour by the people to whom the children look up and are attached. Provide these ingredients and it is probable that the maturation of children's minds will do the rest.

The other principal feature of moral development, which equates almost to the autonomous will to behave morally, is the recognition and understanding of the concept of responsibility. Indeed, the ability to function as a responsible being is thought by many theorists to be the factor which distinguishes the moral from the non-moral. Research into the moral development of children has shown that the acquisition of the concept of reciprocity is a key stage in the journey towards moral maturity. At a very simple level, reciprocity can be understood as 'You scratch my back and I'll scratch yours'. At a rather more sophisticated level, reciprocity equates to:

 What is hateful to you, do not do to your fellow man. (Jewish)

Love your neighbour as yourself. (Christian)

No one of you is a believer until he loves for his brother what he loves for himself. (Islamic)

Do not to others what if done to you would cause you pain. (Hindu)

Hurt not others with that which pains yourself. (Buddhist)

Given such universal backing, it is surprising how often school rules are purely heteronomous and imposed without consultation or any hope of linking rights with responsibilities. Heteronomy, you will recall, does not necessarily lead to moral development for it may contain no elements of reflection or moral reasoning. In the next chapter, I consider further the question of rights and responsibilities in the context of citizenship. Citizenship has moral elements and constructive engagement with issues of

FIG 7.1
Definitions of moral
development

NCC
The will to behave morally
Knowledge of moral codes of society…statutory and non-prescribed
Knowledge and understanding of the criteria which are the basis for moral judgment
The ability to make moral judgments

SCAA
Knowledgable about standards of right and wrong
Skilled in moral reasoning
Willing to be responsible
Prepared to be responsible for actions

OFSTED
Pupils' knowledge, understanding, intentions, attitudes and behaviour in relation to what is right or wrong.

citizenship will not be possible without a basic vocabulary and conceptual framework of moral development. It is unlikely that education in citizenship will proceed very far in any institution where the spiritual, moral and cultural development of the pupils is not high on the agenda.

Reciprocity was an element singly lacking in Mandy's life. Such moral failure, however, has an undeniable logic to it. Why should Mandy behave well to anybody else when everybody else behaved so unpleasantly towards her? There is clearly a 'chicken and egg' situation here and it is for this reason that we owe children the benefit of the doubt. Ultimately, rights are prior to responsibilities and all children have the right to expect us to facilitate their moral development. This might well mean that we have to defend the Mandys of this world. The highest ideal in this respect is that of unconditional love and you might reflect on the meaning of this term and the degree to which you might be able to commit yourself to it in the interests of spiritual and moral development. During my long years of sorting out children's quarrels, one thing I came never to allow was the 'But she started it' routine. This leads nowhere. I always made it a priority to persuade my classes of the wisdom of adopting the maxim, 'We're not interested in blaming the person who started it, we're interested in praising the person who stops it'.

To conclude this section on moral development, you might like to consider the degree to which the definitions of moral development given in Figure 7.1 are reflected in the account that has been given. You might also like to reflect on what is missing from them as prescriptions of moral development. Reflection 2, which follows, may prompt further thought.

Reflection 2

A Year 4 class was taken swimming by a supply teacher. The class consisted of 29 white pupils and one black pupil whom we shall call Isaac. The teacher was surprised when Isaac insisted upon having a changing cubicle to himself, whilst all the other boys changed in the communal school cubicle. On querying this, the teacher was assured by the other boys that this was permitted and normal practice, so the teacher allowed Isaac to have a cubicle to himself. Not certain that he had done the right thing, however, the teacher later checked with the parallel class teacher and was informed that this was indeed the normal practice, since it alleviated the difficulties that arose when the boys teased Isaac about his skin colour as he undressed.

- Is this a suitable case for the 'We do that when it crops up at playtime' approach?
- Do you agree with the solution to this problem of racial harassment imposed by the school?
- Would you say that the school teaches the values of racial equality and respect for individual differences effectively?
- Would you say that pupils are developed spiritually, morally and culturally by the school's approach?
- Are the reactions and attitudes of the white pupils inevitable?
- Are the feelings of the black pupil of any consequence?
- Is it reasonable to expect the black pupil to develop a strong will to behave morally as a reciprocal response to the respect and care shown for him?

Cultural development

Twelve year old Amy is a member of her youth club committee. We were discussing the possibility of including cultural and recreational activities in the forthcoming programme that was being planned. What, I asked, was culture or a cultural event? 'Culture's all to do with understanding other people, it's all about how different people live, like knowing about people from different races or religions' was Amy's erudite reply. This wasn't quite what I had in mind. You might guess that the meaning I had attached to the word was one which encompassed activities such as planning a visit to a concert or play, perhaps to the cinema. The meaning which Amy attached to the word, however, was one which we might imagine could have had its origins in the fact that pluralism or multiculturalism was a clearly explicit value of the primary school she had attended. If no other purpose is served, Amy's little story reminds us of just how important it is in the social-constructivist tradition, to engage us in dialogue in order to achieve a shared meaning.

Is cultural development concerned, however, merely with the transmission of the values of tolerance and the acceptability of multiculturalism as a principle? What does it mean to be a 'cultured' person? Can this question be answered without consideration of the role of 'cultural' activities? What activities are to count as 'cultural'? Amy's understanding does not seem to encompass the notion of the appreciation of art, music or literature as 'culture'. It does not even begin to address the question of whether such qualities as a fascination with number, a delight in the natural world or the pursuit of scientific insights are to count as 'culture'. If such values are absent from Amy's definition, are we to assume that they are also largely absent from the values being taught by her school?

We are confronted here by the problem of *relativism*. Consider what is meant by the terms 'high' and 'low' culture. We might conceive of 'high' culture in the form of ballet or 'classical' music whilst we might conceive of 'low' culture in the form of a television soap or the music of whatever group is currently popular amongst young people. We might imagine an association between 'high' culture and the broadsheet newspapers and 'low' culture and the tabloid newspapers. Is there also an association between mass consumption and the high/low culture continuum? How true is it that Channel Three television caters for mass audiences with 'popular' programmes, whilst Channel Four caters for small audiences by showing programmes which appeal to a 'cultured minority'? Is 'popular' culture necessarily 'low' culture?

This is the problem of relativism because it involves value judgments about what is 'good' in culture. If schools exist to promote that which is 'good', then who is to decide what is 'good'? To the cultural relativist, this is not a problem, since cultural values are entirely a matter of individual choice. If my friend likes a 60s pop group and I like the music of J. S. Bach, then that is his or my business respectively. There are no absolute cultural standards which might enable us to judge one or other of these cultural forms to be the more worthy. Indeed, to the cultural relativist, the only absolute value is cultural relativism itself. The only unacceptable value is to suggest that an attempt be made to teach children to value one cultural form more highly than another, even if this is done simply by not teaching certain cultural forms (values transmission by omission).

What, then, is to count as cultural development? Is it to be the teaching of the absolute principle that all forms of cultural activity are of equal worth and that none is to be preferred to another? Is cultural development to be defined simply as teaching children that there are other people with different views and that our primary moral obligation is to be tolerant of those views? Alternatively, does cultural development entail the identification of cultural values and attitudes deemed to be worthwhile and the subsequent transmission of those values? If you reflect seriously enough on this question, you will come to realise just how convoluted a problem relativism is. You may, of course, already hold certain values or attitudes which predispose you to a certain answer. You may feel that tolerance is the only absolute value and that the obligations of teachers and schools are to be defined primarily as the transmission of this value, combined with a view of cultural development that emphasises breadth of experience; in other words, the exposure of children to as many different forms of culture as possible.

On the other hand, you may feel that certain aspects of culture are more worthwhile than others. You may feel that, as a teacher (or parent), you have a duty to uphold practising the violin or training for the swimming club to be more worthwhile ways for children to spend their time than watching a popular television soap. You may indeed feel that you would be failing children if your work with them never lead them to reflect upon whether striving to attain fulfilment from a cultural form other than mass entertainment might be worthwhile.

If moral development has the capacity to unite by working towards those aspects of greater moral law that are common to all cultures, religions and belief systems, then cultural development has potentially the opposite potential. We need to reflect upon how many conflicts in the world are in fact cultural ones. You might consider the extent to which divisions in society are really cultural ones. A 'youth culture' in conflict with a 'middle-aged, middle-class culture' or 'deviant sub-cultures' in school, for example. To the extent that history is sometimes said to give us our cultural identity, was the conflict in Northern Ireland a cultural one?

Cultural development and spiritual development are often confused. One possible reason for this is that we sometimes use cultural 'artefacts, such as music, as a means of communicating or articulating feelings which we call spiritual. For some people, a walk in the Lakeland Fells can achieve what for other people is achieved by art or literature. Equally, it may be the case that you may enjoy any of these things at a deep level yet not call them spiritual. Spiritual development transcends mere entertainment or recreation. It transcends art and it transcends social boundaries. For religious believers, spirituality might be an encounter with the deity. For non-believers it might be the power of the human spirit to transcend insurmountable challenges. Yet believers and non-believers alike may need a culture to articulate and communicate their spirituality.

Cultural artefacts are thus linked intimately to outward social identity and intimately to deep, personal feelings. We have a real challenge in cultural development to satisfy two criteria. We must not uphold the culture of one ethnic or socio-economic group as 'better' than another. At the same time we must provide standards by which children come to recognise particular cultural activities as worthwhile. Ultimately, we cannot communicate with children spiritually without culture. Yet dogmatic adherence to a sociocultural identity can block spiritual and moral development. It is little wonder that we dodge thunderbolts as we walk across eggshells.

Cultural development might be seen to include:
■ Development of tolerance towards the outward identities of different social groups.
■ Increased capacity to be moved by art, music or literature reflected in dissatisfaction with the banal.
■ Recognition of the intrinsic as well as the functional value of science and mathematics.

Cultural development is not, therefore, the transmission of knowledge about other cultures. As are spiritual and moral development, cultural development is about the growth of the individual. In that cultural development involves a maturation of emotions, values and attitudes, it is closely related to spiritual and moral growth, and the linking of the three together might well be considered appropriate. It may be apposite to refer back to the brief chronology of breadth and balance in the primary curriculum that was given in Chapter 1. The liberal democratic ideal of the development of the whole child has been, ever since the 1902 Balfour Act and the 1904 Public Elementary School Code, one of the most formative influences on the values of primary education throughout the twentieth century. Although other values may have changed, the twenty first century seems set to continue the tradition. The wise, reflective teacher will see spiritual, moral and cultural development as something which grows from within the individual, not a set of targets to be imposed from without.

References

DAWKINS, R. (1994) 'Growing up in the universe', Royal Institution Christmas Lectures, Lecture no. I *Waking Up in the Universe*.

HAWKING, S. (1988) *A Brief History of Time*, London: Bantam.

HOLM, A. (1963) *I Am David*, London: Mammoth.

HOUGHTON, J. (1997) *The Search for God: Can Science Help?* Oxford: Lion.

NCC (1993) *Spiritual and Moral Development: A Discussion Paper*, Hayes: National Curriculum Council publications.

ORR, D. (1994) *Earth in Mind: On Education, Environment and the Human Prospect*, Washington: Island Press.

SCAA (1995) Discussion Paper No. 3 *Spiritual and Moral Development*, Hayes: School Curriculum and Assessment Authority Publications.

Further reading

Best, R. (1996) *Education, Spirituality and the Whole Child*, London: Cassell.
This book deals in greater philosophical depth with many of the issues covered in this chapter. Similar areas are also covered by the Smith and Standish book listed at the end of Chapter 1.

Hay, D. and Nye, R. (1998) *The Spirit of the Child*, London: HarperCollins.
This book is an account of a research project into the spiritual dimension of children's personalities. It pursues the notion that spirituality is biologically natural to the human species and examines ways in which cultural conditioning represses the spiritual instincts. In highlighting relational consciousness (centrality of the awareness of others) it makes an interesting contrast with the Thatcher view of individualism discussed in the next chapter of this volume.

Inman, S. and Buck, M. (eds) (1995) *Adding Value? School's Responsibility for Pupils' Personal Development*, Stoke on Trent: Trentham.
A useful general reader on the question of values and the development of the whole child. Chapter 7 by Lynne Broadbent, entitled 'Making sense of the spiritual and moral', is of particular relevance.

Chapter 8	Citizenship: a new word for humanities?

Martin Ashley with Steve Barnes

> ❝ *The English people believes itself to be free. It is greatly mistaken; it is free only during the election of members of parliament. Once they are elected, the populace is enslaved: it is nothing. The use the English people makes of that freedom in the brief moments of its liberty certainly warrants their losing it.*
>
> (Jean Jacques Rousseau, 1762)

> *Active citizens are as political as they are moral: moral sensibility derives in part from political understanding; political apathy spawns moral apathy.*
>
> (Hargreaves, 1994)

The French enlightenment philosopher, Jean Jacques Rousseau, clearly held the English in some contempt. It is interesting, 200 odd years after the French Revolution, to reflect on the situation Rousseau described. Until very recently, the UK has been one of the very few European states which does not teach some programme of civics. Yet now the Qualifications and Curriculum Authority is happy to quote the second rather challenging statement, made by Professor David Hargreaves in a Demos pamphlet, *The Mosaic of Learning*. It is true that an earlier attempt was made to introduce citizenship as one of five cross-curricular themes almost at the inception of the National Curriculum. It is also true, however, that few schools took much of the cross-curricular guidance seriously, largely as a result of the much publicised curriculum overload. Yet times are changing and new priorities are emerging. History and geography have been downgraded, whilst citizenship appears to have the really serious backing of the government.

In this chapter, we take the view that without history or geography, there would be no citizenship. In that sense, history and geography can hardly have been downgraded at all.

In the absence of any tradition in the UK of education in philosophy, religious education also has some role to play. An understanding of the concept of citizenship is not possible without a sound background in history and geography. Neither is it possible without a sound and systematic development of the spiritual, moral and cultural. The ability to make rational value judgments, rather than to be governed by ill-informed and emotionally driven prejudice, is an intellectual freedom at the core of citizenship to which all children ought to have right of access. That, in itself, is a political statement.

Introduction

If you are of a certain age, you may have noticed the virtual disappearance from the English language of a whole series of words beginning with the letter p. For example, passenger, patron, patient, purchaser, plaintiff. Most important of all, to us as teachers, are perhaps the very words *pupil* and *parent*. All of these words have tended to be replaced by the universal 'c' word, *customer*. People travelling in railway trains or flying in aircraft are no longer *passengers*, they are *customers*. Theatre, concert and cinema goers are no longer patrons, they are customers. If you fall ill, you may well not be a patient of your local NHS Trust, you are more likely to be a customer. If you have recourse to the legal system, the word customer may even be used in place of the word plaintiff. The children who may sit in front of you tomorrow, and their parents, are now regarded by many as the customers of the education service.

This is more than a mere 'dumbing down' of the English language. Behind this superficially innocuous exercise in semantics lies a powerful political ideology which itself espouses a powerful and partisan ideology of citizenship. The word 'customer' is itself the gentile veneer for the value laden word consumer – a word which has somewhat greater power to provoke passions. Consumerism was bequeathed to the nation mainly by the Thatcher government. Indeed, through the right wing Thatcher/Reagan alliance, consumerism has become a powerful global force which is by no means spent at the beginning of the twenty-first century. If you have any concerns over the degree to which consumerism seems to have displaced many of the spiritual, moral and cultural features of our national life, you may not be a whole-hearted supporter of Thatcherism.

Whatever your political views, however, as a person responsible for the development of attitudes and values in young children you need to have some insight into the relationship between consumerism and citizenship, both in the recent past and in the near future. Closely associated to the notion of consumerism is a particular aspect of citizenship which was very dear to the heart of Margaret Thatcher's successor, John Major. This is what is known as *charterism*. As a 'citizen', you may well be familiar with the Patient's Charter. You may even have obtained redress from a recalcitrant provider of rail services through the Passenger's Charter. As a teacher, you must be aware of the Parent's Charter. The Parent's Charter gives all pupils, irrespective of their background, the right of entitlement to the whole National Curriculum. It places upon you, the teacher, a clear duty to deliver this entitlement. In terms of political ideology, the Parent's Charter is indicative of a substantial shift from the 'Ps' to the 'Cs'. From Professionals and Providers to Customers and Consumers.

This political ideology, with its emphasis upon consumption and consumer entitlements, is the same ideology that is behind the shift in culture from the professional to the manager. You may feel that the Health Service has improved considerably since power was taken from consultants, doctors and nurses and placed in the hands of a new breed of professional administrators and managers. You may feel that school meals have improved since the introduction of contractors and competitive tendering. Alternatively you may feel that this is not the case, particularly if you have had a bad experience of conflict between 'market forces', or the profit motive and the value judgment that a school has responsibility to promote healthy eating. Issues such as these stem from the political belief that policy, management and provision should be discrete functions separated by business style contracts. The legacy of the long period of Conservative administration is an emphasis upon deregulation and individual choice which can sometimes be hostile to social and environmental controls which impede economic efficiency. It is the charterist vision of citizenship in which consumer rights are the most dominant theme and the protection of these the most dominant function of the state.

The reflective teacher will wonder about the degree to which the business and management led ideology should permeate education. She will wonder whether head teachers who have served their apprenticeship as classroom teachers should be replaced by professionally trained school administrators and managers who have little or no experience of classroom teaching. If the reflective teacher is committed to such values as open-mindedness and acceptance of the need for change, she is likely to contemplate such radical possibilities seriously. She will also wonder, however, how the arrival of a 'New Labour' administration affected these matters, and how, as a (managed) professional she should communicate to young children the attitudes and values that underpin or promote something called 'good citizenship'.

An immediate answer is that much of this wondering is now done for her. New Labour boldly proclaimed the vision of citizenship that is to replace John Major's charterism. In 1988, under the Conservatives, the National Curriculum Council wrote

> ❛ *The Education Act does not prescribe how pupils should be taught. It is the birthright of the teaching profession, **and must always remain so**, to decide on the best and most appropriate means of imparting education to pupils.*

This long cherished value was swept aside by New Labour in a welter of initiatives which promoted literacy and numeracy hours, guidance on the best and most appropriate way of teaching ICT and the foundation subjects, and unprecedented guidance on what our new national values are. You may not realise it, but if you have qualified in recent years, or are about to do so, you have been trained by means of a prescriptive set of 'competences' which are themselves part of the ideology of charterism and the management and accountability culture. The response of New Labour to this Conservative initiative was to change the term 'competency' to 'standard', thereby promoting and selling a public image of 'raising standards' – with the clearly explicit belief that this is done most effectively by central government.

It is not our position in this book or chapter to give an opinion about whether educational standards will genuinely rise or fall when driven by such ideologies. It is, however, very much our intention to draw to your attention the fact that these are all key issues of citizenship. We also wish to draw to your attention the vital fact that without a knowledge of history, you would have no freedom. We are suggesting that without history, you would understand neither the recent political changes I have outlined above, nor the profound political changes in the past which have created our modern concepts of citizenship. Liberty is a fundamental concept of citizenship and there can be no liberty if people are kept ignorant of history. Citizenship requires more than a knowledge of where we have come from. It requires a knowledge of where we are now which, combined with a knowledge of our past, informs our vision of where we are to go in the future. The metaphorical ambiguity surrounding 'place' here is deliberate. I am referring both to our physical location in the world of political maps, and our 'place' in global society as an economic and political player. So we need geography too.

Behind all of this is what the philosopher Giroux (1983) has called 'dangerous knowledge'. The charterist vision of education sees an *entitlement* to receive the prescribed National Curriculum. This must be 'delivered' by an 'effectively managed' teaching force, subservient to and responsive to the wishes of parents and pupils as 'consumers' of education. The charterist vision does not see an entitlement to challenge what is prescribed by the National Curriculum, or the right to receive an education which is not the version of the National Curriculum rigidly enforced by the OFSTED inspection system. Such rights and entitlements may be part of the UN Declaration of Human Rights, but they are not currently available to parents, pupils or teachers in British maintained schools. Knowledge of this fact is indeed 'politically dangerous'. It may bring the reflective teacher into conflict with the dominant ideology or the agents of its enforcement. The possibility of such conflict is at the heart of the citizenship debate. In the next part of the chapter we review very briefly the history and definitions of citizenship. We also look at some work with children in school. Finally, we consider at some length the 'European problem'.

Citizenship: the historical background

In the United States of America, elections are normally contested between the Republican and the Democrat parties. For the student of citizenship, this is possibly less confusing than the British system. The English language is often quirky. For example, the hills of south eastern England are called 'downs', and foreigners might be excused for thinking the British a little eccentric when they talk about going for a walk up the downs. As we shall show shortly, similar linguistic difficulties attach to such words as 'liberal'. The terms republican and democrat do not have such difficulties and conveniently indicate two broad traditions in citizenship. The republican tradition has its ancient roots in classical Greece, and its more recent roots in the French Revolution, where it was particularly associated with the philosopher Rousseau (1712–1778). The democrat tradition is much associated with the English philosopher John Locke (1732–1704), whose ideas were very influential on the founding fathers of the American constitution. You may well have taught The Greeks at Key Stage 2, as this has until recently been a compulsory part of the history Orders. If you have, you may have been attracted to the idea of introducing children to the idea of democracy and citizenship as an element of this study unit.

If you have done, or plan to do so again, we would urge some degree of caution. By our modern standards, the ancient Greeks were anything but 'democratic'. Modern day usage of this word implies some kind of universal suffrage. We have come to associate democracy with everybody having a voice in government. In ancient Greece, however, the citizen was a superior and exclusive class. Women were not citizens and slaves were not citizens. We would not consider that democratic today. Another very important difference between modern Britain and ancient Greece is that modern British democracy is representative, whereas ancient Greek democracy was participatory. In a representative democracy, we vote for a member of parliament on the basis of a manifesto, and entrust our hopes and aspirations to that person for a period of five or so years. In a participatory democracy, we each vote on issues as and when they arrive.

Representative democracy has run into some difficulties of late. We have an ongoing debate about such matters as a 'first past the post' electoral system as opposed to proportional representation. We also have a prevalent distrust of politicians and a lack of interest in voting amongst the 18 to 25 age group which was sufficiently widespread to alarm, amongst others, New Labour's first Education Secretary. This loss of confidence in representative democracy has become associated with the rise of single issue politics, of which green campaigning against road building and suchlike became a force to be taken seriously during the last two decades of the twentieth century. We should not idolise the ancient Greeks, however. Their participatory democracy operated in small city states, such as Athens and Argos, which bear no comparison with a modern nation state. You may recall the notorious debacle of the national television debate of 1996 on the future of the monarchy, which gave some indication of the difficulties faced by popular participatory democracy. Electronic home voting may be many years away, in spite of modern interactive communications technology.

The possibility would almost certainly have interested the French political philosopher Rousseau, had he been alive today. Rousseau believed that there was something called the 'general will'. You may have noticed that, even to this day, the French seem much more amenable to the idea of a referendum or 'plebiscite' than do the British. A referendum is thought necessary in the republican tradition of the French Revolution to discover what the 'general will' is. Roussau's views on this are interesting. Apart from his contempt for English democracy (quoted at the head of the chapter) Rousseau became famous for the quotation 'Man (sic) must be forced to be free'. He believed that the general will is what is best for the state. If a person is clear headed and thinks according to reason, that person will agree with the general will. People who do not agree with the general will are either ignorant or not thinking according to reason. In such cases, it is legitimate to force them to obey the general will – to force them to be free in other words.

You may think that this sounds somewhat 'undemocratic' – totalitarian even. If you do, bear in mind that in the United States, the electorate has a choice between republican and democrat. Why should anyone want to choose republican if that means voting for 'forcing people to be free'? If we go back to the ancient Greeks, we find an idea that was very attractive to Rousseau. This is the idea of *civic virtue*. The ideal Greek citizen put public duty before family and was incorruptible through the code of honour that went with civic responsibility. The citizen owed the State duty in return for the privileges and protections of citizenship. Civic virtue tended to stress such ideals as communitarianism rather more than individualism. It has given us our idea of the 'good citizen'. The current enthusiasm for citizenship in our schools arises in part from a concern about public ignorance and apathy towards our democratic institutions. It also arises in part from alarm that we no longer have 'good citizens' who pick up litter and take part in voluntary community activities. The moral element of citizenship is very important to the republican tradition and it is particularly appealing at a time when an unprecedented focus on individualism has left us with a society which some people regard as lacking in moral virtue and civic responsibility.

We began this chapter with a review of John Major's Charterism in which we pointed out the degree to which a focus on consumer rights was associated with the supremacy of individualism. You will be able to understand the position at the beginning of the twenty first century better when we have considered the other great tradition of citizenship, that of liberal democracy. Republicanism is of course incompatible with the idea of monarchy, since sovereignty in a republic rests with the people and their general will, not with an heredity monarch. In the United Kingdom, our tradition is strongly liberal democratic. The British, in general, are not republicans. Whether Conservative, Labour or Liberal, of 'Old' or 'New' varieties, the concept of a parliamentary democracy with a 'loyal opposition' is in stark contrast to Rousseau's notion of a single party state in which everyone follows the general will. The 'loyal' in loyal opposition of course means loyal to the monarch, who is sovereign, and gives rise to an interesting anomaly.

The ideas of John Locke can be identified here. Locke believed in the existence of inalienable individual rights: the Right to Life, the Right to Liberty, the Right to Property and the Right to Rebel against unjust rulers and laws. For Locke, these rights were inalienable because they were ordained by God. The ruler of Locke's 'civil society' had no divine right, since all men were created equal by God. The primary purpose of the ruler was to protect the rights of the individual subjects, who had the right to remove any ruler with aspirations to absolute power. In his influential works *Two treatises of government* (1690) Locke proposed the notion of checks and balances within the state. The influence of the English civil war is evident in his proposal that, in place of absolute monarchy, there should be separate executive and legislative powers. The legislative power, which was the elected parliament was supreme. The monarch, or president, as the executive power, must act according to the wishes of the legislature, the people having the inalienable right to remove a monarch or president who did not do so, by force if necessary.

Locke is thus considered by many to be the father of modern liberalism. The word liberal in this context unequivocally refers to the inalienable rights of the individual. Thomas Jefferson regarded Locke as the spiritual guide of the American Constitution and the principles of his political philosophy are plainly evident in that constitution. The unwritten British Constitution, with its 'loyal subjects' and 'Her Majesty's Forces', whilst operating in principle on a Lockean model, is perhaps more ambiguous about the rights of the people to depose an unsatisfactory monarch. In stating that 'the great and chief end of men uniting into commonwealths and putting themselves under government is the preservation of their property' (1690) Locke revealed a disposition to the ownership of private property which we might associate with the individualism of the Thatcher years. It is wise also to remember that Locke's inalienable rights no more applied to women, the poor or slaves than did the rights of Greek citizenship. Indeed, as secretary to the Board of Trade and Plantations, Locke profited out of such individual property as human slaves.

Ambiguity would seem a word that can be used in describing the unwritten British constitution and the position of British subjects in relation to the status of citizenship. It is also a word that can apply to the term 'liberal' in British politics. The existence of a political party calling itself 'Liberal Democrats' is a case in point, particularly when it is appreciated that the British Conservative party is also 'liberal' in the tradition given to us by Locke. Liberal can mean 'moderately progressive'; or 'favourable to democratic reform', in which case liberal with a small 'l' is broadly compatible with Liberal with a big 'L'. It can also refer to the *laissez faire* tradition of free trade and free market capitalism, in which case Conservative with a big 'C' is actually liberal. This is confusing for the uninitiated who has only a passing acquaintance with British economic and political history. Conservatives and Liberals are both liberal in that they share a common disdain for traditional socialism which is illiberal in its desire to nationalise and increase central planning and state control. Now there is 'New Labour', which is a liberal version of socialism.

Liberal is also a pejorative term in that it can mean 'excessively permissive' as in the 'free sex swinging sixties', in which case many Conservatives would be anti-liberal. Such Conservatives tend to portray the liberal emphasis upon 'moderately progressive' as 'woolly' or 'do-gooding' and you can hardly be unaware of the pejorative meaning that has now become attached to the 'progressive' child-centred primary education that was endorsed by the Plowden Report of 1967. Liberal bishops are sometimes similarly pilloried by the tabloid press for not believing in God, through naïve and simplistic reporting of complex issues.

The core value of liberal democracy, however, is that of the freedom and consequent rights of the individual. Liberal democracy is seen as the liberation of the individual from an oppressive state. If you are a British subject, then you can presumably look to Her Majesty's forces to protect your liberty. The concept of liberal democracy is the first resort in confronting the difficulties encountered by a person who sincerely believes that the general will is wrong, and who acts according to reason in sound mind and good conscience. Rousseau did not allow the existence of such people. In contrasting the republican and liberal democratic traditions since the time of the French Revolution, we perhaps need to bear in mind our experiences of totalitarian states and stands taken against tyrants by 'liberal thinkers' such as Bonhoffer. The very notion 'democracy' is interpreted in the liberal tradition as opposed to the idea of a general will in that it allows dissenters and minorities to co-exist with majorities. In this sense, liberal democracy sits more comfortably with the idea of pluralism and the value of multiculturalism than does civic republicanism.

The latter idea might concern you very much as a teacher in a pluralist society. The former might well be a starting point for young children who need to learn about democracy. One of the most difficult lessons for children of primary age is coming to terms with the fact that you may not get what you personally want when the class or group takes a vote. This dilemma confronting teacher and child is in many ways a microcosm of the dilemma confronting modern European states as they try to embrace the best parts of both civic republican and liberal democratic traditions. We return to this question in the next section of the chapter. In the mean time, we conclude with some reflections and an enquiry task, which we hope will assist you in placing the guidance on citizenship with which you now have to work in its historical and political context.

Reflection 3

What is the right balance between liberal individualism and civic responsibility?

Margaret Thatcher once said 'There is no such thing as society'. David Blunkett made scarcely veiled threats about what will happen to schools and teachers who do not follow the prescriptions of the literacy hour.

- How true is it that Thatcher's emphasis upon individualism and consumerism has contributed to a lack of community responsibility in today's society?
- How far can community responsibility be promoted in a liberal society through the making of threats in the manner of David Blunkett, or the use of an enforcement agency such as OFSTED?

FIG 8.1
The domains of
citizenship

- Freedom and Authority
- Democracy and Government
    workplace
    local
    national
    European
    global

- Law and Justice
- Rights and Responsibilities
- Public Virtue and Morality
- Institutions
    State and Civic

Enquiry task 1

The earlier National Curriculum Council cross-curricular guidance on citizenship attempted a very wide ranging definition which encompassed most of the areas in Figure 8.1. The Qualifications and Curriculum Authority have produced a more narrowly focused definition of what they mean by effective education for citizenship. They summarise it as 'three heads on one body':

(a) *Social and moral responsibility*: children learning from the very beginning self-confidence and socially and morally responsible behaviour both in and beyond the classroom, both towards those in authority and towards each other.
Guidance on moral values and personal development, concepts of fairness, attitudes to the law, rules, decision making, authority, local environment and sociability. Developing awareness of whether or not their society is democratic.

(b) *Community involvement*: learning about and becoming helpfully involved in the life and concerns of their communities, including learning through community involvement and service to the community.
In and out of school, the development of political skill through 'non-partisan' voluntary bodies exercising persuasion, interacting with public authorities, publicising, fund-raising, recruiting and activating members.

(c) *Political literacy*: learning about, and how to make themselves effective in, public life through knowledge, skills and values.
Realistic knowledge of and preparation for conflict resolution, decision making related to main economic and social problems, expectations of and preparation for employment, discussion of public resources and taxation, formal and informal, locally, nationally and internationally.

- Which traditions of citizenship (republican or liberal democratic) are represented in the above definitions?
- Have elements of each tradition been combined?
- Would you say that the above definitions, if carried out as intended, are preparing children for an entitlement to 'consume' passively that which is prescribed (e.g. the National Curriculum) or for an entitlement to participate actively in changing and developing that which is to be prescribed?
- Read the *Parents' Charter*. How does it compare as a document about citizenship with the above guidance?
- Would you say that, for an 8 year old, joining the Cubs or Brownies satisfies the need for community involvement as it is defined in (b) above? Discuss, if possible, with a colleague who has experience of the Scout Organisation.
- Make a list of community organisations for children of primary age which you think would promote citizenship as it has been defined. Be specific in stating how each organisation promotes the aspects of citizenship that have been defined.
- In what ways would you say that your school makes children aware that their society is democratic? Make a list and discuss with colleagues.
    Ask some children which of their school rules they have been involved in formulating.
- Interview a leader of a community organisation for children. Endeavour to find out whether children are involved in policy making, or whether the view is that children should be taught conformity to the organisation's rules, constitution and objectives.
- Does a 10 year old have the right to privacy in his or her bedroom, including the right to keep their things as he or she wants (i.e. untidy)? Discuss this question with a range of parents of different aged children.

Putting citizenship into practice

I was recently questioned at the end of a lecture I gave which was entitled 'Children as miniature citizens?' The question went something like . . . 'Suppose you have a democratic classroom and the children vote that the National Curriculum is boring?' This is a very good question. The answer I gave went something like this.

 Children have to learn the limits to democracy and to formulate realistic expectations in relation to their own relationships with their workplace, community and country. One of the most important lessons they have to learn is that they can't always have what they want, but that they have the right to make their wants known and the right to question authority. They need to learn that there are appropriate ways of questioning authority. They need to learn how to use these, how to formulate and present good arguments, and that when the appropriate channels are pursued, peaceful change is achieved if the arguments are good enough.

I added the caveat that, in my experience, children most commonly justified the National Curriculum on narrow and utilitarian grounds. 'It will get us a good job.' Is that *all*? I find this a damning indictment of English primary schools.

I have heard the idea of democracy in schools dismissed by cynical teachers on such grounds as that it 'raises false hopes'. I find this depressing for two reasons. First, it shows an ignorance on the part of such teachers of the true nature of education for democracy and many of the aspects of citizenship we described in the previous section. Second, it simply isn't true where there are cases of good practice. For example, in Richmond-upon-Thames, 22 schools participating in a joint exercise with Richmond Borough Council have a pupil parliament which has brought first-aid teaching to the school curriculum, contributed to the borough's anti-racist policy, commissioned a booklet on pet care by a local vet, established a nursery garden to provide trees for the borough's schools and saved an area of rain forest the size of Richmond. The pupils visit the town hall and gain first hand experience of real institutions of government at work. Pupils at a school in Somerset voted with considerable enthusiasm for an environmental parliament. Through this they learned that it was not possible to save money for sports equipment by conducting an energy audit and saving electricity because the electricity supplier places the school on a Peak User Tariff which acts as a financial incentive to waste energy. This is real learning through citizenship about economics and the environment and counteracts the kind of emotional environmental indoctrination that we discuss in Chapter 10.

If you are unaware of the ultimate experiment in freedom and school democracy, you might find it interesting to read about A. S. Neill's Summerhill School, in his book by that name (Neill, 1962). Another interesting case study is that of the William Tyndale affair (see list for further reading). William Tyndale was a school in London which broke down through the rather radical views on freedom and authority that were held by the senior staff. The Tyndale affair was one of the key events that signalled the beginning of the current trend for greater government control of education. We are by no means suggesting that either Summerhill or William Tyndale are models for democracy. A critical reading of them might, however, help you to formulate your own views on proper authority in schools in a democratic society. You might also find the following research focus of interest:

Research focus

Pupils in Year 6 and Year 9 at four different schools were asked whether they would be willing to pay for education if it were not available free of charge, the alternative being not going to school. They were also asked about their willingness to pay for other services such as a public library, a public park, the provision of health and sanitation services.

Education came second only to health services – 60.6 per cent of pupils said they would be willing to pay to preserve schooling, as against 74.9 per cent who would pay for a doctor and 14.2 per cent who would pay for a public park.

These are average figures for the whole sample of 388 pupils. Of considerable interest is the fact that 83.3 per cent of boys in an urban primary school were willing to pay for education. This compared with 64.3 per cent of girls in the same school. By age 14, in an urban secondary school, these figures had changed to 50.0 per cent for boys and 54.5 per cent for girls. In the more rural environment, the figures were at Year 6: boys 62.0 per cent, girls 68.0 per cent. At Year 9: boys 27.2 per cent, girls 42.7 per cent.

These figures would seem to indicate that in general, children value education much more highly than a park to play in. Children in an urban environment seem to value it more than in a rural environment. Primary school children seem to value education more highly than

---

secondary school children. The greatest falling difference in value is for boys. Eighty-three per cent at Year 6 in an urban school, down to 27.2 per cent at Year 9 in a rural school.

These economic data might well be indicative of children's voting intentions. We need to remember the close relationship between economics and citizenship, and how the needs and aspirations of citizens are prioritised within a national economy.

We might conclude that there is good evidence that children might vote to go to school and to learn, but in terms of voter satisfaction, there is a problem. The older the children become, the less satisfied they are with their schools and the process of learning.

Rights and responsibilities

If you promote active citizenship through school and classroom democracy, you are bound at some stage to confront the question of rights and responsibilities. The following is an example of a Year 6 class's 'charter' of rights and responsibilities. It was negotiated with the children during circle time. You will probably detect the degree to which the teacher focused the children's minds upon the reciprocal nature of rights and responsibilities and the fact that it is difficult to have the former without the latter. You may also be encouraged by the insight and reasonableness of the children's ideas. There is little to suggest in this classroom that children are obsessed by a selfish preoccupation with their own rights.

If you promote moral development through this kind of participatory responsibility within a democratic classroom, you will soon learn that children are generally a lot harsher than adults when it comes to sanctions against offenders. Dealing with the question of *reasonable punishments* in a

FIG 8.2
6W Charter of Rights and Responsibilities

Right	Responsibility
Not to be bullied at school.	Not to hit anybody or say mean things.
Not to be disrupted in my work.	To get on with my work and be polite to people.
To be taught well.	To work hard and do what the teachers ask.
To be treated fairly.	To tell the truth and not get other people into trouble.
To have good facilities at school.	To look after things and respect school property.

similarly democratic way opens huge learning opportunities for citizenship, philosophy and religious education.

If you have a school forum for debating rules, there are certain themes which tend to occur quite regularly. 'The dinner ladies aren't fair' is one of them. You can dismiss this or you can consider involving your school meal supervisors in inservice training for citizenship. This rather depends upon your own attitudes, values and priorities for spending the school budget. Another might well be 'Why do we have to wear school uniform?'. I once worked in a school where boys could wear short or long trousers as they wished. There were no problems until one year it became fashionable for the older boys to wear dark navy shorts which came to just above the knees. This was perceived by the senior management as a major threat to authority, so a total ban on the wearing of shorts was imposed. This included the youngest boys who had continued to wear standard length grey shorts and were therefore 'innocent' of this particular affront to authority.

Issues such as school uniform do indeed take us into the area of 'dangerous knowledge'. Article 13 (Freedom of Expression) of the UN Convention of Children's Rights confers upon children the right to dress as they please. Were you to make your children aware of this right and its implications, you might conceivably end up with an interesting court case which could attract a lot of publicity and possibly even set legal precedents which upset the cosy status quo of school uniforms in the United Kingdom. You might consider such action tantamount to professional suicide, which says something about issues of freedom and authority. Article 14 (Freedom of Thought, Conscience and Religion) raises the question of whether enforced attendance at a denominational school is in breach of a child's rights. Such a possibility is clearly a threat to the very fabric of institutionalised education in the United Kingdom, but it is unlikely that we shall see many serious attempts by children who are socialised into these institutions from an early age to have this right upheld.

You may wonder whether this matters. There are numerous other Articles, including the right of Freedom of Association and the right not to be subjected to degrading punishment. It is interesting that this last mentioned now seems to have become part of our social fabric (contrary to strong resistance in some quarters, particularly independent schools) whereas the right of freedom of expression tends to be ignored. The point at issue is that of how selective we can be in defining citizenship and formulating our aims and objectives for citizenship education. The next enquiry task may help you develop your views on these more controversial areas. Before attempting this enquiry task, you might like to reflect upon two very important court judgments which have set precedent in English law:

The Cleveland Judgment

A child is a person and not an object of concern.

The Gillick Judgment

Parents have no rights over their children other than those rights necessary to their discharging their responsibility to promote the child's welfare.

Enquiry task 2

Obtain a copy of the UN Convention of Children's Rights. (You may find the book The UN Convention and Children's Rights *by Newell (1991) helpful).*
■ Read this and give each article a score out of ten for each of:
  Reasonableness
  The degree to which it is upheld in the UK
  The importance you attach to it for your own teaching, your relationships with the children you
    teach, their parents and your school governors.

Your reflections on the history of citizenship and the difficulties and dilemmas of putting it into practice in British primary schools may well have led you to realise the problematic nature of citizenship education. The list of suggestions for further reading is unlikely to simplify the task or make it any easier for you. Hopefully, you may rise to the challenges with enthusiasm rather than search for cynical excuses. There is one final area of difficulty to consider, however. This is an area of both historical and geographical concern. In the last section of this chapter, we discuss what we have termed The Problem of Europe. How do we cope with British and European notions of citizenship across a continent of constantly changing national boundaries, of which we are supposed to be part? Can economic issues really be kept separate from issues of national sovereignty? Why is Europe not included in the National Curriculum for geography at Key Stage 2? Why are British primary school children alone in Europe in not learning a modern foreign language? What values and attitudes are behind all this?

The problem of Europe

Steve Barnes

The National Curriculum demands that we educate/encourage children to become 'active citizens', yet at the same time it fails to provide any real developmental programme for the study of Europe. The European question, in its various facets, has dominated public thoughts, efforts and actions for the greater part of the twentieth century and it is probably the single most important issue which will determine the quality and style of our lives for the next century. In order to consider the possibilities for teaching about Europe, the 'problem of Europe' needs exploring. A number of factors must be considered. Firstly, the concept of Europe; secondly, the uniting of Europe and finally, the nature of European citizenship.

The concept of Europe

At the time of the signing of the Treaties of Rome and of Maastricht, there appeared to be and still remains, a general ignorance about the implications of membership of the European Community. This lack of information spreads across all levels of European society and is particularly prevalent within the insularity of the UK. Every strengthening of ties with our European partners seems to create deeper divisions and more bitterly entrenched attitudes. The base roots of these prejudiced attitudes may be traced to long forgotten, distant tribal feuds and rivalries. More recently, they are seen in the desire to preserve the Nation State against the perceived incursions of the European SuperState: the championing of the individual against the multinational. Perhaps a major factor in creating this atmosphere is that Europe as a geophysical entity has had a fluid and ill-defined history. Notions of a unified Europe have only arisen at times of conflict and war: White, Christian Europe as defender of the faith of the Holy Roman Empire against invasion by Infidel, Mongol and Moslem – or Europe uniting to preserve liberal democracy against dictatorship, fascism, fundamentalism and communism.

Europe has in reality no unified distinctive history, neither on its eastern edges nor on its internal borders has it any fixed long-term geography. The consequence of this lack of clear definition means that future aims for the expansion of the European Union can be seen in antagonistic terms of inclusiveness and exclusiveness, 'fortress Europe', rather than in terms of a movement for the furtherance of peaceful cooperation. The euphoria with which the world greeted the sweeping aside of the Iron Curtain during the late 1980s has gradually been replaced by a general unease. The conflict between capitalism and communism may now in part be seen as a veneer which, for a short time, covered that older conflict: religions, cultures and ideologies at the borders of East and West.

Until 1918, most of south eastern Europe was dominated by the Turkish Sultancy. That the old rivalries between Sunni Islam, Roman Christianity and Orthodox Christianity remain can be clearly seen in the events which have so recently shattered the former Yugoslavia. The Western European States only felt safe when they were cushioned by buffer countries against invasion from the Eastern hordes. The conventional but arbitrary geographic limit of Europe is the Ural Mountains. The Urals are very low lying and would not be an effective barrier against a serious assault. Russia itself has been seen as semi-Asiatic and the turbulent history of the Middle European zone has only served to reinforce fears of a perceived threat from 'outsiders'. Hence, the mistrust of the non-Aryan: the Mongols, the Jews and the Muslims.

The consequence of these long held fears is that, with the evolution of the Nation States, Europe has formed a loose collection of armed tribalistic camps whose cultures and interests have frequently collided. Notions of modern Europe have arisen out of the violence of the two World Wars and the post-war colonialism which led, since 1945, to Europe itself acting as a buffer state between the USA and the Soviet Union. Post Cold War, there is little in the history of the nation states or within the diverse cultures to cement European unity. The removal of trade and customs restrictions have themselves created more dissension. In order to create some cohesion, the European Union has therefore, had to turn outside of itself in order to attempt to forge common bonds. You may feel that this has been done by operating within an adversarial framework of opposition to the developing, tigerish economies of the Far East and in being less than enthusiastic in dealings with the Muslim countries of the Near and Middle East.

A mark of the latter condition might be read into the apparent reluctance with which Europe intervened on behalf of the Muslim community in Bosnia. The present status of Turkey, which has slipped a long way down the waiting list for entry to the European Union since the more recent claims of some former Iron Curtain countries, might be taken as further evidence of this tendency.

The uniting of Europe

Present versions of the aims and limitations on a future united Europe are many and varied. A union based purely on economic convenience and commercial organisation might also carry with it the possibility of bankruptcy and liquidation when real conflicts of interest arise. The tensions that arose during the Falklands and Gulf wars, as well as the wrangling during the Bosnian crisis, might serve to remind us of the potential fragility of the present monetary union. It can be argued that a Europe which is to benefit meaningfully the mass of its citizens, needs to carry with it a set of agreed, adhered to declared aims and intentions. The equality of opportunity and rights as well as the equality of responsibilities and commitments needs to be extended to all citizens according to this argument.

We have already alluded to the importance of such rights and responsibilities for a modern, liberal democracy in the earlier part of this chapter. To achieve such citizenship status arguably has a transfer of sovereignty from nation state to federation which goes further than many people feel comfortable with. This then is the nub of present political tension.

A Europe founded on a clear declaration of liberal democratic aims and practices is likely to be an inclusive federation. The boundaries of its member states would have no necessity to be in physical proximity. Rather, such a federation might become increasingly global. In this case 'European Union' could, in time, even itself become an anachronistic encumbrance. The desirability of the globalisation of Europe might be relatively attractive when other possible future worlds are considered, for example a world dominated by five or six super federal fortresses, each with its own set of self-interests and conflicting regulations.

Without the real commitment of the hearts and minds of its people, it is improbable that any association or union will last for a significant period of time. The problem for politicians, for educators, for us all, is how to create an enduring European citizenship. A citizenship which is not marked just by the fact that we shop in the same stores, nor just because we all happen to support Europe F.C. The notion of citizenship has always been problematic. The collapse of the Roman Empire and of the Soviet Union may be attributable to a failure to recognise that formal citizenship is not itself sufficient to guarantee loyalty or to weld empires into durable entities. If Europe is to survive as an entity, then common cause must be found which generates a feeling of togetherness. Raymond Williams discussed this point in his paper 'The Importance of Community'. He states

> *A nation once was unproblematic, with its strong connections with the fact of birth, the fact that a nation was a group of people who shared a native land ... A people on the other hand, was always slightly problematic: a mutual term to indicate a group which then at a certain point went through a very significant development in which there were people and there were others within the same place who were not people or who were not the people.* (Williams, 1989)

The development of European citizenship

How then to join the people of Europe? How can we start to overcome the centuries of jealousy and conflict and create some meaningful union? How can we involve people and remove the negative feelings of estrangement and alienation which many people feel towards the centres of power within modern societies? A present point of interest is the antithesis between the twin movements for greater centralisation and the increasing demands for more localised autonomy. More openness of information and a greater empowerment of the ordinary individual might turn out to be essential conditions for a successful and lasting movement towards an extended European union.

Education is likely to be one of the ways forward, but not necessarily just education in the limited sense of schooling. People need to be encouraged towards greater dialogue through information technology and the sharing of concerns. Literature, music, art and humour are all means by which a people might become more closely bonded. Levi Strauss (1963, 1973) and Clifford Geertz (1973) are amongst the many authors who have stressed the need to suspend our own cultural values and attempt to see the world through other people's eyes if we are really to empathise with and ultimately benefit from their wisdoms, their achievements and their lives. Many educators have, for some time, felt a particular obligation to counter unhelpful stereotypes and work against bias and discrimination.

Teaching about Europe

The National Curriculum up until 1998 may not have enabled the European dimension to be fully explored at Key Stage 1 or Key Stage 2. However, many schools and many teachers are working in innovative ways within subject constraints and are exploring useful avenues of knowledge and understanding. Whether or not the relaxation of the statutory requirements for the humanities subjects from 1998 turns out to be associated with a more flexible approach to teaching about Europe may, to some degree, depend upon the values held by teachers and other educators. The remainder of this chapter examines ways in which European issues have become part of our national consciousness and it will also consider how the problem of Europe is being or could be tackled in primary schools.

Children up to the age of 11 years have a considerable, if disparate, world knowledge. A number of studies, for example Wiegand (1992) or Kimber et al. (1995), have shown that by and large, children's most complete knowledge of other countries centres on Western Europe. The likely explanation for this is the increasing frequency with which British families holiday abroad, especially in France, Spain, Greece and Italy. Added to this have been the rising number of shopping day trips and cheap short breaks to the Continent which many people take during the low season. Such was the competition for the cross-Channel trade between the Channel Tunnel, the airlines, the ferries, the catamaran and hovercraft services, that during the months after Christmas 1998 some national newspapers offered return fares for a family and car for as little as £12 plus newspaper tokens. It is a fact that many people in the south of England are closer in travel time, distance and cost to the northern coasts of France and Belgium than they are to Northern England.

The drip, drip effects of first hand experience, increased daily awareness through television, the internet, trade, town twinning and so on are helping to demystify foreign cultures. Most particularly, these effects have relevance to our attitudes towards our neighbours in Europe. There seems to be a growing willingness among the majority of young people to cooperate on equal terms with their counterparts on the mainland.

Educational initiatives have probably helped in this process. Many secondary schools have long standing pupil exchange programmes. Equally, teacher training institutions have been involved in programmes such as Tempus, Socrates and Comenius which promote long and short-term exchange visits for both teacher trainees and for qualified teachers. In South Gloucestershire a Comenius link with French, Italian and Polish schools established through a local comprehensive school, has mushroomed to include the feeder primary schools. A number of staff and pupil exchanges have taken place and joint curricular projects have been successfully undertaken.

How much might primary schools contribute to the development of European citizenship? The British National Curriculum, almost uniquely in Europe, sees no value in pupils of primary school age learning a modern foreign language. You may feel that this reflects a certain attitude on the part of the British government to European citizenship. However, attitudes and values may not be formed purely through the teaching and learning of foreign languages. European days and European topic weeks are fairly well established in some primary schools. Activities emphasising European links and achievements can include the arts, dance, music, and literature. Topics in humanities and science with similar European emphasis have been explored. For instance comparative studies of the local areas of primary

Reflection 5

To what extent is the learning of a modern foreign language during the primary years a principal or necessary means of developing the attitudes and values that might lead to a sense of European citizenship?

- What are your own views on the general failure of British primary schools to teach a modern foreign language?
- What ways other than teaching a language might promote European awareness?

schools have been made, environmental concerns and action have been discussed, historical events and personalities have been debated from different viewpoints.

Case Study 1

The Avon International Education 'No Borders' project linked schools in Poland, Romania, the Slovak Republic and the United Kingdom. Underlying this project was the insistence that linking with other schools and exploring European dimensions should not mean an additional burden to already overstretched teachers. The aim was to enhance the existing curriculum. Its main aims were (1) to help young people gain knowledge and understanding of other places and people through direct communication, (2) to enhance the curriculum, (3) to increase awareness of the interdependence between countries, (4) to widen the audience for students' work in different areas of the curriculum, (5) to challenge prejudices and narrow stereotypes, (6) to enhance opportunities for student exchange and work experience and (7) to enable teachers to communicate about professional concerns.

Avon International Education (1995)

Case Study 2

Luckwell Primary School in Bedminster, Bristol

This school has for many years made extensive use of the e-mail networks as an inexpensive way of providing first hand information about other places, other peoples and other events. These connections provide a major resource with which to support existing curriculum work, especially work in the humanities.

The extension of the internet and the strengthening of the place of ICT within the National Curriculum can only mean that global communication will become a feature of daily life in most schools. Our increasing ties with Europe will of necessity mean that the greater percentage of this electronic communication will be with our European partners. The timorous way in which the UK adopted the metric system caused and still causes uncertainty and confusion in the calculation of quantity. To fail to appreciate the significance and the impact of the Euro and, as a people, to blunder into a fuller European partnership in ignorance, may well cause this country yet more damage and loss. The primary teacher is in a position of some influence over children's developing attitudes towards the metric system and the Euro.

The history of the National Curriculum since 1995 has been one of increasing prescription over literacy and numeracy, but greater freedom over the teaching of the humanities. The values and attitudes of teachers, particularly where the teaching of the humanities is concerned, may yet prove decisive in determining the degree to which the ideal of European citizenship becomes in any sense a reality. If we fail, at this point in history, to ensure that European issues feature significantly in our planning, will we be failing to provide a 'broad and balanced' curriculum which meets the needs of future citizens? Will we, by such omission, restrict the ability of children to become active citizens who are the 'problem solvers of the future'? (Dewey, 1916).

References

AVON INTERNATIONAL EDUCATION (1995) *No Borders*, Bristol: County of Avon Education Department.

DEWEY, J. (1916) *Democracy and Education*, New York: Macmillan.

DELANTY, G. (1995) *Inventing Europe*, London: Macmillan.

DfEE (1995) *The National Curriculum*, London: HMSO.

GEERTZ, C. (1973) *The Interpretations of Culture*, New York: Basic Books.

GIROUX, H. (1983) *Theory and Resistance in Education: A Pedagogy for the Future*, London: Heinemann.

HARGREAVES, D. (1994) *The Mosaic of Learning*, London: Demos.

KIMBER, D., FORREST, M., MENTER, I., CLOUGH, N. and NEWMAN, E. (1995) *Humanities in the Primary School*, London: Fulton.

LEVI-STRAUSS, C. (1963, 1973) *Cultural Anthropology*, Vols 1 and 2, New York: Basic Books.

LOCKE, J. (1690) *Two Treatises of Government*, edited by LASLETT, P. (1960) Cambridge University Press.

NEILL, A. (1962) *Summerhill*, Harmondsworth: Penguin.

NEWELL, P. (1991) *The UN Convention and Children's Rights in the UK*, London: National Children's Bureau.

ROUSSEAU, J.-J. The Social Contract (1767) in Cress (ed.). (1987) *Rousseau*, Bk3, Ch15: Hackett Publishing Co., p. 198.

WEIGAND, P. (1992) *Children and Primary Geography*, London: Cassell.

WILLIAMS, R. (1989) *Resources of Hope: Culture, Democracy and Socialism*, London: Verso.

Further reading

JOHN, M. (ed.) (1996) *Children in Charge: The Child's Right to a Fair Hearing*, London: Kingsley.
This is an edited collection which contains a number of chapters which usefully illuminate further key ideas from this chapter, including Sarah McCrum on children's voices in the media; Penny Townsend on work with children's rights in Devon; Jaqui Cousins on empowerment and autonomy and Rudi Dallos on the paradoxes of autonomy and socialism.

GRETTON, J. and JACKSON, M. (1976) *William Tyndale: Collapse of a School or a System?* London: Allen and Unwin.
A documentary account of the William Tyndale affair. Tyndale was the inner London school where the extreme liberal views of the management team lead to a state of anarchy in the school, which remained national headline news for several months and was a turning point in the movement away from progressive, child-centred philosophies.

KINGDOM, J. (1992) *No Such Thing as Society? Individualism and Community.* Buckingham: Open University Press.
This book is a critical study of the Thatcher years and provides a strong critique of the values of consumerism and individualism.

VAN STEENBERGEN, B. (ed.) (1994) *The Condition of Citizenship*, London: Sage.
A useful general reader which provides further information and ideas about most of the key concepts dealt with in this chapter.

Chapter 9

ICT and the humanities
Martin Ashley and Gaynor Attwood

6 *Remember IT is a tool. In some ways*
the government has tried to make it a subject.
I don't see a curriculum area called
pens and pencils.

Send for Giles!

By the time he was 5 years old, Giles could programme the family video. That is to say, he could set it up to record a sequence of four different programmes on three different channels during the week his family was away on holiday. This was just as well, as neither his mother nor his father had yet managed to master even the basic technique necessary to record one programme whilst they watched another. By the time he was ten years old, Giles was acting as his school's IT consultant. Regularly, he was sent to other classes to perform 'complex' operations such as formatting discs. 'Send for Giles' became a phrase on every junior teacher's lips when confronted with a programme that would not run, or an error message that could not be comprehended. This was again fortunate, for amongst the staff of Giles's school could be found the junior teacher who had attempted to insert a floppy disc by removing it from its plastic cartridge, or the infant teacher who had used the printer cable as the suspension for baby Jesus's crib because she thought it was part of the packaging.

You may be no more inclined to believe these stories than to believe that it once took 20 or 30 minutes to load up a simple programme from a cassette tape because early microcomputers did not have magnetic floppy discs (let alone CD ROMs or on-line links). They are all true stories, however. Furthermore, you may have noticed that the notion that children somehow have an innate 'computer intelligence' that is inaccessible to adults is still part of popular folklore. There may even be some primary schools where 'Send for Giles' is still the principal means of keeping Information and Communication Technology going in the classroom. All this is changing rapidly. Older teachers may find this change unsettling or challenging. This may be partly due to the resistance we all have when faced with change, particularly if it strikes at the heart of our self-esteem or feelings of professional competence. There is another reason, however, which we wish to make the main point of this introduction.

When microcomputers first appeared in schools, computing was definitely the province of the technical expert or 'buff'. We talked about the merits of BASIC, COBOL or FORTRAN and how 9 year olds were to be taught the introductory steps of programming. Pre-programmed software that could be loaded ready to run was the first major revolution in primary computing. Unfortunately, many of these early examples of software were crude and far from what is termed 'user friendly'. A thorough mastery of them still required some knowledge of programming and 'Giles' was undoubtedly a useful person to have around. In many ways, ICT was its own worst enemy because early equipment did behave unpredictably and disrupt lessons. Much of the early software, furthermore, was what we would now refer to as 'drill and kill', by which we mean a crude form of programmed rote learning. It is also doubtful whether much of this early software seriously enhanced the quality of teaching and learning in the mainstream curriculum. If teachers were unconvinced of the value of ICT for enhancing teaching and learning in the primary curriculum, they had good reasons.

If you feel in any way that children are more adept at using computers than you yourself might be, it might be that you have experiences of these early days, which are the source of your misgivings. The only advantage that the children have over you is a lack of such memories. Modern hardware and software is quite different. Apart from being an incredibly powerful and creative tool for the enhancement of teaching and learning, it no longer requires the user to be a specialist in the technology. In banks and building societies, in vicarages and fire stations, in railway ticket offices and yoghurt factories, the ubiquitous micro sits on the desktop no more remarkably than a pencil or a paperweight. Millions of people drive motor cars or operate microwave ovens with little inkling of how they work, and millions of people similarly use computers. The issue is, therefore, not one of how to set up and use the hardware. That is the easy part. The developments in hardware and software over the last 10 or so years have all been in the direction of making this aspect easier and easier. To this may be added the realistic expectation that the general level of personal computing skills in the population is rising all the time, and teachers are certainly not exceptions in this trend.

This chapter is not going to be about how to use a mouse or how to plug a cable into a port. Of course, in primary schools we do have to teach children how to read and write. The mechanics of literacy, however, are merely a means to an end, whether that be the appreciation of literature or the use of language in work or study. The terms 'IT capability' or sometimes 'IT literacy' are used in a way analogous to the mechanical basics of literacy. ICT, on the other hand, refers to the higher level application of this capability in the process of teaching and learning in curriculum subjects. Just as we do have to teach basic literacy, so we do have to teach all children such basic IT capability as how to use a mouse and navigate a windows environment. Some children have already learned some of these skills at home. Equally, some children have already acquired aspects of literacy and numeracy at home.

Reflection 1

In the early years of motoring, one had, amongst other things, to master the exacting skill of 'double declutching' in order to change gear. Nowadays, manufacturers make cars easy to drive. Most people drive cars with little knowledge about how they work and even less thought about the 'interface' between driver and vehicle. Learning to drive can still be something of a challenge for some people. It is a challenge that almost everyone overcomes, however, because driving capability is such a valued and useful feature of modern life.

- How far can this statement be taken as an analogy for the microcomputer?
- Are you clear about the difference between IT capability and the use of ICT in the humanities?

Ideally, all children will have had some exposure to adult reading books at home. It is probably more likely, however, that all children will have had some exposure to IT in the home, through the television, through devices such as programmable washing machines, even through programming the video! Crucially, in this book, we have adopted the attitude that basic literacy is a necessary part of the curriculum but not sufficient for a full primary education. Similarly, we are adopting the attitude that *IT capability is necessary but not sufficient.* IT capability is like basic literacy. It comprises the knowledge, skills and understanding needed to employ ICT appropriately, securely and fruitfully in learning, employment and everyday life. This chapter is not about IT capability. It is about ICT in the humanities.

The key point here is that ICT in the National Curriculum is not an end in itself. It is merely a means to an end. For the increasing number of teachers who have comfortably progressed beyond the 'send for Giles' stage, it is a highly valued means to an end. It is important that we take time to reflect on what that end is, and how IT capability can help us to achieve it. This is our main purpose in the next section of the chapter. We conclude this introductory section with a quotation from Gabriel Goldstein (NCET/OFSTED, 1997), reported in a commentary on OFSTED inspection findings:

❛ *Too often pupils' confidence with, and enthusiasm for, IT are mistaken as evidence of high achievement and pupils' work with IT is recorded simply by referring to items of software and hardware they have used, rather than tracking the skills, knowledge and understanding they have gained.*

If, as a teacher, you are in any way awed by IT, there is a danger that you may be one of those who mistake a superficial confidence and enthusiasm for IT for high achievement in the application of ICT. We hope that by the end of this chapter you will have reflected on the gravity of such an error. Children are in urgent need of guidance about how to apply IT capability. IT has become far too powerful a tool to misuse. You, the teacher, with your professional knowledge of the difficulties children have in progressing from 'barking at print' to being effective readers and writers, are the best person to help children progress from being mere possessors of IT capability to being competent, discriminating and imaginative users of ICT.

We would summarise the position as follows:
■ Modern software does not present the difficulties of use that have become associated with first generation software, such as that written for the early BBC type school microcomputers.
■ Any professional person, as a matter of course, now manipulates a Windows environment in their daily work.
■ Almost all children and adults refer to some ICT functions in their daily lives.
■ It is necessary, but not sufficient, that primary schools teach effectively the basics of literacy and numeracy, and the basics of IT capability.
■ IT capability is a means to an end. Evidence of IT capability must not be mistaken for evidence of quality teaching and learning through the application of ICT across the curriculum.

ICT: a highly valued means to a humanitarian end?

In Chapter 1, we used the argument that reading and writing are valued because they serve to make our children more human. It would be logical to extend this argument to ICT. Does this kind of technology dehumanise people or does it humanise them? If you have ever visited a motorway services area and watched children of primary age playing video arcade games, which trivialise violence, it is possible that you may incline to the former view. The ubiquitous cash machine is undoubtedly a great convenience. Yet you may have pondered on the degree to which a

Reflection 2

A new multimedia PC for a classroom might cost in the region of £1000.

- What proportion of your school's capital budget would this represent?
- In what other ways could you spend £1000 to promote human welfare or humanitarian concerns such as global justice or environmental conservation?
- Given the degree to which ICT has been forced upon schools with very limited budgets, are you happy that this economic prioritisation is a true reflection of your own values?
- How much do you actually need to spend on software to make ICT worthwhile in your school?

'conversation' of bleeping electronic monotones is just one of the thousands of ways in which technology threatens to dehumanise society. Did the friendly passing of the time of day with the bank clerk have any value? What human values have replaced these old social customs? Which do you value more highly, social contact with persons outside your family and work, or the convenience of rapid service?

To develop further another of our themes from Chapter 1, ICT cannot possibly be 'value-free'. The mere existence of disproportionately expensive equipment in schools is a hugely powerful statement about value and the values of society. We would contend that as a reflective teacher you have no option other than to make ICT a positive humanitarian force in proportion to the resources devoted to acquiring the hardware and software. This makes ICT the most significant humanitarian force you have at your disposal. To ignore the potency of this resource is to abrogate humanitarian responsibility. It has been said that for evil to triumph, it is sufficient for good men and women to do nothing. Perhaps this statement could be reinterpreted for the twenty first century as 'For evil to triumph, it is sufficient for good humanities teachers to do nothing about the development of ICT'. There, perhaps, you have your answer to the question of the dehumanising effects of video arcade violence.

How then is the reflective teacher to use ICT as a humanising force in the context of the humanities subjects? Teachers have a wide range of ICT available to them to use with their pupils. The types of software and applications available can be categorised as:
- Generic packages
- Subject specific packages
- Reference packages
- Communications technologies
- Emerging technologies

Generic packages offer teachers the ability to use them with their own contextual material or that collected by pupils. Examples of such packages include: word processing, spreadsheets, databases, graphic representation of data, drawing and desktop publishing. The subject specific packages offer software that is written to cover a particular topic, subject or area of the curriculum. Reference packages offer a collection of sources of information, commonly on CD-ROM. These provide teachers and pupils with an enormous bank of information to use, such as the contents of encyclopaedias or a world atlas, powerfully enhanced by search tools. There is a range of communications technologies that allow teachers and pupils real-time communication with others, both inside and beyond the world of education. This range currently includes e-mail and the internet. There are also a number of emerging technologies that are becoming affordable for school use, such as digital cameras or speech recognition technologies that will play an increasing role in education during the early part of the twenty first century.

You need to bear in mind that ICT is not purely for pupils. The use of ICT in the preparation and presentation of classroom displays has been well established in many schools for some time. Routine administration and more specialised tasks such as electronic record keeping to monitor pupil progress and set appropriate learning targets, is part of an essential revolution in the efficiency and effectiveness of primary schools. A revolution in curriculum development is imminent at the time of writing as internet pages provide the means to disseminate inspiration and good practice as never before. You may already be able to access a virtual teachers' centre or an on-line conference group for your specialist area of the curriculum. Let us conclude this section with some important words of caution, however.

Technology is only as good as the people who use it and the need for wise human judgment, far from being displaced, has never been greater. In the hands of a skilled teacher, even technically bad software can be put to good use. It by no means follows, however, that technically good software will automatically be put to good use for teaching and learning. This is so for ordinary generic software. It is even more so for emerging techologies and, above all, the internet. In the hands of skilled professional teachers, the internet can be a tool for spreading good practice rapidly. The possibility for epidemics of poor practice or dangerous ideas spreading via the internet has to be seriously contemplated. Teachers need to be prepared to confront this disturbing possibility.

Enquiry task 1

*You may be familiar with the idea of **systematic observation**. By this we mean the gathering of data for educational purposes by means of an **observation schedule**. Typically, an observation schedule may ask you to note down what a given pupil is doing at regular specified time intervals, such as once a minute or once every quarter hour. The observation schedule will normally prescribe the categories of activity you are to note. For example, reading/writing/listening to teacher/answering question/on-task/talk to peers and so on. Although systematic observation has well documented limitations, it is also a powerful means by which the reflective teacher can assess classroom activity in order to bring about improvements in teaching and learning. In this task, we are going to ask you to observe, not a pupil, but a classroom computer.*

- Use a modern word processing package to generate an observation sheet similar to the example below.
- Use a spreadsheet to produce a pie chart, which shows how the computer was used throughout the day.

Computer status categories:
A switched off.
B switched on, not in use.

C In use by pupils for time filling activity e.g. games or activity not specified as learning intentions in curriculum plans.

D In use by pupils for planned and directed curriculum activity.

E In use for instruction involving adult/pupil interaction.

F In use by adult for administration or similar.

Application categories	**Pupil categories**
a Word processing	**I** Single pupil
b Data handling	**2** Pair of pupils
c Spreadsheet/modelling	**3** Small group
d Information source (including multimedia)	**4** Large group
e Producing graphs/tables	**5** Whole class
f Generating artwork (including text/graphic merger)	
g Communication (including e-mail)	
h Control technology (including logo/turtle)	
i Subject specific package (State which)	

Example of recording sheet

Time	Coding	Notes
10.45	D&2	*Weather observation*

In this instance, at 10.45 two pupils are using a data handling package such as Grass to input simple weather observations they have made as part of their planned work in geography.

Effective ICT in primary humanities

If you use an ICT application to analyse the data from your Enquiry task 1, it is likely that you will rapidly identify patterns of computer use in your classroom. This alone should confirm the power and potential of ICT. The reflective teacher, however, should find much information that will be of value in improving teaching and learning in the humanities through the use of ICT. In this section of the chapter, we intend to anticipate and comment upon a few patterns or tendencies that you might find in your results, and then to develop our main theme in some depth, which is the degree to which generic packages feature as effective ICT in primary humanities.

The first point to look for is a dominance of Computer Status observations (Category C) – software application which is described as 'games or activity not specified as learning intention in curriculum plans' and which might be considered a relic of the Giles era. A 'C dominance' can signify quite a challenge for the teacher who wishes to develop effective ICT in primary humanities. In the early days of primary school computing, large numbers of programs were produced which were largely 'stand alone'. By this we mean that they were fully self-contained and not designed to be adapted by a teacher to support learning in a given area of the curriculum. Some of these programs were in reality little more than games; not dissimilar in principle from the types of electronic games some pupils might have had at home. Paradoxically, the electronic games available to wealthier pupils at home rapidly outgrew in sophistication the rather crude first generation school computer games, which did little for the credibility of school computing in the eyes of such pupils.

Other 'stand-alone' software claims to be more directly educational. There are numerous programs, for example, which are designed to promote learning in mathematics. For example, the computer will draw a sector of circle and invite the pupil to estimate the angle in degrees. Such software is clearly of some value, and its value probably increases if it is used at a time when the class is pursuing work involving angles. In identifying good practice in ICT, however, you will be looking for more Category D than Category C observations when you analyse the results of Enquiry task 1. The key question to ask is whether or not the software that is in use is an integral part of a planned and directed curriculum activity. Following this, two further questions need to be asked. The first is that of whether the software is actually the best means of achieving the planned learning outcome. If the pupils could have learned the same thing as easily or more effectively by another means, then it is possible that you are not looking at good practice in ICT. The second is that of whether the teacher has had to adapt the lesson to fit the software, or whether the software has supported points or developed skills the teacher judged appropriate to the learning needs of her pupils. Good practice is more likely to be associated with the latter than the former.

At this point, you might look at the Application Categories on your observation schedule. How often does the letter 'i' appear? It is our belief that, as teachers become increasingly confident users of IT and the repertoire of expertise in primary schools grows, the letter 'i' will appear less and less frequently. The relative usage of subject specific software, in other words, will decline. In its place, we will see greater and more versatile use of generic software. It is the generic software, which, once mastered, can become a powerful tool for enhancing teaching and learning in the humanities and allowing the teacher to meet planned objectives more effectively. It is the subject specific software, which is less likely to be seamlessly integrated with the planned curriculum and identified learning objectives for the humanities. This might at first seem a strange claim. How, you might ask, could it be that a data handling package, which could be used equally in a maths, PE or history lesson, better support the teaching of history than a program written specifically for history?

As the National Association of Advisers for Computers in Education (NAACE) (1997) make quite clear, subject specific software frequently represents someone else's perspective, a culture with which the pupils are unfamiliar, or a view of teaching which is not shared by the teachers using the software. It also has pre-set routines and levels of difficulty which, whilst superficially appear to meet needs for differentiation, soon turn out to be limiting and restrictive. To integrate these criticisms with our own argument, how often does the pre-set content of subject specific software really support the learning needs of the pupils or genuinely reinforce the methods of the teacher? How well does the content of subject specific software really match the content of the curriculum? How often could the teacher himself achieve a better match by other means? Some highly specialised subject software can be useful in a strictly limited situation. An example might be a simulation program, which draws cross-sections from, or allows pupils to view three-dimensional projections, of a contour map. You will need to judge whether a given piece of subject-specific software teaches a specialised skill such as this more effectively than any other means.

In making such judgments, you will need to consider the degree to which the software is *interactive*. Interactive software generally requires pupils creatively to input data or make a response which itself affects the response of the computer and the way in which the program develops. Many of the crude, early programs merely asked pupils questions, and awarded a score out of five or 10, often to the accompaniment of admonishing hisses or approving bleeps. This is merely using the computer as a teaching machine. If teaching machines were a better means of promoting children's learning and development, they would surely by now have replaced teachers. The fact that they have not might be indicative of the shortcomings of this kind of non-interactive software. Another not insignificant failing of subject specific software, is also pointed out by NAACE. Subject specific software generally fails to develop pupils's IT capability. This has overtones of the entertainment or 'game' element again. A subject specific program more often than not is somebody else's product with somebody else's agenda. The pupil is merely the passive recipient, much in the same way as he or she would be the passive recipient of television entertainment.

Generic software, on the other hand, requires pupils to understand how word processing, data handling, modelling and control packages work. It requires pupils and teachers to use a program as a creative tool in their teaching and learning. Pencils, paints and paper are creative tools. Books and measuring equipment can be. Generic software ought increasingly to figure prominently in this category too, and in many schools it already does. In the most successful schools, the computer has ceased to be a novelty. Through the use of generic software across all the subjects, it has become just another of the creative tools available for curriculum use. So, without dismissing altogether the value of the best subject specific software, we envisage the future of ICT in the humanities very much in terms of the application of generic packages. How might the reflective teacher go about doing this?

It is useful to remember that the National Curriculum for IT specifies four key strands. These are *communicating, handling, modelling* and *control and monitoring*. Each of these strands is associated with particular types of generic software and each has applications within the humanities subjects. The software associated with communicating is word processing, desktop publishing and certain graphic packages, particularly ones that enable text and graphics to be combined. Historically, the communicating strand has had something of a head start in most schools. Word processing software such as *Pendown* has been around since the earliest days of the BBC micro. Most teachers are by now confident users of word processing and it is perceived as a 'safe' classroom activity in which the failure or unpredictable behaviour of equipment is no longer seen as a threat to discipline and class management.

Communicating is, of course, vitally important. History, geography and RE can benefit from the use of word processing to produce reports that are drafted and developed, as well as producing displays on particular topics. Higher level communication skills, such as changing layout, font size and colour, cutting and pasting, file merging and combining text and graphics can be very successfully developed in the context of humanities. An 'historical newspaper' (i.e. produced as though in 1492 etc.) has become a popular activity which does develop these skills and arguably enhances the teaching and learning of history. We would caution, however, against the use of the computer as a 'glorified typewriter'. At this point you might return to the results of Enquiry task 1 in order to see whether you have a dominance of lower case 'a' categorisations. If you have, this may be indicative of 'glorified typewriter syndrome'. An imbalance in the direction of 'a' categories should tell you that you might be under-using many powerful ICT applications in the humanities which fall outside the communicating strand.

The role of empathy has engendered much controversy. Traditionalists favouring a strong framework of knowledge claim it is 'woolly'. Supporters of the empathy approach claim that it motivates primary children and develops an interest in the subject. A third approach emphasises the search for evidence in order to refute myths and promote critical study of the past.

Certain generic ICT packages, particularly ones that include data handling capability and text search facilities have proved immensely valuable in developing this last approach.

- Compare the use of ICT as a means of enhancing communication with the use of ICT as a means of searching, finding out and hypothesis testing.
- Can we have one without the other?

If you are able to obtain an example of an 'historical newspaper' type document produced by some primary school children, reflect critically upon it.

- To what extent does it communicate the results of research and enquiry by the children?
- Does it introduce historical or cultural anomalies?
- What proportion of the information communicated is based upon evidence in the form of primary or secondary sources, and what proportion is pure conjecture by the children?
- Do these things matter?

The communicating strand and word processing within it is only one small element of how ICT can help. On the grounds that the communicating strand is the most developed in the majority of schools, as well as the one with the most obvious applications in the humanities, we intend to focus more on the handling strand, and upon the emergence of communication technologies such as the e-mail and internet. This is because children are already part of an information based, data handling society, and this affects the humanities as much as any other area of the curriculum. It might help to reflect for a moment on your attitude to the teaching of history.

Your reflections may lead you to the obvious, but nevertheless vitally important, conclusion that successful communication depends upon having something to communicate. The search for historical evidence is a painstaking one and a lengthy process. A critical approach to history which allows the educated person to discriminate between myth, conjecture, cultural prejudice and a provisional hypothesis about the past supported by evidence is hard to achieve, yet vitally important. Powerful word processing packages which can incorporate archaic types of font and merge text with historical looking graphics can offer the temptation of letting children rush into print before they have properly researched the topic. The thoughtful teacher will both resist this temptation and reflect upon the use of generic packages such as data handling and large CD-ROM databases with search facilities. The enquiry task below is designed to set you thinking about the creative use of a generic data handling practice to support an investigative approach to history.

Enquiry task 2

Choose a suitable data-handling package to which you have access and set up a database that would support an investigative approach to the teaching of history. An example might be a database on Roman roads, which children might use when learning about Romans, Anglo-Saxons and Vikings in Britain (Key Stage 2, History Study Unit One).
- What fields would you include in the database?

(Possible answers might include name of route, length of route, direction of route, start and end points, settlements passed, regions or counties etc.)
- Where could you find this information out? Is it available on CD-ROM?
- Could the children themselves create, or help to create, the database?
- What sorts of searches could be made with this database?

An example of a hypothesis that could be tested with this database might be: All Roman roads in Britain led to the easiest place for crossing the English Channel.

The study of local history is likely to undergo significant development through the use of ICT, particularly where data handling facilitates an investigative approach. You might, for example, take the class to a local cemetery and gather data on the ages at which men and women died. This could be powerfully processed by a data-handling package. It is quite possible that such processing might reveal localised anomalies, which lead to further questions. A more sophisticated version of this type of enquiry might compare different centuries in order to investigate whether there are any trends such as the disparity between life spans of men and women increasing or decreasing over time. The possibility of sharing such information with other schools via e-mail or the internet opens up revolutionary prospects for children to pursue thematic investigations in history through access to primary sources held locally.

If you have a curriculum responsibility for history, you might consider the possibility of setting up your own database of local history as a whole-school resource. A visit to the local records office might provide an inspirational starting point. You might be able to obtain census data that allowed you to create records, such as family size in your local area. These could be combined through a simple multimedia-authoring package with old photographs of the area. Local collections of old photographs are frequently published in book form available in the bookshops or newsagents of even quite small towns. These can be scanned in if you have the appropriate hardware, software and copyright clearance. Similarly, old maps or plans might be scanned in. 'Then and now' photo contrasts created on screen can be a very stimulating source of ICT work in history. They can be combined with text, reproduced in both original form and modern form. The point we are making is that your own creative use of generic packages will ultimately give much greater satisfaction than the purchase of subject specific software which relates to somebody else's interests or agenda.

You may not immediately have thought of history as a context for data handling. Perhaps geography springs more immediately to mind. Geography, indeed, went through a very data-based quantitative phase during the 1970s and 80s (see Marsden, 1995). Obvious topics such as weather recording or traffic flow analysis perhaps confirm the number based side of geography. Geography will certainly be an area of the curriculum in which pupils apply the graph making capabilities of ICT to the fullest.

A comparison might be drawn here between the use of ICT in the humanities and the use of calculators in mathematics. You will doubtless be aware of the disputes that sometimes arise between those who wish to ban the use of calculators in primary schools and those who see them as an essential tool for developing mathematical skills in the contemporary context. Those who are opposed to the use of calculators in primary schools generally fear a

Reflection 4

- Consider the number of times in which geographical concepts or information are represented in the form of graphs, tables, charts or diagrams.
- Does the time spent by children drawing and colouring in graphs leave too little time for reading and interpreting them?
- Is it sufficient for children merely to repeat in linguistic form information shown on a graph, or are higher level interpretative skills needed?

decline in computational skills and the use of mental arithmetic. Those who support the use of calculators point out that such fears are unfounded in that it is essential to teach children the appropriate use of the calculator. Using the calculator when the competent application of mental arithmetic would have been quicker is *not* an appropriate use. The calculator can open up to children important mathematical concepts which would otherwise have been denied them simply because of the complexity of the task in learning lengthy procedures, or repeating simple procedures a large number of times.

The analogy with ICT stands on both counts. It is essential to teach children the appropriate use of the computer. They must similarly know when ICT use is inappropriate and a book or other information source would have been more effective. The computer can also open up conceptual areas of the humanities which would otherwise have been inaccessible simply because a cumbersome procedural task stands in the way. A spreadsheet that will carry out large numbers of simple calculations is one example. Another obvious example of this is the pie chart. Before the use of ICT, the drawing of pie charts was an exercise beyond all but the oldest and most able primary pupils on account of the relatively complex mathematics involved (conversion of data to degrees of a circle and measuring/drawing angles). Yet once drawn, pie charts are one of the clearest ways of showing proportion, and their effective comprehension is within the grasp of a wide range of primary age pupils. There is a need, nevertheless, to exercise a degree of caution when using graphing packages.

Traditionally, primary and even younger secondary pupils have encountered a conceptual block in moving from discrete categorical variables, such as numbers of cars, buses and lorries to continuous variables such as temperature (DES, 1989). Concepts such as representation of and extrapolation of trends from line graphs are difficult ones, even for the oldest and most able primary pupils. The power of data handling packages to produce instantaneous pictographs, bar charts, line graphs and pie charts is likely to influence this area considerably. Through skilled teaching, pupils might come to a better understanding earlier and gain greater conceptual insights into certain topics within the humanities as a result. Unskilled use of powerful graphing packages, on the other hand, might set pupils back considerably in their understanding of why we have different kinds of graph. Although software provides the instantaneous facility for a line graph or a bar chart, it gives no indication of which it is appropriate to use or why. This is where the teacher must act, and it is obvious that you need to be quite clear in your own mind.

The ability to produce graphs instantly not only relieves pupils of pointless tedium and unproductive 'colouring in', then, it also allows pupils to learn much more about how and why we use graphs. It additionally allows pupils to pursue more sophisticated lines of questioning. Higher level interpretative questions might be asked whereas previously much interrogation of graphs by primary pupils amounted to little more than repeating in words the information actually displayed on the graph. Once you, as a teacher, are confident of your ability to manipulate data and graphs on screen in front of the pupils, possibilities open up, such as showing the pupils how easily data can be distorted. For example, the scale of a graph can be manipulated to make a relatively small variation look far more impressive or significant than it actually is. This sort of thing happens all the time in the world of lies, damned lies and statistics.

Discrete variables are likely to dominate in the earlier stages of primary work, certainly at Key Stage 1. For example, in geography pupils might be studying how many in their class came to school by car and how many walked. In cases such as this, almost any good data-handling package will produce a block graph or a pie chart, which would be appropriate ways of representing such simple categorical variables. Similarly, in studying the weather at Key Stage 1, pupils might use simple categorical variables such as 'rainy' or 'sunshine' and a data handling package will generate pictorial or graphical representations of how many days in the month were sunny and how many were rainy. Given such conceptual difficulties as grasping the meaning of 'month', such a use of data handling is probably both challenging and powerful for early years children.

At Key Stage 2, however, pupils are going to encounter the measurement of temperature in their weather studies. Although a data handling package will instantly draw a line graph, a lot of skilled teaching is needed to put across the concept that temperature is a continuous variable which is changing in between the times at which observations were made. You might do well to consider the difficulties of teaching children of primary age to draw a line graph manually. If you encounter a significant number of pupils showing unusual difficulty in following the procedures for drawing such a graph, it is likely that a lack of conceptual understanding of what the graph actually is and does is behind the problem. It is vital that this is born in mind when pupils have the power to produce instantly almost any kind of graph at the click of a mouse. The last Enquiry task is designed to help you clarify your thoughts on this important issue.

Enquiry task 3

There are a number of topics or themes in the geography curriculum in which data handling is or could be a key feature of an investigative approach to learning. Weather is an obvious example, and we return to this topic in later chapters. In this task, we have chosen the theme of settlement as an example of geographical topic which could involve data handling and which could be supported by the use of ICT. We outline a teaching situation and then ask you to work through some key questions relating ICT.

From Key Stage 2, Programme of Study 9a:

> *In studying how settlements differ and change, pupils should be taught that settlements, e.g. villages, towns, cities, vary in size and that their characteristics and locations reflect the types of economic activities in the settlement.*

- How could you use ICT to help pupils produce a hierarchical classification of their settlements in their home region?

The following data might be useful:
population size;
principal employers;
services available (e.g. how many railways stations, supermarkets, leisure centres etc.).

- Could such information on database support a hypothesis such as *Leisure centres are only found in towns with large populations?*

In adapting any generic package for specific use in the humanities, you need always to bear in mind the following questions:

1 How well did the ICT help you meet your teaching objectives?
2 How well matched was the ICT to the age, stage and prior experience of the pupils?
3 Did the use of ICT raise your expectations of what the pupils could achieve? Were the pupils able to perform tasks that they would have been unable to do without ICT?
4 Were you able to manage the use of ICT so that the contributions of individual pupils could be identified, monitored and recorded against measures of attainment in both ICT and geography?
5 Were you able to demonstrate, through the speed and automatic functions of ICT, teaching points you wished to make?
6 How well did the capacity and range of ICT enable you to gain access to relevant information that made your work with the pupils more accurate and up to date than a paper-based enquiry would have been?

Data handling can enhance teaching and learning in many other areas of the geography curriculum, for example, the study of rivers. Pupils might plot on a spreadsheet the depth of a local stream at intervals of one metre taken by dropping a weighted line over the edge of a bridge. A cross section of the riverbed could then be printed from the spreadsheet by application of the graphing tool. There is no need to use our example of settlements in carrying out Enquiry task 3.

Another specialised application of generic ICT in geography, which we might mention in passing, could be the use of object based graphics packages to enhance pupils' work in drawing simple maps. Control and modelling packages such as Logo can be used. For early years pupils in particular, logo-based packages allow you to extend in effective ways such ideas as 'mental mapping'. For example, can you trace on the screen a line which shows your route to school? If these can be printed off, some stimulating displays might be produced. Whilst we would always advocate the primacy of fieldwork in teaching humanities (see Chapter 6) there are certain topics where a computer simulation or model is the most effective means of teaching. For example, the growth of a river meander. A computer model could show how, over time, the faster current flow on the outside of the bend causes the meander to migrate. It is conceivable that, with the ever increasing sophistication of generic software such as multimedia authoring packages which enable simple animations, you might soon be able to create such a model for yourself, rather than rely upon a piece of subject specific software. Emerging technologies such as digital cameras will almost certainly revolutionise fieldwork in good schools.

We have drawn attention to the relatively well-established position of word processing and associated applications. We have dwelt considerably on data handling applications because we wish to emphasise their importance. Looking to the future, the other major application of ICT in humanities will undoubtedly be communications technologies. The use of communication technologies in humanities is limited only by the human imagination. E-mail can be used to put pupils from different countries and cultures in day to day contact. The fast and immediate nature of the communication means that children's motivation and interest can be maintained. This replaces written pen-friend relationships which often took weeks before the post, or snail-mail to those that use the new jargon, delivered a reply and an answer to a question that was long forgotten. E-mail can also be used by teachers to set up joint work between two or more different institutions with other institutions. Such work could be collecting data about the area's history and/or geography and then sharing and comparing the data. This may be a particularly beneficial activity to schools that are in isolated areas of the country.

The study of a contrasting locality has for some time been an important part of the geography curriculum and is likely to remain so, for good reasons. For children of primary age, however, the quality of learning and level of motivation has often been higher in the case of local studies involving field work than in the study of distant and inaccessible places. If you have used the e-mail with children, you may already be quite enthused about the possibility of exciting change and improvement here. Some schools are already using video conferencing and more will do so. This will add the visual dimension to the sharing of information in an immediate and direct way, allowing pupils to see and talk to one another directly without distance or time being an obstacle. You need to remember also that data files can be attached to e-mail, and given all that we have said about data handling in history and geography, the possibilities for radical improvements in teaching and learning in the humanities are exciting indeed.

The internet, when used in the correct context, can offer endless opportunities for humanities. The access to almost unlimited real-time information on any number of topics is staggering. Pupils can find out the weather in almost any part of the world and can see pictures both still and moving on any part of any country. They can even take visual tours around museums and art galleries. The role for the teacher here is one of supervisor, protector and adviser. Children need to be aware that there is little control over the accuracy of data on the net and that there is some harmful information that they may access. By harmful, we do not necessarily mean the more obvious elements such as hard core pornography. It is likely that schools will be linked to service providers who will be largely successful in filtering such material out. Far greater harm might ultimately result from the fact that there is *no editorial control over content* on the net. This means that there is a vast quantity of material that lacks any kind of authority, accuracy or verification, and it is potentially available to children.

If you have surfed the net much yourself, you may be aware of the potentially harming and corrupting nature of some of the internet debates, many of which are phrased in emotive language which lacks any of the restraints and reserve of authenticated material over which there is editorial control. This means that children will have to come to understand the concept of editorial control. They will need to be able to differentiate between emotionalism or personal prejudice and properly constructed arguments that can be verified or substantiated. How will children know what to believe? Will they believe anything just because it is on the internet? Helping children acquire these skills and attitudes is likely to be a demanding new task for primary teachers during the early decades of the twenty-first century. Children must also understand the difference between quantity of information and quality of information. This will require an understanding of how best to use search engines (the systems that allow them to access the information they require).

If teachers do not structure the activities correctly, then children might simply drift from one page of interest to the next and a search that starts looking for desert in the Sudan might become a look at a desert on a distant planet. This might be a perfectly suitable activity in some contexts but not others. The introduction of CD-ROMs into schools has already provided us with the lesson that, left unsupervised or untaught, children are likely to print out reams of irrelevant material which they don't understand, yet be proud of the result! This is the point with which we began the chapter. It is the difference between making the technology work as an end in itself, and a developed ability to use the technology effectively as a means to an end.

Summary

- Most creative work of quality that both promotes teaching and learning in the humanities and develops ICT skills is likely to be with generic software packages.
- The communications strand, which principally includes word processing, is the most well established use of generic software in primary humanities.
- More time needs to be given to the handling strand. The humanities provide a context for data handling which needs wider appreciation and use by primary teachers.
- The most exciting new developments in humanities and ICT are likely to be communications technologies, including e-mail and the internet.
- These developments, whilst full of exciting potential, are also hazardous because of the lack of editorial supervision. Teachers will have to develop a new set of skills to cope with this.

The evaluation of classroom software

Reflection 5

How valuable is some of the information on the internet? Surf the net to find a website that interests you and download the information provided. Would you pay as much for this information as you would for a book you possess on the same subject?

- In what ways is the net a valuable new tool that provides a facility which did not previously exist?
- In what ways is the net inferior to other sources of information?

Evaluating software and multimedia resources poses similar questions to using any other classroom resource. However, due to the nature of the resource there are also some additional questions. In this section we are using the terms ICT resources to include the hardware and range of software including computer applications, computer programs and multimedia products.

It may help teachers, posed with a multitude of computer applications, software and multimedia resources, to divide the questions they need to ask into a number of groups.

- Educational and classroom management questions
- Technical questions
- Resource support needs

Only when the above questions are addressed can the final all-important question be asked, that is,

❛ *Will the use of this resource with that particular group of children be more beneficial than using traditional resources?*

If the answer to that final question is no, then why use it?

To return to the groups of questions. Each group has a key question and then some subsidiaries.

Education and classroom management questions

Key question
Will the ICT resource be suitable to the age, phase and subject needs of the children and offer a benefit beyond traditional resources?

Subsidiary questions
Does the ICT resource actually suit the age, phase, subject and group suggested by the packaging or marketing information?

Is the language used appropriate for the group you intend to use it with?

Does the ICT resource provide adequate and appropriate feedback to children?

Can the children, with or without your support, use the resource? This will affect how you can then manage the resource in the classroom.

How many children can use the system at the same time or is it only suitable for whole classroom use?

Is the ICT resource appropriate to all children in the class or for a particular sub-set? It may be that the resource is more suitable for the more able or children with special educational needs or to support a particular learning difficulty.

Are the 'hidden values' of the ICT resources appropriate to the group?

Does the ICT resource treat fairly issues of equal opportunities?

Technical questions

Key question
Will it work in my classroom?

Subsidiary questions

Do I have the correct hardware, software platform? (In non-ICT terms this means: is the equipment in the classroom the correct sort of equipment, including sufficient memory in the computer, to actually make the computer application or software work?)

Does the resource provide sound? If so, can I turn it off and would I lose significant benefit by doing so?

Do I need a colour monitor? A question that is less relevant today as most monitors are now colour.

Do I need a printer?

Do I have the correct input devices? Some resources need a mouse or joystick rather than a keyboard.

Do I have the correct licence to run the software in the classroom? This may need to be checked with the distributors. There is a range of licences, individual machine, site licence, and institutional licence.

Resource support material questions

Key question

Do I have the necessary support materials to make using the ICT resource beneficial?

Subsidiary questions

What do I need to do to prepare the children to use this resource? This may be giving them help in technically using the resource, but it is more likely to be giving them background information as to the content and context.

What do I need to do to help the children follow up the material to the best educational advantage?

Do I have a range of books, videos, pictures or play activities to help build on the learning experience?

Conclusion

The emphasis, then, is on teaching, not technology. If you choose your software wisely, you will be in possession of a relatively small number of powerful generic packages that enhance teaching and learning right across the curriculum. These generic packages have particular applications in the humanities where they enable you to do much better the things you have always done. This might be something as simple as asking a child to produce a short piece of writing. It would certainly include the drawing of tables, charts, maps and the production of graphs. At the most exciting level, it might mean virtual field work in a contrasting locality via an e-mail link with another school. ICT enable us to do much better that which we have always done, and opens up exciting new learning possibilities for the future.

References

DES (1989) *Science at Age 11: A Review of APU Survey Findings 1980–1984*, London: HMSO.

MARSDEN, B. (1995) *Geography 11–16: Rekindling Good Practice*, London: Fulton.

NAACE (1997) *Implementing IT* (The National Association of Advisers for Computers in Education), Coventry: National Council for Educational Technology.

NCET/OFSTED (1997) *A Commentary on Inspection Findings, 1995–96*, Coventry: NCET.

Further reading

STRAKER, A. and GOVIER, H. (1997) *Children Using Computers* (2nd edition). Oxford: Nash Pollock.
Of all the books dealing with primary ICT, this is perhaps the most useful to own for personal reference and is as nearly 'future proof' as any book dealing with ICT is likely to be. It is strong on practical suggestions for the effective use of generic packages with children, and provides a comprehensive overview of good practice in primary computing.

CROMPTON, R. and MANN, P. (eds) (1996) *IT Across the Primary Curriculum*, London: Cassell.
This edited collection has been particularly written with the four strands of the UK National Curriculum in mind. It gives clear guidance on how these are to be implemented via suitable generic software. There are also useful chapters on training and staff development and the management of ICT in the primary school.

NCET (1998) *History using IT. Book 2: Searching for Patterns in the Past Using Databases and Spreadsheets*, Coventry: NCET.
Although intended specifically for Key Stage 3, this practical workbook contains many ideas and suggestions similar to the ones we have given as enquiry tasks in this

chapter. Software is provided for you to practise with and we are confident that, working through the examples will help you to set up your own spreadsheets and databases for use with younger children. The companion volume (Book 1) deals with communicating and word processing in history and is also useful.

Chapter 10

Sustainability and the humanities
Martin Ashley

The National Statement of Values tells us that 'We value the environment, both natural and shaped by humans, as the basis of life and a source of wonder and inspiration'. It goes on to inform us that, on the basis of these values we should: '. . . accept our responsibility to maintain a sustainable environment for future generations'. What does the word 'sustainability' mean to you? If you immediately think of 'Agenda 21', the Rio Earth Summit or Kyoto, it probably means quite a lot. If these terms are unfamiliar to you, however, it may be helpful to begin with an explanation as to why we have devoted this and the next chapter in a book on the teaching of humanities for the twenty first century to a concept which is probably a great deal less familiar than such concepts as 'history' or 'geography'.

It may help to appreciate that, as far as primary education is concerned, the word 'sustainability', or at least 'sustainable development education' has grown out of the more familiar term 'environmental education'. The humanities subjects, geography in particular, have much to say about environmental education and therefore, by implication, about sustainability. You might like to refer to the Schools Curriculum and Assessment Authority (1996) publication *Teaching Environmental Matters Through the National Curriculum*. In that, you will find under required coverage, a list of all the geography topics which support environmental education. You will see that geography, along with science, is responsible for most of this required coverage. For science, of course, the coverage is still 'required'. Since 1998, however, those elements of environmental education which are part of the geography Orders can no longer be regarded strictly as 'required coverage'.

However, geographers have for many years been at the driving edge of developments in environmental education. An interest in geography is almost invariably associated to a greater or lesser degree with an interest in the environment. More than this, we might reasonably say that some geographers are driven in their subject by a passion for the environment. For such geographers, environmental education or education for sustainability undoubtedly has the status of required coverage, regardless of who is education secretary. Is this merely a partisan enthusiasm, or is the ability to promote education for sustainability an essential competency for the twenty first century primary school teacher? Does the topic, indeed, merit *two* chapters, and the last two chapters at that?

In these last two chapters, we hope to provide you with a good answer to this question. This chapter begins with a critique of environmental education as it currently stands through which we invite you to look afresh at the subject. Our suggestion in this chapter is that you jettison some of the 'baggage' that has come to be associated with environmental education. We invite you to look afresh at the primary curriculum. We take a very important theme of sustainability, that of climate change, and visit areas of the primary curriculum you might expect, and other areas of the primary curriculum that you might not.

Introduction

The conference hall was hushed with expectation. David Bellamy, Michaela Strachan, Jonathan Porritt and a host of other environmental celebrities had run their course. Now, finally, it was time for the Secretary of State himself. Polite, expectant applause greeted the Right Honourable John Selwyn Gummer as he took the stage. Would he rise to the challenges posed by the delegates to this unique international gathering? Would he condemn the French nuclear testing programme? Would he, indeed, condemn other politicians or just adults in general, for their irresponsible attitudes and the threat they posed to the world's environment? Would he lend his support to this most just of all causes, the welfare of future generations? Would he proclaim, before the world's assembled media, the right of today's children to inherit a beautiful, bountiful, unpolluted and biodiverse planet?

No. This was not his agenda. He lectured the 800 odd 9–13 year old conference delegates, assembled from all corners of the globe, about their failure to wear extra sweaters when it got cold. 'Who?' he enquired 'made the world?' (An embarrassed silence.) 'Ought we not?' he suggested, 'to be thankful to the Maker for a beautiful world?' (murmuring of discontent). 'You must all do something about it', he proclaimed across an atmosphere of thickening hostility. 'You must not turn the heating up when it gets cold, you must put on an extra sweater.' The conference hall resonated to the chorus of jeers and disapproval from many outraged delegates. This was the moment of glory. This was real child power. This, at last, was the ghost of generations to come, rightly haunting the wicked Scrooge of twentieth century environmental abuse. 'GUMMER SHOUTED DOWN' 'ENVIRONMENT SECRETARY TAUGHT LESSON BY CHILDREN', proclaimed the national newspapers the following day.

The occasion I am describing was the world's first International Children's Conference on the Environment, held in Eastbourne in October 1995. I was privileged to attend this auspicious event as chaperone for 12 year old Laura, a pupil at the school I then taught at. Laura had won a free delegate place to the conference by describing for a competition run by the *Radio Times* the environmental work we did at our school. None of her family was free to chaperone her, so the task fell to me. The conference was indeed a unique and prestigious event. Sri Lanka, Australia, Nigeria (thanks to the generosity of sponsors British Airways), child delegates from every continent made it a truly international conference. Delegates were accommodated in Eastbourne hotels with all the trappings of the best party political conference seasons. The conference resolutions (or 'challenges') were carried by the two chief organisers, 13 year old Debbie and 12 year old Dermot, on Concorde to New York where they were presented by the children in person to the Secretary General of the United Nations.

As an advocate of children and their futures, I have to confess to being deeply moved by the spirit of these youngsters. Debbie and Dermot were certainly remarkable young people, as indeed was Laura from my own school. There is some doubt, however, that I would have been alive today to contribute to this chapter, had I voiced the thought 'Mr Gummer did have a point' on board the bus which returned the delegates to their hotels. The parents and chaperones, to say nothing of the children themselves, seethed as the bus wound its way through the streets of Eastbourne. I prefer to think that the virtue of discretion rather than the vice of cowardice was responsible, but I kept the thought 'Mr Gummer did have a point' to myself on that bus journey. Perhaps you might like to reflect on your own thoughts before reading mine?

Recycling and global warming are two of the most commonly reported 'environmental issues'. There is little doubt that many children know that recycling is a 'good thing' which we all 'ought to do'. (See Research Report below.) Indeed, I still have (and use with children) a video of one of the

This is the way we rinse the can,
rinse the can, rinse the can.
This is the way we rinse the can, for
re-cy-cal-ling.

This is the way we smash the can,
smash the can, smash the can.
This is the way we smash the can,
for re-cy-cal-ling.

This is the way we bundle the
papers, bundle the papers, bundle
the papers.
This is the way we bundle the
papers, for re-cy-cal-ling.

- Do you know a tune that
  would fit these words?
- Can you think of some
  suitable actions to accompany
  it?
- Would you teach this song to
  a class of early years children?
- Perhaps you work with later
  years children and are more
  used to textbooks which deal
  in straightforward facts?

The natural greenhouse effect is
essential as without it the Earth's
average temperature would be 33
degrees Celsius lower than it is.
Recent human activity has led to an
increase in greenhouse gases. This is
causing world temperatures to rise, a
process known as global warming.

(Waugh, 1994, p. 28)

- Do you understand the
  science of global warming?
- How would you cope with
  children's questions arising
  from it?
- Would you use this text by
  Waugh in a class of later
  years primary children?

news reports of the Eastbourne Conference. 'Conference organisers' it explains, 'were left red faced when they failed to provide recycling bins.' Indeed they were, and the situation was rapidly rectified after the first day. To committed eco-children, dumping cans in the recycling bin is almost a form of religious ritual.

Does this mean, then, that environmental education has been an unqualified success? My answer to this question would involve consideration of what is meant by the word 'education'. You might find it quite useful to draw a parallel between religious education and environmental education. There are certain practices which are considered undesirable or even repugnant in religious education. These include training and instruction, evangelisation and indoctrination. Training is the provision of instruction in procedures which can be carried out without an understanding of underlying principles. Evangelisation is the winning of converts to your particular religion or world view. Indoctrination is the attempt to inculcate an adherence to a doctrine (usually established by dogmatic argument rather than scientific enquiry) through bypassing the process of reason. I imagine that you would be opposed to all such practices and alarmed if you felt that a religious group were carrying them out within your school.

You may well have come across the terms 'education *about* the environment', 'education *through* the environment' and 'education *for* the environment'. They were introduced in 1976 by a Schools Council initiative known as *Project Environment*. They crop up with unfailing regularity in the literature on environmental education and sustainability. The National Curriculum Council lent authority to them by including them in the Cross-Curricular Guidance no. *7 Environmental Education*. Education *about* the environment consists of providing knowledge about matters pertaining to the environment and perhaps the notion of sustainability. Much of this happens in science, but geography is perhaps the subject most associated with the provision of information about the environment. Education *through* the environment consists of using the environment as a first hand learning resource. I hope that you have read the chapter on field work by Don Kimber and Maggie Smith. Effective field work lies at the very heart of the unique contribution of the humanities subjects in making good primary schools the lively, vibrant centres of activity they are.

Education *for* the environment as Palmer (1998) reminds us, supposes that pupils might come to engage in certain more pro-environmental behaviours (recycling perhaps?). If education *about* the environment is to do with *concepts* and education *through* the environment is to do with *feelings*, then education *for* the environment is left to deal with *values*. As such, it might be a core theme of this book. We must proceed with some caution, however, because there is rather too much evidence that over-zealous approaches to education *for* the environment have sometimes led to the activity ceasing to be education at all. There is, for example, an American programme of pseudo-ecological education available to British schoolchildren which actually uses the techniques of a catechism (rote learning of 'correct' questions and answers). You may well, on reflection, regard such techniques as instruction or indoctrination rather then education. One writer has attacked what he calls the 'evangelical' approach to environmental education, pointing out the similarity of the 'establish guilt-portray retribution-demonstrate salvation cycle' of doomsday environmentalism to Victorian religious evangelism.

You would probably not countenance instruction, indoctrination or evangelisation in religious education and it is surely reasonable to apply similar standards to history and geography when they deal with environmental education and sustainability. Perhaps 'looking afresh' requires us to step back from established notions of environmental education and ask anew what are the implications of educating for sustainability. What does this term mean to children and teachers in schools?

Research focus 1: Children and sustainability

1   Some key ideas from recent research
Pupils of both primary and secondary school age feel that schools are in general doing a poor job in educating them for the future and informing them about humanitarian and global values.

Children appear to bring with them a naive humanitarian concern and orientation to fairness in global affairs. This is not always developed by schools into an informed, realistic and mature view.

Where schools *do* work consistently hard to implement a particular value, there is evidence of success in producing a lasting and positive effect on pupils. This is manifest mainly in attitudes to racism and cultural equality.

Children's hopes and fears about national and global futures tend to reflect currently popular and short-term media images rather than a long-term strategy. These are generally pessimistic. Paradoxically, hopes

---

and fears about personal futures show an orientation, largely consistent over time, towards an optimistic and traditional future (house, car, partner and increased material well-being). There is a need for schools to provide children with a credible and authoritative long-term overview which links personal futures to national and global futures and focuses on lasting values rather than current media fashion.

(Richmond and Morgan, 1977; Tizard, 1986; Hicks and Holden, 1995; Symons, 1995; Morris and Schagen, 1996)

2 Case Studies

The aim would seem to be for schools to respond to the above research by providing an authoritative overview which pupils recognise as a worthwhile education about an humanitarian future, more worthy of their attention than either media hype or pressure group campaigning. How are they to do this?

One 9–13 middle school responded to the challenge of a new millennium by setting up a whole school project on sustainability. The following is taken from the school's *action research* evaluation of the project. It is interesting because it took place a week after the act of worship theme had been 'sustainability'. The whole staff had received inservice training on sustainability and had explored on a training day the question of developing a whole school ethos on sustainability through assemblies. The children's responses represent different age level understandings of Acts of Worship experienced by the school and therefore provide an interesting snapshot of progression. We can see the degree to which sustainability as a concept is understood by children in a school where it is taken seriously.

Case Study I

Some views of pupils on sustainability

Year 5 pupils. 'Kind of doing something everyone can do without hurting the environment . . . saving animals, stopping pollution . . . trying to keep greenery in Britain.'

Year 6 Pupils. 'Caring for the Earth . . . extinction, rubbish . . . Keeping the world the same as it was before . . . just as beautiful . . . but finding new ways of heating and lighting.'

Year 7 Pupils. 'To keep things longer . . . not to use everything up straightaway . . . If you have a forest and you cut down the trees you have to plant them again.'

Reflection 2

- How do these teachers' understandings of sustainability compare with your own?
- To what degree are the pupils' understandings of sustainability informed by appropriate subject knowledge and to what degree are they influenced by popular conceptions of environmentalism?

Year 8 Pupils. 'Using other methods of making energy so that we can carry on and the Earth's resources won't be depleted . . . to do with endangered things, especially countryside threatened by pollution . . . turning lights off when not needed . . .'

The understandings of the teachers
To me, education for sustainability means . . .
. . . an improved way of living for all.
. . . developing a whole school approach which encourages awareness of environmental issues and the importance of such issues for the future.
. . . taking time to adapt and modify what we do within school and the curriculum to enforce and enhance sustainability within children's minds and our own.
. . . increasing everyone's awareness of the fact that our lifestyles at present are not sustainable and increasing our awareness of what we can do to change our lifestyles to help sustain the planet and its resources.
. . . changing attitudes and practice to creation and the resources in the universe.
. . . the process by which children's attitudes are fostered and reinforced to appreciate the appropriateness of sustainable development.
. . . bringing home to children the realities of future resources.
. . . (1) giving pupils the opportunity to understand environmental issues and (2) giving pupils a role/voice in the use of natural resources in the twenty first century.

Children and teachers in this school are both trying to come to terms with what is meant by sustainability. There are clear patterns of development in the children's responses. The younger children have a tendency to perceive sustainability as undifferentiated from a naïve form of environmentalism. It is to do with 'good behaviour' towards the environment, saving animals, not making pollution and so on. Saving animals and not making pollution were also concerns more common amongst girls than boys, irrespective of age. None of the youngest children mentioned ideas which might begin to indicate a dawning insight into sustainability, such as scarcity, new technology, setting limits to growth or utilising renewable cycles. Conversely, an appreciation of these topics begins to feature more in the responses of the older children. The idea of a renewable cycle is first mentioned in Year 7, beyond the age of primary education. However, the partial misconception that sustainability has to do with a 'no change' scenario is also more associated with the older children. It perhaps betrays the conservative influences of an environmentalism which appeals to saving animals rather than developing human ethics and value systems.

These children need to understand more about the social and technological changes that have happened in the past in order to learn more about the fact that their lives will change in the future. They need to understand that sustainability is not a naïve form of conservation. They need to understand also about aspects of continuity in human nature that might affect the future, for example, tendencies towards greed or social inequality. The question is *when*? The children of older primary age in this middle school tended, in spite of an emphasis upon understanding sustainability, to be more influenced by popular environmentalism than by relevant subject knowledge. This has clear implications for the primary school teacher. An ill-informed approach to educating for sustainability in the primary school runs the risk that the subject knowledge will be both over-simplified to the point of naïveté yet still misunderstood. In the absence of understanding and the ability to exercise reason, children may revert to emotionally driven misconceptions derived from popular environmentalism and little real education will have occurred.

The above research seems to give us one possible answer to the question of when. It was in Years 7 and 8 that some understanding of the key concepts of sustainability began to emerge. A key point we wish to emphasise in these chapters is that it is vital for you, as a reflective practitioner, to keep in mind an overview of the whole curriculum from age 5 to age 16/18+. Educating for sustainability, to coin what is probably becoming a cliché, is a process of lifelong learning. It is also the business of whole communities and not just schools. Local councils, perhaps through their Local Agenda 21 officers, where appointed, have at least as big a role to play as educational institutions. We are not saying, however, that primary schools have no role to play. This is far from the case. In the remainder of this chapter and throughout the next chapter, we attempt to outline what we see that role to be. We begin by exploring further the notion that knowledge and understanding (education about) are not the reasons for action.

Research focus 2: Knowledge and understanding are not the reasons for action

In a perfectly rational world, we might expect everybody to behave as television's *Mastermind* presenter Magnus Magnusson might like. Giving the keynote address to the 1994 Association for Science Education Scotland Conference, he explained how when scientists detect warning signs that the Earth is under stress, they measure, monitor and analyse the signs. They make public their results and . . . the public does the rest. The research evidence we refer to here and in the next two chapters suggests that this is simply not the case. We do not change our attitudes or behaviour simply in response to the fact that scientists or other experts say in effect 'x is happening, if we all do y the result will be z'. In other words, education about the environment, in spite of our critique of certain aspects of education for the environment, is not likely on its own to lead to movements towards sustainability.

Some key ideas from recent research

1   There is only very small correlation between knowledge and actual behaviour and the level of scientific knowledge is not generally one of the variables that influences environmental behaviour.

(Ashley, 1998; Duit and Haeussler, 1994;
Hines, Hungerford and Tomera, 1987; Laneheime and Lehman 1986)

2   Children do not understand the science of global warming and hold many misconceptions, for example about the effects of car pollution.

(Boyes and Stanisstreet, 1993; Plunkett and Skamp, 1994)

3   Most adults, including teachers, don't understand this science either.

(Boyes et al. 1995; Dove, 1996; Rudig, 1995)

4   There is, in any case, no simple progression from knowledge to informed behaviour.

(Breckler, 1984; Chaiken and Yates, 1985; Gigliotti, 1992; Hungerford and Volk, 1990)

5   Giving pupils the facts and letting them make up their own minds doesn't work.

(Slater, 1994)

An idea in a little more depth

If knowledge and understanding are not the reasons for action, then what are the reasons for action? How do we explain the popular perception that children are in some way 'green'? Why do children engage in pro-environmental behaviours such as walking or cycling to school, or recycling waste?

Approximately 400 children, aged 11 (end of Key Stage 2) and 14 (end of Key Stage 3) in a sample of primary, middle and secondary schools in rural and urban locations were questioned about their knowledge, understanding and intention to act in relation to two key issues of sustainability: transport and the recycling of waste. The pupils were first questioned to determine the level of knowledge about what the 'correct' pro-environmental behaviour is thought to be. They were then questioned to ascertain their level of understanding of some basic scientific and economic reasons which could justify such pro-environmental behaviours. Finally, they were questioned about the degree to which they would be prepared to make small changes in their behaviour in response to the knowledge.

88.8 per cent of the children held a level of knowledge equivalent to that of a well-informed adult about what is the appropriate pro-environmental behaviour for transport. For waste recycling, the figure was 84.2 per cent. However, only 20.7 per cent of the children could justify the pro-environmental behaviour for transport scientifically, and only 16.7 per cent could provide any kind of scientific justification for recycling waste. No relationship was found between the three variables of knowledge of pro-environmental behaviour, understanding of the science and intention to carry the behaviour out. In other words, the results clearly confirm the conclusions summarised above.

This research was followed up a year later with 162 of the former Year 6 pupils who were asked, by means of a whole year census conducted by Year 7 form tutors, about whether they actually undertook certain pro-environmental behaviours including cycling to school in preference to car, and recycling waste.

The results for recycling were particularly interesting, not least in the light of the reflection box for the Eastbourne Conference above. Sixty-three per cent of the pupils claimed in the census that they regularly recycled waste. A sample of 45 of the pupils were then interviewed individually in depth by a researcher who sought to find out whether the behaviour claimed actually took place, and the reasons behind it.

The pupils were asked about whether they separated rubbish at source at home, what they actually recycled and how in practice they got the materials to the recycling point. They were asked questions about why they did it and the attitudes of the roles played by the various members of their families.

Compared with the 63 per cent who claimed in the whole year census to recycle waste, only one pupil interviewed was found to have initiated the behaviour himself and to have persuaded his family to support recycling. In all other cases, it was found that when a pupil claimed in a survey to 'recycle waste' he or she was merely a participant, often passive, in a family activity. The most frequent reason for recycling was that it was a family activity undertaken during shopping trips to the supermarket. Mothers were the family members most frequently cited as initiating the activity (50 per cent), both parents/whole family (25 per cent) and big sisters (16 per cent).

Three significant factors thus emerged during interview. The first was that in 100 per cent of cases the behaviour was actively supported by parents or other family members who undertook a regular journey to a recycling point, encouraging their children to help. The second was the number of times the existence of such a facility in a supermarket car park was mentioned, without prompt, in response to open-ended questioning. The third was the influence of the popular children's television programme 'Blue Peter' which was mentioned without prompt by 23 per cent of subjects interviewed.

The issue of transport was complicated by parental worries over safety. In the census, children were given the opportunity to state whether they actually cycled, or whether they wished to do so but were not generally permitted to by their parents. In spite of this, considerably fewer children cycled to school than recycled waste. During the detailed interviews, the children described their reasons for cycling to school, which are summarised in the table below. (The observed column refers to the children who were actually observed to cycle to school, the conditional column refers to the children who said they wanted to but their parents wouldn't let them.)

TABLE 10.1
Operative value of cycling

	Frequency		
	Observed	conditional	all
Enjoyment:	3	0	3
Health:	1	1	2
Quicker than walking:	1	3	4
New bike:	1	2	3
Cars bad for environment:	1	0	1
Council will provide track:	1	0	1
Taxi expensive:	0	1	1
Walking boring:	0	1	1
Parent needs car:	0	1	1

The significant finding here is that, in spite of the fact that these children were taken from a sample, 88.8 per cent of whom had a knowledge of pro-environmental behaviour equivalent to that of an informed adult, environmental reasons for action were mentioned only twice (and then only in response to an 'are there any other reasons you haven't mentioned?' prompt).

> The conclusions are clearly that behaviour which is apparently
> pro-environmental occurs in the children, mainly for social reasons
> such as integrating in family life, recreation or personal convenience.
> Knowledge and understanding are not, as all the research summarised
> earlier seems to confirm, the reasons for action.

Clearly we are presented with something of a challenge by this research.
Behaviour changes are not going to come about simply through the provision
of greater subject knowledge. Whether or not the next generation behaves in
a way that would be considered sustainable would seem to depend most of
all on their socialisation into our culture. If, as a culture and society, we
recycle resources, our children will be more likely to recycle resources. If, as
a culture and society, we are economical in the use of energy, our children
will be more likely to be economical in the use of energy. We will not
become economical in the use of energy, however, simply by providing
children with scientific and geographical facts about resources or energy and
expecting them to behave differently when they are grown up on the basis of
this knowledge. Neither will we change things through moral exhortation or
even through attempted indoctrination.

A recent critique of environmental education (Aldrich-Moodie and Kwong,
1997) makes this point. The point about recycling as a pseudo-religious
practice rather than a rational response to scientific and moral reasoning is
dealt with in particular depth. Given that this report is the work of the
Institute of Economic Affairs, we might not expect it to be entirely unbiased
itself. This is a point we discuss further in the last chapter. For the present,
the claims it makes that children in both the USA and the UK are being
presented with biased information about the environment through textbooks
which present controversial theories as facts demanding an immediate
response from children, merit serious consideration. Kwong claims that
teachers sometimes respond to a lack of subject knowledge by bringing
'experts' into the classroom. The 'experts', however, turn out to be fervent
young environmentalists whose understanding of science is probably no
greater than that available in the school anyway and whose understanding of
children and *education* is considerably less than the teacher's.

I suspect that this practice may be more widespread in the USA than
the UK. My concern here is with another source of dubious 'expertise'
which I anticipate being much more of a threat to a sound education for
sustainability over the next two decades. I am talking about the World Wide

Web. You are probably familiar with the National Curriculum Orders for ICT. I quote from the Key Stage 2 Programme of Study, 2d Communicating and Handling Information: 'interpret, analyse and check the plausibility of information held on ICT systems . . .' I quote also from the National Curriculum for Initial Teacher Training:

 *14biii Trainees must demonstrate that they know how to judge the accuracy of the information and the **credibility of its source**; e.g. discussing the fact that anyone can set up a website and there is no quality control over its content.*

The question of subject knowledge is as problematic as the question of emotionalism and indoctrination. Not only are children and their teachers potentially at the mercy of 'emotional spin' on issues of sustainability, they are also at the mercy of scientific misinformation. The combination of the two is potentially a highly potent force and the professional primary teacher must know how to deal with it, even if she is not herself a scientific expert. In the remainder of the book, we put forward the argument that the problem of subject knowledge and scientific misinformation must be confronted by looking afresh at the curriculum in order to discern what is relevant and of value. We simultaneously pursue the argument that there is a vital difference between emotionalism and emotional education. A sound emotional education must develop side by side with the learning of subject knowledge. We would remind you also that the culture into which children are socialised is by and large the greatest determinant of their behaviour. If you want children to recycle or save energy, then you must first do that yourself and your school must do it as an institution. The behavioural implications of educating for sustainability then become more a matter of explaining why adults are already doing it.

Towards a balanced approach in primary school

Let us begin by establishing an appropriate area of the curriculum upon which to focus.

Enquiry task I

For this task, you will need a copy of Teaching Environmental Matters Through the National Curriculum *(SCAA, 1996), the old 1995 Dearing version of the National Curriculum; DFE and the newer Curriculum 2000.*

Imagine that you are writing a new scheme of work for your school. Your headteacher has asked you to 'slim down' the geography curriculum so that fewer topics will be covered, but in greater depth and to a higher quality than before.

- Make your own list of *essential topics* in geography. (You may assume that map skills will continue as a core theme.)
- Now compare your own list of essential topics with SCAA's required coverage for environmental education.
- How many geography topics, defined by SCAA as required 'environmental' coverage, have you included in your list of essential topics?
- Which ones are the same?
- Have you left any 'environmental' ones out?
- In what ways are any of the topics you have included 'environmental'?
- What were the value judgments that informed your exercise in curriculum design?
- Compare your curriculum with Dearing's and the new Curriculum 2000, using the criteria developed in this enquiry task.

We would argue that there are certain key ideas in geography that an imperative of educating for a sustainable society demands primary school children learn about. We would include on our own list the topics of weather and climate; use and misuse of resources; economic activity, for instance farming or communications and transport; and some understanding of conditions in other countries, particularly developing countries. Of these, the topic of weather and climate is arguably as important as any because it is fundamental to understanding the issue of climate change, one of the most significant and controversial issues of sustainability. Popular environmentalism often begins with the assumption that we can talk about global warming and climate change because we all know what climate is. Is this assumption justified for children of primary school age? Hopefully your knowledge of the geography curriculum and your knowledge of children and their learning, will lead you to answer *no* to this question.

Let us consider for discussion in a little more detail the topic of weather from the geography curriculum. How will children come, as adults, to make rational decisions about global warming if they have never been taught about weather and climate? How, indeed, will children recognise climate change if they do not know what the climate is now and what it has been in the past? Why should children consider the topic to be of any importance if they have no understanding of such relationships as that between climate and agriculture? and between agriculture and trade? The National Curriculum Orders for geography at Key Stage 2 specified the following:

 In studying how weather varies between places and over time, pupils should be taught:

    a) how site conditions can influence the weather e.g. temperatures in the shade and in the sun, wind speed in sheltered and exposed sites;

    b) about seasonal weather patterns;

    c) about weather conditions in different parts of the world e.g. temperatures, rainfall and sunshine conditions in the localities studied, extremes of weather in other parts of the world.

Reflection 3

- If the water cycle is not in the geography curriculum for Key Stage 1 or 2, why teach it?
- If the water cycle is in the Key Stage 2 science curriculum, who is right, the scientists or the geographers?
- What is the difference between the water cycle in science and the water cycle in geography?
- Why did the Secretaries of State for Education during the late 1980s allow insufficient time for consultation between the different subjects in drawing up the National Curriculum?

The word *climate* does not appear. To find it, we must turn to the Orders for Key Stage 3 which specify:

 In studying how and why weather and climate vary, pupils should be taught:

a) *how weather and climate differ;*

b) *about the components and links in the water cycle;*

c) *how and why aspects of weather and climate vary from place to place.*

We would not want to advocate an approach to the curriculum which is either reductionist, behaviourist, linear, developmentalist or in any other way ignoring of the principles of social constructivism. We would not deny that some children of primary age will have the word 'climate' in their vocabulary. However, there might be sound reasons for keeping climate until Key Stage 3. The primary teacher will do well to reflect upon problems faced by secondary school teachers of geography and science arising from misconceptions about the rivers, mountains and the water cycle which seem to be acquired through poor work in primary schools. Equally, you might like to reflect upon the ignorance many children in Years 7 and 8 in micro-climatology. Could this be a result of the failure of some primary schools to make effective use of the school grounds and ICT in teaching a topic many scientific and geographical educators would regard as vital for an informed basis for the subject of climate?

If there are sound reasons for keeping climate until Key Stage 3, there may be equally sound reasons for proceeding with extreme caution over the provision of 'information' about climate change and global warming. The 9 year old boy who informed his father that he must demolish his greenhouse to prevent London from being flooded might be one of them. The 8 year old girl who believes that driving cars will cause the sun to go red, which will cause the world to blow up might be another. (Examples quoted by Storm, 1990.) Perhaps we should interpret QCA's emphasis upon children being able to explain causes (*Maintaining Breadth and Balance*, 1998) with a degree of caution. Naivety and over-simplification in this area seems to resonate with our earlier criticisms of reductionism (see Chapter 7). There is no need for this if we are thoughtful about what is really involved in work on climate at primary level.

In guiding the development of children's attitudes and values, there are not one but three domains of thought to which we need to attend. These are the domain of knowledge and understanding (cognitive), the domain of feelings and emotional reasoning (affective) and the domain of intentions to act (conative) which is closely associated with the child's cultural and social environment. What is the difference between emotionalism and the kind of emotional education that we believe is necessary for a proper response to education for sustainability? Hopefully, you are now fairly clear about the link between emotionalism and indoctrination. To summarise this, emotionalism is the desire to use untutored feelings to bypass reason, and it is one of the key techniques of indoctrination. Emotional education, on the other hand, demands that we help children to articulate their feelings and reason about them. This is very much the domain of spiritual, moral and cultural development, which was discussed at some length in Chapter 7.

In adding to that discussion, however, we would draw your attention to the fact that, at the time of writing, the standards for newly qualified teachers refer to spiritual and moral development twice. One reference requires that you should *exploit opportunities* for spiritual and moral development. The other requires that you should *plan systematically* for spiritual and moral development. There is a less than subtle difference. The former undoubtedly has its place, but if it is the only approach you use, then you may be guilty of the 'We do that when it happens in the playground' approach of which I was critical in Chapter 7. Planning systematically means that you incorporate in your lesson plans appropriate learning objectives that lead to emotional development, which hopefully avoids the kind of emotional hype and scientific misconception quoted in the previous paragraph.

To assist you with this process, there follows an expanded list of possible learning objectives for weather and climate (Figure 10.1). The list includes objectives for cognitive understanding, objectives for the development of skills and objectives for emotional development listed as 'spiritual, moral and cultural'. The list is extensive and might encompass progression across the first three key stages of the National Curriculum (possibly extending even into Key Stage 4). The enquiry task which precedes it invites you to consider and map out such progress.

Enquiry task 2

Sort through the below learning intentions and allocate them to each key stage of the National Curriculum. (They can, of course, appear in more than one key stage.)

Attempt to identify and map out a scheme for emotional development on the basis of the learning intentions which shows progression and development. Expand one or more of the intentions into a detailed lesson plan or sequence of plans which shows clearly:
a) Assumptions made about children's prior knowledge, skill, and spiritual/moral development.
b) Exactly what you will do (including the use of resources and first hand experiences) to promote new learning of knowledge and skill and genuine progression and development in the spiritual/moral realm.

Learning intentions: Development of concepts

- Children will identify the main phenomena of weather (wind, rain, etc.)
- Children will have some understanding of the relationship between weather data and conditions that can be experienced (e.g. a temperature of 30 degrees is very hot, a temperature of 2 degrees is quite cold).
- Children will recognise predictable and unpredictable elements of weather.
- Children will appreciate that there is an element of uncertainty in predicting weather.
- Children will be aware of the effects of extremes of weather.
- Children will have some understanding that climate describes likely weather patterns over a period in a given region, based on analysis of past weather data.
- Children will understand that there is a relationship between climate and vegetation, and between climate and the animals that live in a place.
- Children will have some understanding that there is a relationship between the success of agriculture and the nature of climate.
- Children will appreciate that there are significant differences in climate between different regions in the world.
- Children will understand that the global climate is subject to significant change over long periods (e.g. thousands of years ago there was an ice age when much of Britain was frozen like the Arctic is now).
- Children will demonstrate awareness that the climate continues to change and that scientists do not fully understand how.
- Children will demonstrate awareness that there is evidence that the world's climate is currently becoming warmer, and that some scientists believe that human activity may be a contributory factor.

Learning intentions: Skills

- Children will be able to perform simple measurements and observations of weather phenomena (e.g. rainfall, temperature, wind speed and direction, cloud cover and sunshine, visibility, ground condition).
- Children will be able to record and represent weather data in tabular form.
- Children will be able to represent weather data by appropriate graphic methods (e.g. block graph for rainfall, line graph for temperature).
- Children will be able to use good English to communicate effectively simple information, such as a weather forecast.
- Children will be able to use ICT software, such as a spreadsheet to record their weather observations and produce graphs.
- Children will be able to input weather data into a computer database and query the database.
- Children will be able to extract information about weather and climate from books and ICT sources.
- Children will be able to suggest whether the weather in a place is seasonal or unseasonable on the basis of given data.
- Children will be able to attempt a simple interpretation of the climate of a place on the basis of given data (e.g. 'It is a very hot place and it has a dry season').
- Children will be able to use ICT such as e-mail, fax or the internet to compare weather conditions in different parts of the world.

Learning intentions: Spiritual/moral/social/cultural

- Children will be able to recognise and articulate emotions connected with the impressions of weather.
- Children will have some knowledge of how the weather affects the lives of people who work outdoors (e.g. farmers, construction workers, sailors etc.).
- Children will recognise that man cannot yet control the weather, showing some wonder or awe at the place of human beings within nature.
- Children will be able to respond with some consideration of human needs to the inequitable global distribution of climates which allow reliable agriculture.
- Children will exhibit a sense of wonder and questioning of the existence of apparent injustice in nature.
- Children will be able to join in discussion of whether it is right or wrong that people should experience the effects of famine if these are avoidable.
- Children will show some understanding of the way in which different cultures and ways of life have arisen as human beings have adapted to different climates.
- Children will show some appreciation of the richness of cultural diversity associated with climatic and weather patterns.
- Children will recognise, with some empathy or appreciation, cultural representations of weather and climate (e.g. in painting or through music or literature).

FIG 10.1

Preparation for understanding climate change: learning intentions for weather and climate

Reflection 4

You might like to try compiling a similar list of learning intentions for resources and waste management in the primary school.

Can you identify opportunities for including the systematic planning of learning objectives for spiritual, moral and cultural development in relation to the topic of resources and waste management?

Reflect critically on the topic of waste and recycling. Can you identify:

a) elements that are better left to secondary or higher education?
b) assumptions made about prior knowledge which primary schools could but, in reality often don't, teach?

Education for sustainability (as opposed to indoctrination) is a lengthy process and the primary school is only the beginning. It is important that primary teachers at least acknowledge the need for an overview of the whole curriculum before endorsing any activities which might be open to criticism as potentially indoctrinating. If in doubt, a thorough brain storming of any 'environmental' topic should open up at least as many legitimate learning objectives for primary education as did my consideration of weather and climate. In the next and final chapter, we take further our consideration of climate change, placing it in a global context and reflecting upon the role of the educated value judgment in coping with uncertain futures.

References

ALDRICH-MOODIE, B. and KWONG, J. (1997) *Environmental Education*, London: Institute of Economic Affairs.

ASHLEY, M. (1998) *Value as a Reason for Action*, Unpublished PhD thesis, Bristol: University of the West of England.

BOYES, E., CHAMBERS, W. and STANISSTREET, M. (1995) 'Trainee primary teachers' ideas about the ozone layer', *Environmental Education Research*, **3**, 3, pp. 269–282.

BOYES, E. and STANISSTREET, M. (1993) 'The Greenhouse Effect: Children's perceptions of causes, consequences and cures', *International Journal of Science Education*, **15**, 531-552.

BRECKLER, S. (1984) 'Empirical verification of affect, behaviour and cognition as distinct components of attitude', *Journal of Personality and Social Psychology*, **47**, pp. 1191–1205.

CHAIKEN, S. and YATES, S. (1985) 'Affective-cognitive consistency as thought induced attitude polarisation', *Journal of Personal and Social Psychology*, **49**, pp. 1470–1481.

DFE (1995) *The National Curriculum*, London: HMSO.

DOVE, J. (1996) 'Student teacher understanding of the greenhouse effect, ozone layer depletion and acid rain', *Environmental Education Research*, **2**, 1, pp. 89–100.

DUIT, R. and HAEUSSLER, P. (1994) 'Learning and teaching energy' in FENSHAM, P., GUNSTONE, R. and WHITE, R. (eds), *The Content of Science: A Constructivist Approach to its Teaching and Learning*, London: Falmer.

GIGLIOTTI, L. (1992) 'Environmental attitudes: 20 years of change?' *Journal of Environmental Education*, **24**, 1, pp. 15–26.

HICKS, D. and HOLDEN, C. (1995) *Visions of the Future: Why We Need to Teach for Tomorrow*, Stoke: Trentham.

HINES, J., HUNGERFORD, H. and TOMERA, A. (1987) 'Analysis and synthesis of research on responsible environmental behaviour: a meta-analysis', *The Journal of Environmental Education*, **18**, pp. 1–8.

HUNGERFORD, H. and VOLK, T. (1990) 'Changing learner behaviour through environmental education', *Journal of Environmental Education*, **21**, 3, pp. 8–21.

LANEHEIME, R. and LEHMAN, J. (1986) *Die Bedeutung der Erziehung Fuer das Umweltbewusstein*, Kiel: IPN.

MORRIS, M. and SCHAGEN, I. (1996) *Green Attitudes or Learned Responses?*, Global Environmental Education, Slough: NFER.

NATIONAL CURRICULUM COUNCIL (NCC) (1989) Curriculum Guidance Seven: Environmental Education, York: NCC.

PALMER, J. (1998) *Environmental Education in the Twenty-first Century: Theory, Practice, Progress and Promise*, London: Routledge.

PLUNKETT, S. and SKAMP, K. (1994) 'The ozone layer and hole: children's conceptions', Paper presented to *Australian Science Education Research Conference*, Hobart, Tasmania.

QUALIFICATIONS AND CURRICULUM AUTHORITY (QCA) (1998) *Maintaining Breadth and Balance*, Hayes: QCA Publications.

RICHMOND, J. and MORGAN, R. (1977) *A National Survey of the Environmental Knowledge and Attitudes of Fifth Year Pupils in England*, Ohio State University: ERIC Science, Mathematics and Environmental Education Clearinghouse.

RUDIG, W. (1995) 'Public opinion and global warming', *Strathclyde Papers on Government and Politics, no. 101*. Glasgow: University of Strathclyde.

SCHOOLS CURRICULUM AND ASSESSMENT AUTHORITY (SCAA) (1996) *Teaching Environmental Matters through the National Curriculum*, Hayes: SCAA Publications.

SLATER, F. (1994) 'Education through geography: knowledge and understanding, values and culture', *Geography*, **79**, 147–63.

STORM, M. (1990) 'The evangelical approach to environmental education', *Annual Review of Environmental Education*, **4**.

SYMONS, G. (1995) *A Window to the Future: Young Peoples' Visions of the Year 2012*, Godalming: WWF Education.

TIZARD, B. (1986) 'Can children face the future?' *New Society*, 12 September.

WAUGH, D. (1994) *Key Geography for GCSE: Book 1*, Cheltenham: Stanley Thornes.

Further reading

PALMER, J. and NEAL, A. (1994) *The Handbook of Environmental Education*, London: Routledge.

This is a comprehensive general text on the subject of environmental education. The main emphasis is upon approaches to implementing and managing environmental education in primary and secondary schools.

PALMER, J. (1998) *Environmental Education in the Twenty-first Century: Theory, Practice, Progress and Promise*, London: Routledge.
This book is a comprehensive, scholarly review of the environmental education scene at the end of the twentieth century and covers the key concepts we have addressed in this chapter in greater depth.

HUCKLE, J. and STERLING, S. (eds) (1996) *Education for Sustainability*, London: Earthscan.
This book is a collection of critical and analytical essays which state the case for educating for sustainability. It is one of the most authoritative summaries of the issues currently available. The chapter by John Huckle entitled 'Realising sustainability in changing times' is a succinct summary of the key issues and of particular relevance to the humanities. Sterling's chapter 'Education in change' is more controversial in tone and develops further the type of discussion that has been initiated in this volume.

ALDRICH-MOODIE, B. and KWONG, J. (1997) *Environmental Education*, London: Institute of Economic Affairs.
A reaction against some of the more extreme elements of environmental education is now well established. Furthermore, the impact of environmentalism has been sufficient for most large organisations to take seriously the need both to appear 'green' and to exploit with hard evidence weaknesses in the environmentalist case. This volume is critical of environmental education. A dispassionate reading of it in conjunction with the other suggestions will help you to form an overview of the whole debate.

Chapter 11

Towards uncertain futures?

Martin Ashley and Malcolm Hughes

In the previous chapter, we considered the importance of subject knowledge in teaching about sustainability and the environment. Looking afresh at the geography curriculum may have helped you to see how relevant many of the traditional topics of geography are to a curriculum for sustainability and the twenty-first century. There is so much that a primary teacher needs to do if children are to have the necessary background of knowledge and understanding to become informed citizens, capable of intelligent participation whenever environmental issues are debated. Yet a question remains. Mere 'book learning' has always been thought insufficient by the practically experienced. To echo the theme of an earlier chapter, subject knowledge is 'necessary but not sufficient'.

This final chapter compares the power of book learning with the power of learning from first hand experience. Drawing upon the discussion of the importance of the affective domain and the education of the emotions in the previous chapter, it highlights the problem that attitudes, values and above all emotions cannot be very effectively learned from books or worksheets. It also raises another difficulty; that of the risk and uncertainty which is part of educating for sustainability. We cannot talk about sustainability without some attempt at visioning the future, and this inevitably takes us into the realm of uncertainty. Add to that the vexed problem of present day scientific uncertainty, and it will be seen that a clear set of knowledge objectives for sustainability is hardly possible. Perhaps that is why the subject receives limited consideration in a knowledge centred curriculum. The context for our discussions in the final chapter is a global one, for reasons that will become apparent as the discussion proceeds.

Introduction

Jamie was caught by the water police. The water police were feared, ruthless and thorough. Nevertheless, Jamie's custody may well have saved him from a far worse fate, for had the angry mob got to him first, he would surely have been in for a lynching. Law and order on the island were under severe stress. Democratic ideals had been discarded in favour of an authoritarian regime. Corruption was rife. When members of the water police were found to have concealed a horde of water bottles under the beds in their dormitory, it looked as though authority might break down altogether. Complete anarchy looked imminent. Golding's awesome prophecy seemed about to be realised. It was time for the Navy to step in.

Jamie received a fair trial. His crime had been to flush the toilet without paying. The moral outrage of the witnesses against him was palpable. Jamie remained defiant to the end. Anger, indignation and resentment seethed beneath the surface, but gradually, as the islanders learned more about how to manage their water supply sustainably, their attentions became more profitably directed. Jamie became once again, not the quarry of an angry lynch mob, but the irritating school pupil everybody knew too well. The water police became increasingly the benign guardians of a system the islanders had come to understand. Once fear of thirst had been allayed, acceptance of necessary limitations on toilet flushing and other extravagant uses of water became part of island life.

David Hicks, in his book of classroom ideas *Educating for the Future* (Hicks, 1994), describes various scenarios, one of which he calls 'Brink of Disaster'. The story we have just related has some of the hallmarks of Brink of Disaster – political and social breakdown in the face of a serious and genuine scarcity of a vital resource leads to urgent and decisive political action. A social and environmental catastrophe is averted, but only just and in the nick of time. You may be forgiven for wondering why we should introduce this chapter with a story seemingly inspired by William Golding and Arthur C. Clarke. You may also have a suspicion that the 'story' might actually be a true account of a school field trip. If you do, you are right.

I had taken 15 pupils to stay on an island nature reserve for a week. The island was uninhabited save for a resident warden, a PhD student studying gull's eggs and my school group. The island had its own water supply, based upon a roof catchment and underground tank. We examined the island's

Reflection 1

History gives us a sense of the past, and from that sense of the past, we can develop a sense of the future. History shows us how often our society has pulled back from the brink of disaster in the past. We learn, from this sense of the past, the vital lesson that we need a sense of the future. We learn, from having lived through disasters in the past, or having come to the brink of such disasters, to take action to avoid them in the future.

Geography gives us a sense of place, and from that sense of place we develop a sense of the global present. From geography too we develop a sense of future. We know where many of the world's people are today living on the brink of disaster. We learn, from watching other people living through or on the brink of disaster, to take steps to secure our own future well-being.

- Write down all the places in the world where people are currently, or within the last 10 years, living on the 'brink of disaster'.
- Would you say that a sense of 'brink of disaster' is stronger in the developed world or in the developing world?

rainfall records and we measured the area of the rooftop catchment. We calculated the probable quantity of water that might be collected during the month we were on the island and arrived at a total budget of water. We had a lively debate about how we would ration it. We were to have a token system of 'water money' consisting of items such as 50 litre notes and 1 litre coins. The liveliest debate was over whether we should all receive the same 'salary' or whether our ration should be differentiated according to status. Some intelligent and perceptive debate about needs and wants ensued. We opted for equality.

The events which followed were largely as described in the opening paragraph. The children genuinely believed that they might not have enough to drink. The results were frighteningly Darwinian. Their behaviour might be dismissed as childish, were it not for the uncanny resemblance it bears to newsreel footage I have of American citizens fighting at the petrol pumps during the 1971 world oil crisis. No amount of classroom discussion or theoretical debate can approach the apparent reality of how people brought up in the rich nations behave in a resource scarcity. On the more positive side, the quality of learning about water consumption that took place on the island was in all respects probably greater than anything that could have taken place in a classroom. It was certainly more real and it certainly fully engaged the pupils' interests. I have repeated the activity with adult groups and discovered that the technique has surprising social power. Intelligent adults have become really concerned when faced with genuine scarcity and have very rapidly adapted to the demands of sustainable management.

Another real example of the Brink of Disaster scenario was the Clean Air Act of 1954. It is not always realised that approximately 4,000 Londoners died during one particularly bad London smog. If you did not know this, you might find it hard to believe, but it is true. The result was firm and decisive political action to create smokeless zones within a short time scale. 'Brink of Disaster' seems to obtain results where political rhetoric, media attention or inspired education often seem to fail. You may be wondering, however, if it is wise to operate permanently on such a footing. If you are interested in environmental issues, you may even be concerned about the possibility of a 'disaster too far'. Is it possible that our resource rich lifestyle, our continuous economic growth and our escalating demands for energy might one day take us irredeemably over the brink?

The above reflection box may well have brought home to you the fact that, for millions of people in the developing world, brink of disaster is not an alternative future which it is preferable to avoid. It is the real present. Brink of disaster is the normal mode of existence for millions of people in the third world. In the introduction to this chapter, we drew attention to the extremely rapid and effective response of the British government to the environmental disaster of the London smog crisis. In answering the obvious question of why it is that the governments of third world countries do not respond in a similar manner to the environmental disasters that befall their peoples, we have to bear in mind such elements covered by the humanities subjects as the history of imperialism and exploitation, and the economics of present day trading relationships.

Unfortunately, education for sustainability often goes astray at this point. A lack of focus on the global issues of history and geography can lead us to a preoccupation with issues such as digging out the school pond, organising litter picks or promoting campaigns for more cycle ways. Worthy though these activities are, on the global scale they are insignificantly trivial. The real value of them lies in teaching children the maxim 'Think globally, act locally'. If our enthusiasm for 'muscular environmentalism' leads us to forget the ultimate global dimension, however, we are probably doing more harm than good to the cause of sustainability. The classic misconception that *'they should stop cutting down the rain forests'* should set alarm bells ringing. One excellent outcome of the Eastbourne Conference which I critiqued in the previous chapter was the presentation by two Nigerian boys, aged 9 and 11, of the tremendous work they were doing against difficult odds to preserve their local rain forest. *They are* stopping cutting down the rain forests. Hopefully better global understanding through e-mail and the internet may yet lay this perennial misconception to rest.

The lack of global thinking is evident in our *National* Statement of Values. We have taken the liberty of composing a 'fifth column' of values:

The World

We value all the peoples of the world, irrespective of colour, religion or place of birth as having an equal entitlement to flourish as human beings.

On the basis of these values we should:

- accept our responsibility to promote peace, justice and equality between all nations of the world;
- understand the need to reduce third world debt;
- understand our responsibilities toward innocent victims of war, famine and disease;
- ensure that fair trade is practised whenever possible;
- repair, where possible, human and natural habitats damaged by western exploitation; and
- control and where possible, reduce, our emissions of those toxins and noxious substances which are likely to stray across national boundaries.

Reflection 2

- Would you say that the above values could be 'sincerely denied by any person of goodwill'?
- Can you imagine situations which would justify the exclusion of The World from the National Statement of Values?
- Should morally mature people take into consideration the rights of all people or the rights only of their own community?
- Is it possible or desirable to construct a hierarchy of value obligations beginning with the self and immediate family and moving outwards through local community, nation to international boundaries?

Given that we have pointed out the omission of any form of global perspective in our National Statement of Values, do you think that the Statement should be just what it claims to be (a *national* statement), or does the lack of consideration for other nations imply a degree of xenophobia or national selfishness?

Our fifth column of values may stimulate your thinking about this last question by focusing your mind more on what is *not* in the National Statement of Values. We are told that we value *ourselves*, that we value *our* relationships, that we value *our* society and that we value (presumably) *our* environment. We do not, it appears from this, value people outside our own society or those parts of the world environment where those people live. The case for significant elements of humanities curriculum time to be given to the study of distant places is a strong one. I was alarmed recently, when teaching some able Year 7 pupils on a curriculum enrichment course, to find that they had no conception at all from primary school of what an economically developing country was. We must be careful, of course, to avoid stereotyped images of starving refugees (true though some of these images may be). Children nevertheless need to know some very basic facts about world geography. Once again, we are in danger if we unthinkingly raise popular environmentalist ideas within children's minds before they have the necessary background in the 'basics' of the humanities.

The myth of 'resources running out'

Questions such as resources running out or global warming are highly complex scientifically and economically, strongly subject to uncertainty and therefore highly controversial. Let us return briefly to the question of Jamie and his friends, trying to live sustainably on their little island. Let us place it in the global context of Article 25 of the Universal Declaration of Human Rights:

 Everyone has the right to a standard of living adequate for the health and well-being of himself and of his family, including food, clothing, housing and medical care and necessary social services . . . all children whether born in or out of wedlock shall enjoy the same social protection.

A myth which seems to be quite prevalent amongst school pupils is that, at some time in the future, the world will run out of resources. The origins of this myth may well lie in the fact that for three decades, some

environmentalist pressure groups attempted to promote the need for
sustainable development through the notion of *hypothetical future scarcity*.
There are, we suspect, plenty of adults whose thinking has not progressed
much beyond this naïve 'resources will run out' view of sustainability either.
The persistency of this idea perhaps owes something to the impact of the
widely read and publicised report *The Limits to Growth* which was
published by the Club of Rome in 1972. The report has subsequently been
extensively critiqued, including by its own authors (Meadows, Meadows,
Randers and Behrens, 1992). We shall not take further our discussion of this
now. There is plenty of literature, both academic and popular, available if
you wish to explore the complexities of the *resources will run out* scenario.
(See suggestions for further reading.)

Instead, we turn to the reality of the child's social world with which we
work as teachers. This is, quite simply, that *there is no scarcity*. Few children
born in the western world today (other than Jamie and his friends, perhaps)
have ever experienced a scarcity of water. There is enough high quality
drinking water freely available to waste on virtually unlimited toilet flushing,
bathing, car washing and other such uses as to render the notion that there
might be a scarcity faintly ridiculous, at least as far as the child as a rational
consumer is concerned. Neither is there a scarcity of other vital commodities
such as food or energy. The supermarket shelves present to the western
child a cornucopia of virtually infinite consumption opportunity. Practically
unlimited amounts of energy flow out of the electric socket almost as
cheaply as water flows out of the tap. A hypothetical future scarcity of such
commodities, even if it were a scientific and economic certainty, makes little
impact upon the minds of children whose conceptualisation of the past let
alone the future is, to varying degrees, fairly limited. It is not surprising then
that, faced with such competition from reality, some environmentalists have
tempted to exaggerate or sensationalise the hypothetical future scarcity
scenario.

If we turn to a global perspective on Article 25, however, we find a rather
different picture. Millions of children world-wide live on the brink of
disaster. Millions of children world-wide do not receive their entitlement to
the benefits of Article 25. They do not have adequate food, clothing, housing
or medical care. They do not even have access to an adequate supply of fresh
drinking water. Why, other than because we have no global awareness, do
some of us ignore the pressing present reality and instead worry our children
about hypothetical future scarcities of luxury goods for the West? There is
no need to generate misconceptions through chasing hypothetical future
scarcities when data can be brought via the internet into every classroom on

real scarcities. Looking afresh at a humanitarian curriculum for the primary school might lead us to consider the value of doing this.

If we do engage children with real issues via the World Wide Web, we have to be prepared for real emotions. This might mean being in contact with a development agency which is into educating sponsors and donors as well as recipients. A school or class project to support the development of water supplies in a village in an under-developed country can have benefits which work both ways. There are, of course, various published materials available on world studies. To my mind, few of them escape the look of a 'worksheet'. You may feel that worksheets have their place, but in my experience they seldom do much to engage the two vital elements of emotional commitment and *practical* understanding. I have never encountered a worksheet, however glossily produced, which has engaged the hearts and minds of the children anything remotely like as much as living sustainably on a small island.

Present certainty, future probability

A view which has emerged during this book sees history and geography as a continuum of human experience. We create futures out of our pasts. Not all geography teachers have grasped the significance of this comment. Not all geography teachers have even realised just how significant it is that the present for many developing countries is the past for us and other developed countries. We discussed earlier in the book the importance of history in giving us a sense of citizenship. In concluding this book about humanities in the primary curriculum, we want to emphasise how vital this continuity of past to future is, by including an exercise on visioning the future. Given all the comments made earlier about the problems of subject knowledge, we conclude this chapter with a summary of what it is reasonable for a primary teacher to know about global warming. This is knowledge at your own level, not knowledge for the children. You will need this knowledge to undertake the enquiry task on visioning the future which follows.

Enquiry task I

Climate change: a global humanitarian perspective
Global warming is, first and foremost, an ethical issue at the heart of human value systems. Natural disasters such as earthquakes or volcanic eruptions have been accommodated since time immemorial as 'Acts of God'. Such disasters, alongside a climatic catastrophe such as the arrival of another ice age, are not ethical issues because they are outside the remit of human control. Global warming is different, because most informed scientific opinion believes with little doubt that human actions are more significant causes of present trends than natural cycles.

Global warming is an ethical issue that concerns the humanities because it involves the wilful perpetration of a fundamental human injustice of the first magnitude. One and a half millennia after the time of Christ saw the initiation of the process of oppression and exploitation of three-quarters of the world's people by western imperialism. Many primary school children will be familiar with the story of the Aztecs, Hernando Cortés and 'Spanish' gold. Some may know of the story of slavery and its abolition. Some may have heard that the United States of America contain only about 6 per cent of the world's population yet consume between 50–60 per cent of the world's energy resources with the associated pollution.

Two millennia after the time of Christ, an humanitarian view of a 'preferable future' would look forward to an end to this great global inequality and the values of greed, nationalism and racism which allowed it to come into being. Yet our 'probable future' seems to suggest the very opposite. Climate change is unlikely to be bad for everybody. The biggest impact will probably be upon the world's water supply. In regions where rainfall is heavy, it will become heavier and catastrophic floods will occur more frequently. In regions where rainfall is light, it will become lighter and the incidence of drought will increase. This will affect mainly those countries which are already disadvantaged by unpredictable and unreliable climates. Wealthy nations will probably be stimulated to replace their ageing nineteenth century infrastructures and enjoy better than ever water supplies.

The next biggest impact may be upon world food production. There will almost certainly be significant changes in the location and nature of agricultural production. Wealthy nations will probably accommodate these to their advantage. Overall, food production has been estimated to rise relative to the needs of the population by 5 per cent in the wealthy nations and to fall by 10 per cent in the developing nations. After changes in food production come changes in employment patterns and, associated with these, massive migration patterns and movements of 'environmental refugees'. Low lying areas such as the Ganges and Nile deltas will very likely be overwhelmed, enforcing major losses of quality agricultural land and an unprecedented flight of rural populations.

*Wealthy nations will probably create new employment opportunities as technology rises to the challenge of adapting to rapid climate change. Quite possibly unimagined leaps forward in automation may yet bring about the 'leisure society' that we were falsely promised for the closing decades of the twentieth century. Whether or not wealthy nations admit environmental refugees is likely to be one of the bigger political issues of the next one hundred years. Another issue is the spread of tropical diseases as warmer and more humid conditions encourage mosquitoes and other parasites to migrate northwards. It seems likely that western medicine will be able to come up with an answer to this for the wealthy. At the same time, we have not yet solved the problem that western ethics has been unable to find an answer to the fact that millions of children in developing countries die **now** of entirely preventable diseases.*

For people in the western world, there will undoubtedly be some difficulties. Global warming is not an event which will one day occur. Many scientists believe that it began some time ago. The decade 1960–69 saw insured losses due to windstorm catastrophe of 5 thousand million US dollars (adjusted to 1992 prices) in the western world. This had risen to 8 thousand million in 1970–79 and 19 thousand million for 1980–89. The equivalent figure for the ten year period 1983–92 had climbed to 52 thousand million. The insurance industry has already begun to identify houses which are 'uninsurable'. We may well expect to see a resurgence of negative equity in some regions, this time induced by climate change.

The poorer members of western society may suffer a little if economic resources are diverted to flood defences and the construction of new and better water supplies. The poorest members of western society are likely to be the losers in a new round of internal migration. Areas of urban deprivation may arise as the wet parts of Britain become considerably wetter and the wealthy migrate to the parts of the country that have the most desirable climate (possibly more 'desirable' than at any time in recorded history). Possibly an influx of 'environmental refugees' displaced from third world countries with major flood water problems will add to racial tensions in these newly created ghettos. History certainly informs us about the consequences of enforced migration in the past, although we are left to speculate on how the world will cope with a projected figure of 150 million environmental refugees at a mean rate of 3 million per annum until the year 2050.

*All this constitutes our 'probable future' because we do not think about the future in humanitarian terms. A 'preferable future' might envision western countries educating their children so that value systems of greed, nationalism, racism or plain ignorance of the 'economically inconvenient' become less prevalent. Our biggest mistake is to allow children to imagine that global warming is in the distant future. Global inequality and injustice is **now** and the values of the western world that created it and seem set to perpetrate it have existed at least since the fifteenth century. What, after all, is the fundamental difference between annihilating an indigenous culture by stealing their land for cattle ranching and annihilating an indigenous culture by flooding their land through unrestrained output of greenhouse gases?*

Enquiry task 2

Messages from the future: This task is not a model for one which could be undertaken with children. It is aimed at your own level.

Here are two imaginary articles from *The Times*, published in what is currently the approximate time in the future when the pupils you are now teaching have reached your age.
■ Read them through, then discuss with colleagues the questions which follow them.

The Times 2030 CE
Ignorance of history is dangerous and inexcusable. Fewer than 1 in 3 adults, according to the latest zango-poll understood that, in spite of race and colour differences, people claimed to believe that all humans were somehow 'equal' in the twentieth century. But we ignore the lessons of history at our peril. The great revolution that happened at the beginning of the twentieth century could happen again. In spite of the fact that we now have a colony on Mars, terrorism on Earth still hasn't been defeated. How much faith can we place in mind control technology? One failure, however improbable, could result in the under-humans hacking into our defence network and over-running the civilised world.

The Times 2030 CE
Ignorance of history is dangerous and inexcusable. Fewer than 1 in 3 adults, according to the latest zango-poll, understood the degree to which the twentieth century world was a world divided by class, privilege and the economic exploitation and suppression of the poor. But we ignore the lessons of history at our peril. The great revolution that happened at the beginning of the twentieth century could happen again. In spite of the fact that inhuman poverty has been eliminated and everyone in the world now has access to fresh water, sanitation and health care, greed on Earth still hasn't been defeated. How much faith can we place in an education system that has failed, after twenty years, to agree on a World Statement of Values?
■ Are either of these two futures possible? Which do you think the more likely?
■ According to your present level of scientific knowledge, is the concept of *under-humans* pure fantasy, or is it based upon current developments in science?
■ What views of humanities teaching are implicit in each?
■ Construct two 'futures editorials' of your own. Make one of them reflect the future you currently regard as most probable. Make the other reflect your vision for a preferable future.

David Hicks (Hicks and Holden, 1995; Hicks, 1994) has written considerably on the subject of assisting children to vision the future, and uses the terms 'probable futures' and 'preferable futures', thereby raising the whole question of an understanding of *probability* in relation to the future. He has also pointed out how often the humanities element is left out of visions for the future. At the time of writing indeed, *Mega* (*The Times* Saturday supplement for children) of 14 March, 1998, asks 'What does the future hold for you?' The article is all about high technology and the excitements and benefits this is likely to bring to the most privileged children in the wealthy nations. It does not consider humanitarian futures such as greater justice in international affairs or the cultural enrichment of those whose lives are currently at subsistence level, or the spiritual development of those whose excess of wealth has blinded them to their humanity.

By this argument the spiritual and moral development of primary pupils, therefore, has to be an essential foundation for later consideration of such difficult issues as global climate change (see Chapter 7). The other essential point concerns probability. Probability is the key to understanding why the kind of enquiry task we have asked you to complete at your own level may not be appropriate for children of primary age. An OFSTED criterion for the quality of science education is that children should be moving towards an appreciation of the *powerful but provisional nature of scientific explanation.* The scientific critique of energy consumption is certainly powerful, but it is also provisional. You will have realised, from reading this and the previous chapter, that we are opposed to the process of influencing children's attitudes and values through environmental scare stories masquerading as incontestable scientific 'fact'.

Before rushing headlong into the ending of childhood innocence, the wise, reflective teacher will pause to consider the nature of children's understanding of probability and uncertainty. He or she will ask whether children of primary age have the intellectual maturity necessary to assimilate concepts which are based upon uncertainty and estimations of probability. If he or she appreciates the importance of 'risk literacy' as an attribute of citizenship for the twenty first century, then he or she may ask how the foundations of risk literacy may be laid in the primary school. The context of global warming and climate change remains a good one, since weather is an excellent context for children of primary age to learn about the concepts of risk, uncertainty and probability. The Dearing 'slimming down' of the National Curriculum was not a universally good thing. The old 1991 Orders for mathematics were helpful in giving teachers appropriate contexts for the study of probability, whereas the 1995 Orders left many teachers floundering when asked to explain why children need to learn about probability.

In the absence of appropriate national guidance, we could do worse than to suggest that weather is an eminently suitable context of risk for the teaching of probability. If we hold the school sports during May instead of July, do we increase or decrease the risk that they will be rained off? If you hold records on a database of how many days it rained during each May and how many days it rained during each July since you introduced ICT and data handling to the teaching of geography, you will be well on the way to the kind of synthesis we have alluded to. You still retain the considerable advantage over your secondary colleagues who have to cope with the fact that probability is likely to be taught in mathematics at a completely different time and place to the teaching of climate in geography. You may find the following guidance on probability from a mathematics colleague helpful, now that you are clearer about its potential relevance to sustainability and the teaching of humanities.

Probability in the primary curriculum

Malcolm Hughes

 Probable impossibilities are to be preferred to improbable possibilities.

(Aristotle, *Poetics*, Ch 24, 1460a)

The inaccuracy of much of the language we use, when trying to describe comparisons of risk, is well illustrated by the quotation from Aristotle's *Poetics*. The definition of what is probable and possible appears to have been the subject of some discussion, even in ancient times. To some this may appear mere word games, or perhaps the kinds of confusions that we seem bent on creating for children by the way we introduce and develop the teaching of probability in mathematics lessons. How do children make sense of what is or is not probable? We now intend to explore some of the ways that notions of risk and likelihood are introduced to children and to highlight some of the common teaching practices.

Case Study 1

The trainee teacher stood next to the chalkboard at the front of the classroom and called for order from her Y5/6 class. Obediently, the children fell quiet and transferred their attention away from the visiting university tutor sitting at the back of the class. On the board was drawn a horizontal line marked with numbers:

0————¼————½————¾————1

This was the second lesson on probability. The first lesson, yesterday, had been a discussion of more and less likely events in the lives of children. Now the teacher explained that the line represented the probability or likelihood of something happening and that 0 was impossible and 1 was certain.

'What is the half? Hands up, no calling out.'
'50 per cent.'
'Well, yes, Jane, and I can write that above the half.' (Writes 50 per cent above the ½.) 'But what does it represent?' (Pause. Silence. Nervous glances at the tutor.) 'Come on, what does the half mean as a chance of something happening?'
'A half chance, fifty-fifty.'
'Yes, excellent, Jane! I can write that under the half. Now somebody else, what does the quarter mean?'
'Does it mean less likely?'
'Yes, Paul, that is exactly right, a quarter means less likely and I can write that there.' (Writes 'Less Likely' under the ¼.) 'Now Beth what must three-quarters mean?'
'More likely.'

'Well done! If something is more likely, then it has a three-quarters chance of happening and a quarter chance if something is less likely to happen. Good . . .'

Making sense of it all

Does the world of primary probability as glimpsed here make much sense? Does it relate in an intelligible way to the scientific world of risk management that lies behind major issues of sustainability, such as the probability of environmental harm through climate change? Would you say that the lesson described in the above case study was teaching the 'basics' of risk literacy? How *do* we begin to make sense of the world of chance around us? How do we learn to make fine scale judgments of the likely occurrence of seemingly incomparable events? How does our school-type learning of concepts, facts and skills contribute to our ability to make decisions about what we will or will not do?

It becomes clear to a child from a very early age that some things, actions and places are riskier than others. It is unwise to cross the playground by the old climbing frame because that is where the big children play. Some roads are more dangerous than others because they are bigger and sound and feel very busy. If I go too near the fire then my mum is likely to shout at me.

Judicious probability

These experiences and many thousands like them, create a common sense or judicious sense of the probability of certain outcomes given a similar context. The judgment about likelihood is based upon applying an existing model of experience to a situation and then acting in accordance to the extent of the congruence that is discovered. This judicious sense of probability is hardly refined. It is content to provide a working understanding that some things are certain, some things more or less likely, or sometimes even impossible. We teach probability to children in an attempt to provide them with the language, symbols and techniques to make more and more refined judgments about events within their experience.

We also want them to make sense of anything they may read or hear about the likelihood of an event outside their experience. What is the increased probability of developing lung cancer if you smoke 20 high tar cigarettes a day? We cannot apply our judicious sense of probability to this question, except to say that people tell us we are more likely to develop the disease. Developing the disease is not within our experience, nor is smoking that number of cigarettes, yet we must make sense of information that you are eight times more likely to develop the disease or there is a one-in-three chance of dying before the age of 60.

Experimental probability

The process of teaching children probability is to build upon their judicious sense of likelihood by first providing them with empirical experiences using everyday objects and play objects of chance. This is often referred to as experimental probability. Either using structured apparatus (the DIME materials for example) or coins, cards and dice, the children are encouraged to count the number of desired outcomes from a pre-determined number of events and then to compare the two amounts. As the children develop an understanding of the concept of ratio and other related abstract notions, and the associated language and symbols are learned, then more and more sense can be made of the results.

 I got 14 heads when I tossed the coin 50 times. Mary got 38 heads in a similar experiment. That is OK because we put all of our results together and we got 700 heads out of 1350 tosses of our coins and that is the same as just over 25.9 heads out of 50. There are two possible outcomes when tossing a coin so it makes sense that we tossed a head about half of the time. Therefore the probability of tossing a head is one-in-two, a half chance, fifty-fifty or 50 per cent.

This approach is established in a number of different contexts with an increasing number of possible outcomes and a variable number of desired outcomes. We attempt to allow the children to discover that there is a one-in-six chance of throwing a four or a two with a die, a one-in-eight probability of resting an octagonal spinner on a particular edge or perhaps a one-in-four likelihood of dealing a heart from a complete pack of cards. These are important moments as children construct their own understanding of the relationship between the numbers and the practical outcomes of the experiment. However, the step into theoretical probability is not so straightforward.

Theoretical probability

We can quickly rehearse the principal ideas of theoretical probability: the sum of the ratios representing all the possible outcomes of an event is one, and that we combine the probabilities of a number of events all happening by multiplication and any one of a number of events happening by addition. We often attempt to help children to construct an understanding of these three ideas by using diagrams. Tree diagrams and sample space matrices give a powerful representation of how probabilities can be combined and are very useful for events with a limited number of outcomes.

Reflection 4

Consider the following questions in relation to your understanding of what is happening in Case Study 1.

■ What strategies was the teacher using and why did she use a number line in this way?

■ What did the line represent to the teacher and come to represent for the children?

■ What responses could have been made to the answer of 50 per cent? What other opportunities were there to challenge the children's thinking and provoke discussion?

■ What does Jane understand about probability? What kind of experiences might she have had in the past?

■ What significance would you attribute to the treatment of the quarter and three-quarter positions by the teacher?

■ If you were the university tutor, how would you address your concerns with the student teacher so as to encourage her to reflect upon what had happened?

A number line represents the relational position of different events and can include all the possible outcomes of one event or a comparative display of the ratios representing different events. A number line was the device being used by the student teacher in the Case Study 1 as part of an introduction to probability for Year 5/6 children.

There is a concern about scale when using a number line to represent the outcomes of an event or as a comparison of probability of two or more different events. The probability of a major explosion at a chemical plant may be one-in-a-million, but how can this be represented on a number line or compared with another risk of say one-in-a-thousand? The number line would have to be huge in order to appropriately represent the difference. That is one of the reasons why we would consider it dangerous practice to place any values along such a line other than zero, one and half, and we are very wary of using position along a line to represent any other specific value of probability.

The introduction to probability should be where children can construct a feel for more or less likely events and then begin to ascribe some value to these likelihoods. As their understanding of ratio and proportion increases they can be shown how to use more sophisticated comparative measures to make sense of the world they experience. Then we can expect our children to see the meaning of facts and figures and make informed decisions about the world of chance that they experience.

The precautionary principle for primary practitioners

According to Sir John Houghton, co-chairman of the Science Assessment Working Group of the Intergovernmental Panel on Climate Change and chairman of the Royal Commission on Environmental Pollution, almost all scientists are agreed that we are certain to suffer consequences of global warming (Houghton, 1994). There is great uncertainty, however, over *how much* and *when*. Our present science is simply not powerful enough to give us the answers we need. This uncertainty poses us with huge economic and political dilemmas. If we knew for certain that a definable major climatic catastrophe would happen between the years 2020 and 2030, and that we could definitely avoid it by meeting certain key pollution control targets by the year 2005, then we would meet them. We have seen this in the case of the Clean Air Acts of the 1950s. We, in the West, have the economic means to respond to certain environmental pressures, whilst the world's under-developed countries seem locked into a permanent cycle of debt which results in many of them suffering theoretically avoidable environmental catastrophes as a feature of the present. Primary teachers need to have some awareness of how scientific uncertainty is used by various interest groups.

The problem of scientific uncertainty manifests itself in two ways. On the one hand, it results in the exaggeration of risk by environmentalist pressure groups impatient with the speed of change. On the other hand it results in the playing down of risk by certain sectors of the business community whose economic interests are served by keeping expensive environmental controls to a minimum. The citizen who is ignorant of the most basic principles of risk and uncertainty is potentially at the mercy of either extreme. No discussion of sustainability can be complete without reference to something called the *Precautionary Principle*. As you might imagine, the Precautionary Principle has evolved as a response to scientific uncertainty and you will often find it referred to in the literature on education for sustainability. The precautionary principle states simply that, when there are reasonable scientific grounds for imagining catastrophic consequences, we should take action in advance of scientific proof. This is particularly the case with such matters as global warming or ozone depletion where the effects continue inexorably for some time after remedial action has been taken. Ought we then to be educating our children about the precautionary principle?

The precautionary principle is neither simple nor straightforward. We referred in the previous chapter to the critique of environmental education by Jo Kwong and the Institute of Economic Affairs. You will recall that we were largely in agreement with Kwong over the issue of emotional hype, pseudo-religious rhetoric and scientific misinformation. At the same time, we were suspicious of possible bias coming from an organisation as politically motivated as the Institute for Economic Affairs. The IEA urges us to believe that calls for reductions in greenhouse gases are exaggerated because the scientific evidence is inconclusive. Other right wing economists such as Beckerman (1995) bolster such arguments by the superficially comforting notion that economic growth and development is in any case necessary for the very type of third world welfare that we have discussed in this chapter. It is easy for right wing economic organisations to justify a call for a more conservative approach to reductions in the economic growth of the rich nations on the grounds of scientific uncertainty. Scientific proof, they can always say, is insufficient.

Furthermore, risk, uncertainty and precaution can favour the existing status quo. The increased risks of global warming that would follow from vast populations such as the Chinese developing their coal reserves or the increased risks of nuclear catastrophe that might result from politically unstable third world countries building nuclear power stations are 'good' reasons to keep things as they are. As humanities teachers, we have to consider whether they are just reasons. We have also to consider whether they are sustainable reasons. Can we or should we educate children as though the developing world will never develop? As teachers of humanities, we have to navigate a coherent path through these difficulties. We have to reach some view in our own minds in order that we do not unwittingly mislead children. We know that we cannot do this by value-free facts alone. We know that the science and economics is far too complex. Equally, we do not wish to indoctrinate children. Yet we now have a *national value* for sustainability and this must imply some kind of a response to the precautionary principle.

We seem committed, therefore, to considering *risk and uncertainty* in our teaching. How are we to do this? We could and probably we should couch what we say to children in the language of uncertainty. For example: 'A *majority* of scientists believe that the climate *will probably* become warmer over the next fifty years and that there is evidence to suggest that this *might* be partly due to human activity which we *could possibly* do something about, since the consequences *are likely* to be quite harmful'. You may rightly identify the fact, however, that we have here strayed straightaway into territory that we earlier defined as more likely to be the province of the secondary school. A possible answer to this difficulty might be to look afresh at the primary curriculum and reconsider that cherished value of class teaching and the holistic approach to the curriculum. Are we, in primary education, being just a little arrogant if we sometimes imagine that primary education has the monopoly on the development of the whole person?

In the previous chapter, we pointed out how important it is that the professional primary teacher has an overview of the whole curriculum, from age 5 up to age 16 or 18. We suggested that, in relation to global warming, the role of the primary school was to give children a secure grounding in the basics of weather and climate. Similarly, primary schools have a role to give children a secure grounding in the basics of probability and risk. Later on, in secondary, further or higher education, pupils and students will begin to *synthesise* their knowledge of such apparently disparate areas as mathematical probability, the study of climate and the study of ethics or world religions into a coherent conceptual understanding of global climate change. If you are unfamiliar with the seminal work of Bernstein (1971) on curriculum integration, you may find that reading this (see list of suggestions for further reading) causes you to look afresh at this long running debate.

The real issue is that of just how many 'basics' there are. A broad and balanced curriculum can still be very basic.

Conclusion

The view of education for sustainability and the role of humanities that has emerged can really be summarised thus. Sustainability is a global humanitarian issue. If, by educating for sustainability, we imagine an emphasis upon making our streets litter free, recycling our fast food containers and persuading an extra 15 per cent of the population to cycle to work, we are wide of the mark. Educating for sustainability is a complex task which lies within the domain of life-long learning. The role of the primary school is to ensure that the basics are understood. The basics include not only literacy and numeracy, but the basics of humanities and the basics of philosophy and ethical reasoning. Educating for sustainability without some kind of vision of the future is impossible, yet we are failing to give children such visions. If our schools are producing young people who imagine that at some time in the very distant future (probably after their lifetime) 'resources will run out' and the 'people in Bangladesh will be flooded', we are even further from the mark. The future is tomorrow and tomorrow is a world of rising insurance premiums in the West, rising unpayable debt in the third world and increasing inequality between human beings at national and global levels.

Children need realistic, humanitarian visions operating over realistic time scales. In history, the first five years of a child's life is often considered conceptually appropriate for introducing early years children to chronology through time lines. What future, then, is contained in the five years between a child leaving primary school and taking his or her GCSEs? Will the next five years see significant progress towards solving the problem of third world debt? If not, why not? Will the next five years see the achievement of education targets set in place by the 1992 Rio Earth Summit for 1995 and so far not achieved? If not, why not? The future we get in the year 2030 will be unpredictable. It will, however, be a future which results in broad terms from the values and beliefs that are in place at the turn of the twentieth century. Is it to be, that as a nation expressing itself through a National Statement of Values and a National Curriculum for literacy and numeracy, we appear to have chosen a future of continuing global inequality?

Sustainability demands that schools develop a curriculum model for the twenty-first century. You are very probably aware of the fact that the 1988

Education Act required that we 'prepare pupils for the opportunities, responsibilities and experiences of adult life'. This chapter may have led you to reflect upon whether our National Curriculum is preparing pupils for adult life in a twenty first century or in a twentieth century. It may have led you to reflect on your own values and the type of twenty first century you would like to see. If it has, that is well and good, for we have aimed throughout this book to develop you as a reflective practitioner. You may be wondering, however, what you can do now. If we have a National Curriculum that is set by a government that operates over five-year time periods, how can we consider the world in the year 2030? One answer to that question is that your life as a teacher will, hopefully, be somewhat less short-term than the life of a government or education secretary. Another is that we are suffering from some kind of collective denial if we cannot see that there is a time equivalent of 'think globally, act locally'. It is, of course 'think long-term, act short-term'. Acting short-term might, at the very least, lead us to critical reflection on the assumptions that are embedded in our present National Curriculum and Statement of Values. Five years is a long time in developing sustainable futures.

References

BECKERMAN, W. (1995) *Small is Stupid*, London: Duckworth.

BERNSTEIN, B. (1971) 'On the classification and framing of educational knowledge', in YOUNG, M. (ed.) *Knowledge and Control: New Directions for the Sociology of Education*, London: Collier Macmillan.

HICKS, D. (1994) *Educating for the Future: A Practical Classroom Guide*, Godalming: WWF.

HICKS, D. and HOLDEN, C. (1995) *Visions of the Future: Why We Need to Teach for Tomorrow*, Stoke-on-Trent: Trentham Books.

HOUGHTON, J. (1994) *Global Warming: The Complete Briefing*, Oxford: Lion Publishing.

MEADOWS, D., MEADOWS, D. L., RANDERS, J. and BEHRENS, W. (1992) *Beyond the Limits*. London: Pan.

'WHAT DOES THE FUTURE HOLD FOR YOU?' (1998) *The Times*, Mega, 14th March.

Further reading

BERNSTEIN, B. (1971) 'On the classification and framing of educational knowledge', in YOUNG, M. (ed.) *Knowledge and Control: New Directions for the Sociology of Education*, London: Collier Macmillan.

This is a classic text on the subject of curriculum integration. Given the degree to which environmental education has been seen as a cross-curricular theme and the degree to which we have advocated a grounding in the humanities subjects as a necessary foundation for the synthesis of diverse concepts some years after primary education, it merits careful study by the reader who wishes to understand the shortcomings of cross-curricular approaches.

HICKS, D. and HOLDEN, C. (1995) *Visions of the Future: Why We Need to Teach for Tomorrow*, Stoke: Trentham.
This book is an account of research undertaken into children's views of the future. The authors draw upon their research findings to develop a convincing argument which suggests that a futures perspective in education is necessary if society is to move towards sustainability.

HOUGHTON, J. (1994) *Global Warming: The Complete Briefing*, Oxford: Lion.
If you wish to extend further your understanding of weather, climate and the science of global warming, you will find this book an invaluable reference. It contains a wealth of relevant data and deals with key scientific and geographical concepts at a level that will be appreciated by the well-educated general reader. It also considers some of the ethical and economic questions we have touched upon in this chapter.

MEADOWS, D., MEADOWS, D. L., RANDERS, J. and BEHRENS, W. (1992) *Beyond the Limits*, London: Pan.
If you wish to examine in greater depth the 'resources will run out' question, then this is a classic text. You may also wish to consult the earlier work by the same authors *Limits to Growth* (1972), upon which many of the resource scare stories were founded. The two volumes make an interesting comparison as well as a sober reflection on the risks we are continuing to take with the Earth's carrying capacity.

O'RIORDAN, T. (ed.) (1996) *Environmental Science for Environmental Management*, Harlow: Longman.
This book will provide you with further scientific background to the issues of sustainability we have discussed. As with the Houghton book, an advanced scientific education is not needed. The chapter by Timothy O'Riordan entitled 'Environmental science on the move' will provide you with a succinct but reasonably detailed account of the *precautionary principle*, to which we have referred several times in this chapter.

Notes on contributors

Martin Ashley is a senior lecturer in primary ICT and science at the University of the West of England, Bristol. He taught science and humanities in primary, middle and preparatory schools for 17 years and in 1995 won the World-Wide Fund for Nature Curriculum Management Award. His research interests are in spiritual, moral, social and cultural development, citizenship and values education. He runs the Project for the Scientific Study of Spirituality and Values.

Gaynor Attwood is a principal lecturer at the University of the West of England. Within the Faculty of Education she is responsible for ICT and is currently engaged in a multimedia project based in Latvia. Her research interests include competence based assessment and assessment in ICT.

Alison Bailey teaches geography in the Faculty of the Built Environment at the University of the West of England, Bristol and is a contributor to subjects specialist studies at the Faculty of Education.

Helen Butcher is a senior lecturer at the University of the West of England with responsibility for language and literacy on the primary undergraduate and postgraduate programmes.

Steve Barnes is now a visiting lecturer in humanities and primary education at the University of the West of England. Since 1967 he has taught in primary, secondary, further education, higher education and special needs. He was humanities subject leader at Bath Spa University College where he was European coordinator from 1988–1993. He has been involved in World Studies since 1979 and has published quite widely in educational magazines, journals, course textbooks and children's workbooks.

Nick Clough has taught for many years in primary schools and is now a principal lecturer at the Faculty of Education at the University of the West of England, Bristol where he is Award Leader for the primary undergraduate programme. He is currently developing a long standing interest in citizenship education, environmental education and religious education through research and curriculum development activities in the UK and the wider European context.

Penelope Harnett is a senior lecturer in primary education at the University of the West of England where she specialises in primary history. She is an active contributor to the work of the Historical Association and has published widely in journals and educational materials for children.

Malcolm Hughes taught mathematics and physical education to both primary and secondary pupils for 22 years and was a deputy and then head teacher for over a decade. Since 1997, he has been a senior lecturer in primary mathematics and ICT at the University of the West of England, where he has recently been appointed as subject leader for physical education.

Elizabeth Newman is Award Leader on the primary postgraduate certificate in education programme at the University of the West of England. She teaches humanities and music and has research interests in religious education.

Don Kimber has taught since 1960 in primary, secondary and higher education, with a strong emphasis upon geography and humanities. His research interests and publications have included the assessment of children's understanding of history and geography at Key Stage One and he was co-author of *Humanities in Primary Education* (1995). He has engaged since the 1950s in a long running longitudinal socio-anthropological study of the North Bank at Highbury, North London, the results of which are yet to be published.

Maggie Smith is a coordinator of secondary geography at the University of the West of England and at the University of Reading. She is a practising member of the Geographical Association where she has recently contributed research on the development of field work in primary schools. She is actively involved with the work of the Field Studies Council.

Index

achievement 22, 33, 106, 157–8, 165, 220
active learning 105
Activity Centres (Young Persons Safety) Act 111
act of worship 14–15, 124, 189
Agenda 21 184, 191
Aldrich-Moodie, B. 195, 201, 203
Alexander, Robin 23–4, 32, 38
analysis 12, 30–1, 40, 45, 55, 87, 173, 200, 202
Antouris 90, 99
Aristotle 40, 214
arithmetic 6, 22, 26, 174
art 14, 21, 67, 103–4, 114, 122, 134, 136–7, 157
artefacts 13, 52, 60, 81–100, 136
arts 4, 30, 32, 79, 158
Ashley, Martin 1–40, 119–222
assemblies 93, 114, 119, 124, 189
Association for Science Education Scotland Conference 191
Astley, J. 99
attitudes 4, 9, 25, 27, 37, 70, 76, 82–3, 105–6, 116, 129, 131, 133–5, 137, 140, 142, 148, 152–4, 158–60, 164, 172, 178, 185, 188, 190, 192–3, 198, 201–2, 204, 213

Attwood, Gaynor 162–83
authority 8–10, 122, 148–50, 152, 178, 187, 205
autonomy 83, 132, 157, 161
Avon Agreed Syllabus 115
Avon International Education 69, 159–60
awe 121, 126–7, 200

Bach, J. S. 135
Bagnall, B. 1, 19
Bailey, Alison 58–80
Bailey, P. 117
Baker, Kenneth 2, 5
Bale, J. 62, 80
Barber, M. 33, 38
Barker-Lunn 22
Barnes, Steve 139–61
Barton, David 30, 38
basics 6, 16, 21, 23, 32, 40, 56, 75, 208, 215, 219–20
Bastide, D. 100
Beardsley, G. 53, 56
beauty 18, 79, 124, 127–8
Beckerman, W. 218, 221
behaviour 12, 15–16, 19, 25–6, 31, 44, 66, 116, 123, 128–33, 148, 171, 187, 190, 192–6, 201–2, 205
Behrens, W. 209, 221–2

beliefs 13, 43, 58, 60, 82, 87, 94. 116,
    125–8, 136, 141–2, 220
Bellamy, David 185
Bernstein, B. 219, 221
Best, R. 100, 138
biology 5
Black Papers 23
Bland, K. 108, 117
Blatchford, P. 24, 39
Blue Peter 194
Blunkett, David 2–3, 55–6, 147
Board of Education 22, 43–4, 56
Bohr, Niels 126
Bonhoffer 147
Bourne, J. 39
Boyes, E. 192, 201
Breckler, S. 192, 201
Brember, I. 34, 39
'Brink of Disaster' 205–7, 209
British Humanist Association 8
Broadbent, Lynne 138
Buck, M. 138
Burke, J. 24, 39
Burman, E. 19
Butcher, Helen 20–40

Callaghan, James 23
capitalism 146, 154
Catling, S. 62, 65, 80
CD-ROM 163, 166, 172, 179
Chaiken, S. 192, 201
Chambers, B. 108, 117
Chambers, W. 201
charterism 141–2, 145
church 6, 44, 93–4
circle time 14–15, 98, 124, 151
citizen 2, 11, 18, 20, 31, 44, 46, 70, 78–9,
    139, 141, 144–6, 149, 153, 156, 160,
    204–5, 218
citizenship 3, 10, 44, 105, 114, 132–3,
    139–61, 210, 213
civic virtue 145
civics 139
civilised society 3
Clarke, Arthur C. 205

Clarke, Kenneth 4, 7
Clay, Marie 34
Clean Air Act 206, 217
Cleveland Judgment 153
climate change 185, 197–8, 200–1,
    210–13, 215, 217, 219
Clough, Nick 81–100, 157, 160
Club of Rome 209
cognitive development 84
Comenius 158
communication 30, 32–3, 60, 90, 101,
    114, 159, 166, 168, 171–2, 177, 179,
    197
communism 154
communitarianism 145
community 145, 147–9, 156, 161, 191,
    208, 218
competency 6, 11, 30, 36, 120–1, 124,
    142, 163, 185
comprehension 38, 55
concepts 7–8, 19, 32, 45, 60, 66, 70,
    72–4, 83, 90, 94, 96, 123, 126–7,
    132, 140, 142, 154, 161, 174–5, 178,
    184, 187, 189, 191, 200, 213, 215–16,
    222
confidence 14, 16, 18, 59–60, 83, 102,
    109, 113–14, 122, 125, 144, 148, 165
conscience 7, 123–4, 147, 152
conservation 122, 166, 191
Conservative 141–2, 146–7
consumerism 140–1, 147, 161
Cooling, T. 83, 99
Cooper, M. 19, 57
Cope, B. 31, 39
core subjects 1, 34–5, 55
Cousins, Jaqui 161
creative writing 14, 21, 26
creativity 21, 33
Cress 160
Crompton, R. 182
cross-curricular skills 69, 79, 139
cultural development 3, 8, 12, 16, 19, 30,
    32, 84, 97, 99, 101, 105–7, 116,
    119–38, 140–1, 199, 201
cultural diversity 12, 18, 102, 117, 200

cultural identity 12–13, 136–7
culture(s) 5, 30, 35, 37, 46, 51, 71, 94, 98, 106, 115–17, 134–7, 141–2, 154–5, 158, 160, 170, 177, 195–6, 200, 202, 211
curiosity 33, 107, 121, 126–7
Curriculum 2000 196–7

Dallos, Rudi 160
dance 122, 158
Darwin, Charles 206
data handling 11, 69, 72, 168, 170–9, 213
database 166, 172–3, 176, 182–3, 200, 213
Davies, J. 34, 39
Dawkins, Richard 125, 137
Dearing Report, The 23, 47, 55
Dearing, Sir Ron 2, 4, 196–7, 213
Delanty, G. 160
democracy 14, 143–5, 147–52, 154, 156, 160
democratic society 3, 148, 150
Department of Education and Science 4, 19, 45–7, 54, 56, 80, 174, 182
design technology 63, 67
developed world 207, 209–12
developing world see third world
Dewey, J. 160
DFE 55–6, 111, 196, 201
DfEE 34, 39, 55–6, 83, 99, 160
diversity 18, 22
domain
    affective 198, 204
    conative 198
    cognitive 198
Donaldson, M. 28, 39
Donert, K. 108, 117
Dove, J. 192, 201
drama 14, 29, 48, 53, 77, 122, 124
Duit, R. 192, 201

Eastbourne Conference see International Children's Conference on the Environment
economics 149–51, 207, 219

economy 6, 151, 155
'Educating for the future' 205
Education Act
    1870, Forster 22
    1902, Balfour 22, 137
    1944, Butler 22
    1988 8, 23, 30, 34, 82, 84, 142, 220–1
Education Secretary, see Secretary of State for Education
Einstein, A. 127
Eke, Richard 20–40
11+ 22–3, 103
elite 5, 30
e-mail 70, 114, 159, 167–8, 172–3, 177–9, 182, 200, 207
emotional development 196, 199
emotions 52–3, 124, 129–31, 137, 200, 204, 210
empathy 53, 72, 172, 200
energy 34, 73, 148, 190, 195–6, 201, 206, 209–11, 213
English 1, 8, 15, 21, 23–5, 34, 68, 103, 139–40, 143, 146, 149, 153, 200
enquiry 2, 4, 6, 10–11, 14–15, 21, 25, 27, 30–3, 36–8, 45–6, 48–50, 63–4, 69, 72–4, 79, 87, 97, 101, 105, 107–10, 113, 115, 124, 131, 147–8, 152–3, 167–9, 171–3, 175–6, 182, 187, 196–7, 199, 210, 212–13
entitlement 60, 141, 143, 207, 209
environment 3, 7, 18–19, 37–8, 49, 53, 58–60, 62–3, 68, 70, 73, 75–9, 80, 91, 101–2, 105, 109, 125, 129–30, 137, 148–50, 164–5, 184–9, 192, 195, 199, 204, 208
Environment Agency 110
Erriker, C. 97, 99
Erriker, J. 97, 99
ethics 190, 211, 219
Europe 153–60
European Community 154
European Union 154–7
evidence 9, 11–13, 24, 28, 34, 37, 45, 50, 54, 97–8, 106, 151, 155, 165, 172, 188, 191, 200, 203, 218–19

experience 2, 7, 14, 16–17, 22, 29, 32, 43, 45, 47–8, 53, 55, 67, 70–1, 78, 81–4, 87–8, 90–1, 98, 102, 104–7, 109–10, 112, 117, 120–1, 123, 125, 130–1, 136, 141, 147, 149, 158–9, 176, 181, 199–200, 204, 210, 215–17, 221
expressed value 15–16

facts 5, 12–13, 22, 73, 116, 187, 192, 195, 208, 213, 215, 217, 219
faith 8, 82, 154, 212
family 6, 17–18, 48, 54, 74, 78, 88–9, 92–4, 115, 193–5, 208
Farquhar, C. 24, 39
feelings 33, 52–4, 59, 62, 78, 90, 95, 101, 120, 122, 124, 129–30, 134, 136, 157, 163, 187, 198–9
Fensham, P. 201
Field Studies Council 110
field work 11, 17, 36–7, 65–6, 69–70, 76, 101–18, 177, 182, 187
Fien, J. 80
Fines, J. 53, 56–7
Foley, M. 65, 68, 80, 117
Forrest, M. 157, 160
Foscett, Nick 118
foundation subjects 35, 55, 142
Fox, P. 117
France 146, 152, 158
Francis, L. J. 99
freedom 3, 5, 10, 18, 25, 139–42, 147–8, 150, 152, 160
future generations 18, 76, 184–5

Galton 23
Gardner, Howard 39
Geertz, Clifford 157, 160
genre 30–2, 35, 39
geography 4, 9, 11, 13, 19, 21, 23, 31, 35–7, 58–80, 117–18, 139–40, 142, 153–4, 160, 168, 171, 173, 175–8, 182, 184, 187–8, 196–8, 202, 204, 207–8, 210, 213
Geographical Association 4
Gerber, R. 80

Gigliotti, L. 192, 201
Gillick Judgement 153
Giroux, H. 142, 160
global issues 3, 188, 207, 220
global warming 186–7, 192, 197–8, 202, 208, 210–11, 213, 217–19, 222
Golding, William 205
Goldman, R. 83, 99
Goldstein, Gabriel, 164
government 23, 34, 43–4, 47, 74, 139–40, 142, 144, 146, 148–50, 158, 160, 162, 207, 221
Govier, H. 182
Graham, D. 19
greenhouse effect 187, 201
Gummer, John 185–6
Gunstone, R. 201
Gretton, J. 161

Hadow Reports 21–2, 44
Haeussler, P. 192, 201
Halocha, J. 117
Hamer, J. 54, 56
Handbook of Suggestions for Teachers in Elementary Schools 22, 43–4, 54, 56
Hargreaves, David 139, 160
Harnett, Penelope 12, 41–57
Hawking, Steven 127, 137
Hay, D. 84, 94, 98–9, 138
heritage 46, 48, 66, 110, 210
heteronomy 132
Hicks, D. 189, 201, 205, 212, 221–2
Hines, J. 192, 202
historians 3, 7, 12–13, 43, 45–6, 48, 50–2
Historical Association 5
historical enquiry 12
historical evidence 37, 172
history 2–5, 9, 12, 19, 21, 23, 27–8, 31, 35–7, 41–57, 65, 67, 76, 92, 115, 122, 136–7, 139–40, 142–3, 146, 153–5, 160, 170–3, 177–8, 182–4, 188, 207, 210–12, 220
History Working Group 46–8, 56
HMI 22–3, 43, 45, 47, 54, 56
Hoggart, Richard 35, 39

Holden, C. 189, 201, 212, 222
holism 129
Holm, Ann 124, 137
Holy Roman Empire 154
Houghton, John 125, 137, 217, 222
Huckle, John 203
Hughes, J. 80
Hughes, Malcolm 204–22
human 4, 6, 17, 19, 41, 55, 62–3, 69–70,
    72, 74, 78–9, 80–2, 88, 94, 107,
    122–3, 127, 136–8, 165–7, 177, 184,
    187, 190–1, 200, 207, 210–12,
    219–20
human rights 18
humane society 6, 16
humanity 6–7, 18, 54, 66, 79, 106, 121,
    123–4, 212
humility 119, 128
Hungerford, H. 192, 202
Husbands, C. 57

'I am David' 124, 137
ideals 2, 13, 15–16, 133, 137, 205
ideologies 7, 54, 123, 140–3, 154
individual 10–11, 18, 21, 36, 45, 47, 55,
    66, 78, 81, 86–7, 107, 124, 134–5,
    137, 146–7, 154, 176
individualism 138, 145–7, 161
information and communication
    technology 3, 20, 55, 66, 72, 79, 142,
    159, 162–83, 196, 198, 200, 213
information technology 16, 157, 162,
    164–5, 169–71, 182
initial teacher training 83, 196
Inman, S. 138
inservice training 16, 35, 152, 189
inspiration 1, 18, 167, 184
Institute of Economic Affairs 195, 218
intention 130–1, 133, 192–3, 198–201
International Children's Conference on
    the Environment 186–7, 193, 207
Internet 158–9, 167, 172–3, 178–9, 200,
    207, 209
interview 46, 113, 148, 194
intuition 33

investigation 14, 21, 48–9, 60, 67, 71–2,
    79, 83, 103–4, 107–9, 114, 173
Iron Curtain 154–5

Jackson, M. 161
Janikoun, J. 65, 68, 80, 117
Jefferson, Thomas 146
John, M. 160
John, T. 54, 57
Judd, Judith 5, 19
justice 10, 18, 131, 141, 148, 166, 207,
    212

Kalantzis, M. 31, 39
Kay, W. 83, 99
Kerr, J. 54, 57
Key Stage 1 33, 45, 47, 57, 82, 87, 117,
    157, 175, 198–9
Key Stage 2 35, 47, 57, 68, 82–3, 87, 117,
    143, 153, 157, 172, 175–6, 196–9
Key Stage 3 28, 57, 82, 182, 199
Kimber, Don 17, 58–80, 101–18, 157,
    160, 187
Kingdom, J. 161
knowledge 4–6, 17, 22, 24–5, 28–9, 37,
    43–7, 51, 66–8, 70–3, 79, 83–4,
    86–7, 90, 101, 104, 108, 117, 120–1,
    129–31, 133, 137, 142–3, 148, 152,
    157–9, 163–5, 172, 187, 190–202,
    204, 210, 212, 219, 221
Kress, Gunter 29–30, 39
Kwong, Jo 195, 201, 203, 218
Kyoto Summit 184

Langeheine, R. 192, 202
language 21, 24, 27–8, 30, 32, 38, 45, 81,
    83, 94–8, 114, 140, 143, 153, 158–9,
    164, 178, 180, 214–16, 219
league tables 8, 16
Lee, John 20–40
Leeds Primary Needs Programme 24
left brain 36
Lehmann, J. 192, 202
Levi-Strauss, C. 157, 160
Liberal Democrat 146

liberalism 146

liberty 5, 139, 142, 145, 147, 207

life-long learning 191, 220

life-style 18, 49, 76, 190, 206

'The Limits to Growth' 190, 209, 222

Ling, L. 19

literacy 3, 6, 8–9, 13, 16, 20–40, 55, 58, 60, 66, 70, 72, 79, 148, 160, 164–5, 213, 215, 220

literacy hour 16, 20–40, 55, 142, 147

literalism 126

literature 9, 29–32, 121–2, 134, 136–7, 157–8, 164, 187, 200, 209, 218

Little, V. 54, 57

Littlefair, S. 53, 56

Local Agenda 21 see Agenda 21

local agreed syllabuses 81, 83, 87, 92, 99, 115

Locke, John 143, 145–6, 160

logic 36, 133

look and see 108

Lowe's revised code 22

Luckwell Primary School, Bedminster 159

Maastricht Treaty 154

McCrum, Sarah 161

MacGilchrist, B. 39

MacGregor, John 5

Magnusson, Magnus 191

Major, John 141–2, 145

Mann, P. 182

map work 11, 37, 63, 65–6, 101

Marsden, W. E. 80, 173, 182

mathematics 1, 8, 14, 24, 34, 103, 137, 169–70, 173–4, 213–14

Meadows, D. 209, 221–2

Meadows, D. L. 209, 221–2

meaning 17, 30, 78, 82, 87, 99–100, 121–2, 125, 133–4, 175, 217

Mega 212, 221

mental development 8, 84

Menter, I. 157, 160

Mills, D. 80, 117

Ministry of Education 45, 57

moral development 3, 8, 12, 16–17, 19, 84, 97, 99, 105–7, 116, 119–38, 140–1, 151, 199, 201, 212

moral judgment 12

morality 8, 148

Morgan, R. 189, 202

Morris, M. 189, 202

motivation 54, 105, 113, 117, 177

Murphy, R. 98–9

music 14, 26, 39, 52, 88–9, 111, 122, 124, 134–7, 157–8, 200

Myers, K. 39

mystery 82, 87, 121, 127–8

National Association of Advisers for Computers in Education 170, 182

National Curriculum 2, 4, 19, 23–5, 34, 37–8, 41–2, 46–7, 52, 54–7, 72, 79, 115, 117, 123–4, 139, 141, 143, 148–9, 153, 157–60, 164, 171, 182, 184, 196–9, 201–2, 213, 220–1

National Curriculum Council 120, 129, 131, 133, 137, 142, 148, 187, 202

National Forum on Values 8, 10

National Foundation for Educational Research 34

National Grid for Learning 20

National Literacy Strategy 14, 28, 32, 34, 38

National Numeracy Strategy 14

National Statement of Values 3, 7–8, 10–14, 17, 19, 98, 107, 109, 117, 184, 207–8, 220–1

nature 11, 76, 78, 103–4, 121, 200,

NCET 164, 182

Neal, A. 202

Neill, A. S. 150, 160

New Labour 23, 141–2, 144, 147

Newell, P. 153, 160

newly qualified teachers 83, 199

Newman, Liz 81–100, 157, 160

Nichol, J. 53, 56–7

Northumberland County Council 99, 107

note taking 55, 108

Nuffield Primary History Project 57

number 21, 24, 134, 173–4
numeracy 3, 6, 8, 13, 16–17, 20–1, 26–7, 36, 55, 72, 79, 160, 164–5, 220
numeracy hour 16, 23, 32–3, 142
Nye, R. 94, 98–9, 138

observation 9, 15, 27, 54, 58, 60, 63, 65, 72–3, 101, 105, 108–9, 115, 124, 167–9, 175, 200
OFSTED 16, 35, 54, 57, 120, 133, 143, 147, 164, 182, 213
oil crisis, 1971 206
operative value 15–17, 194
opinions 4, 12–13, 47, 52–3, 63, 66, 98, 102, 106, 116, 125, 142, 202, 210
oracy 69, 96
Orders for mathematics
  1991 213
  1995 213
O'Riordan, Timothy 222
Orr, David 7, 19, 123, 137

Palmer, J. 187, 202–3
participation 18, 83, 204
Patten, John 5
perseverance 123–4
personal identity 46, 55, 107, 122
PGL 110
philosopher 7–8, 139, 142–4
philosophy 9, 45, 125, 129, 140, 146, 152, 161, 220
photograph analysis 11, 37
physical development 8, 84
physical education 14, 21, 26, 103, 170
physics 104
Piaget, J. 28, 83, 99
Plato 40
Plewis, I. 24, 39
Plowden Report, The 2, 19, 23, 37, 45, 147
Plunkett 192, 202
poetry 29–30
political fashion 3
politician 3, 144, 156, 185

Pollard, A. 28, 39
Porritt, Jonathan 185
positive benefits 25
practical work 79
precautionary principle 218–19, 222
prejudice 11–13, 72, 140, 159, 172, 178
Primary Education in England 23
Primary Survey 45
PRINDEP study 24
probability 128, 210, 212–17, 219
problem solving 79, 108, 160, 210
process 2, 8, 12, 18, 30, 34–5, 45, 47–9, 73, 76, 78, 81, 83–4, 90, 108–10, 112–13, 172, 187, 190, 201, 211, 216
PSE 38
psychologists 122, 129
psychology 19, 83, 99
Public Elementary School Code 22, 137
purpose 17, 29, 35, 43, 46, 64, 66, 68, 78, 82, 90, 103–4, 119, 121–2, 134, 152, 164, 167

Qualifications and Curriculum Authority 19, 23, 47, 55, 57, 120, 139, 148, 198, 202
questioning 43, 83, 86, 116–17, 123–4, 175, 194, 200

Randers, J. 209, 221–2
Rawlings, E. 75, 80
reading 6, 14, 22, 25, 27, 29–30, 32–3, 35, 38–9, 48, 53–5, 93, 104, 164–5, 167, 174
reading age 34
Reading Recovery 34
Reagan, Ronald 140
reasoning 13, 19, 33, 36, 39, 59, 129–30, 132–3, 195, 198, 220
reasons for action 191–2, 194–5, 201
recording 65, 72, 105, 108, 113, 168, 173
recycling 186–7, 192–4, 201, 220
reductionism 126–9, 198
Reed, J. 39

reflective practioner model 2, 5
reflective teacher 5, 126, 137, 141, 143, 166–8, 171, 191, 213, 221
relationships 5, 12, 14, 17, 30, 55, 59, 68, 78–9, 91, 94, 96, 98, 107, 109, 120, 132, 141, 149, 153, 177, 197, 200, 207–8, 216
religion 81–2, 84, 93, 99, 116, 120, 123, 125–7, 134, 136, 152, 154, 187, 207, 219
religious diversity 12, 18, 117
religious education 4, 9, 13, 23, 31, 44, 55, 81–100, 115–16, 121, 125, 127–8, 140, 152, 171, 187–8
research 15, 19, 22–6, 34, 45–6, 49, 57, 70, 83–4, 97–9, 132, 138, 150, 172, 188–9, 191–3, 195, 202, 222
resource(s) 9, 15–16, 18, 24, 39, 68–9, 72–3, 75–6, 81–2, 109, 113, 148, 159–60, 166, 172, 179–81, 187, 190, 195, 197, 199, 201, 205–6, 208–11, 220, 222
respect 60, 66, 78, 82, 117, 121, 134, 151
responsibilities 17–18, 44–5, 54, 76, 78, 80, 96, 108, 110, 112–13, 132–3, 138, 141, 145, 147–8, 151, 153, 156, 166, 184, 207, 221
Reynolds, David 34, 39
Richardson, R. 105, 117
Richmond, J. 189, 202
right brain 32, 36
rights 17, 44, 46, 54, 132–3, 141, 143, 145–8, 151–2, 156, 161, 208
Rio Earth Summit 184, 220
risk 33, 111–12, 127, 191, 204, 213–15, 217–19, 222
Robbins Report 23
Roberts, M. 4, 19
role model 44
role play 53, 78
Rose 23
Rousseau, Jean Jacques 139, 143–5, 147, 160
Royal Commission on Environmental Pollution 125

Royal Institution Christmas Lecture 125, 137
Rudig, W. 192, 202
Ruskin College Speech 23

sacred 81, 87, 92–4, 97–9
Schagen, I. 189, 202
Schiller, Christian 22
Schools Council 187
Schools' Council History Project 45
Schools Curriculum and Assessment Authority 8, 28, 39, 82–3, 99, 120, 125–7, 130, 133, 137, 184, 196–7, 202
science 1, 4–5, 14, 21, 23, 31, 34, 39, 67, 72–3, 76, 79, 104, 121, 125–8, 130, 137, 158, 182, 184, 187, 192–3, 195, 198, 212–13, 217, 219, 222
scientific enquiry 12, 187
scientific evidence 11–12, 218
scientists 12, 121, 125–7, 191–2, 200, 211, 217, 219
Sebba, J. 80
Secretary of State for Education 2, 4–5, 144, 185, 198, 221
self-discipline 17, 78
self-esteem 33, 59–60, 79, 102, 107, 114, 122–3, 130, 132, 163
self-respect 17, 78
sensitivity 122–4
Shepard 64
Shepherd, Gillian 2
Simon 23
Skamp, K. 192, 202
skills 5, 9, 11, 14, 16, 34, 36, 38, 45–51, 55, 58–60, 64–6, 68–70, 72, 79, 81, 101–2, 104–5, 108, 114, 131, 148, 164–5, 169–71, 173–4, 178–9, 197, 199–200, 215
Slater, F. 192, 202
Smith, Maggie 17, 101–18, 187
Smith, R. 19, 138
SMSC 38, 99, 107, 119–38, 140–1, 199–201

social development 3, 12, 16, 19, 97, 99, 104–5, 107, 116

social skills 65–6, 68–9, 101, 105, 114

socialism 146–7, 160–1

Socrates 158

source 37, 43, 45, 48, 50–2, 72–3, 76, 87, 121, 166, 172–3, 184, 193, 195–6

South Gloucestershire 82, 87, 99, 158

Soviet Union 155–6

special educational needs 58, 79, 180

spiritual development 3, 8, 12, 16–17, 19, 81, 84, 97–9, 105, 107, 116, 119–38, 140–1, 199, 201, 212

spirituality 94, 98–100, 120–1, 136, 138

spreadsheets 166, 168, 174, 182–3, 200

Standard Assessment Tasks 8, 34, 131

standard(s) 3, 16, 21–4, 28, 32, 34, 36, 39, 55, 99, 124, 133, 135–6, 142–3, 199, 208

Standing Advisory Council on Religious Education 82

Standish, P. 19, 138

Stanisstreet, M. 192, 201

statements of attainment 4

Stephenson, J. 19

Sterling, S. 203

Storm, M. 198, 202

Strachan, Michaela 185

Straker, A. 182

Summerhill School 150, 160

sustainability 72, 74–6, 79, 184–204, 207, 209, 213, 215, 218–20, 222

sustainable environment 18, 184

sustainable society 3, 197

syllabuses 81, 83, 92, 99, 115

symbols 64, 66, 81, 116, 126, 215–16

Symons, G. 189, 202

Talbot, M. 10, 13, 19

Tate, N. 10, 13, 19

technology 31, 52, 144, 163, 165–8, 172, 177, 179, 181, 190, 211–12

Tempus 158

Thatcher, Margaret 4–5, 19, 47, 138, 140–1, 146–7, 161

third world 76, 197, 206–8, 210–11, 217–20

Thomas, A. 108, 117

3R's 5–6

Tilbury, D. 118

time management 24–5, 28, 32–3, 35–6, 40

Tizard, B. 24, 39, 189, 202

Tomera, A. 192, 202

topic work 21, 23, 25, 37

Townsend, Penny 161

tradition 66, 72, 82–3, 99, 106, 134, 137, 140, 143–8

transport 47, 110, 192–4, 197

Treaty of Rome 154

trips 14, 103–4, 110–11, 113–14, 205

truth 3, 5, 10, 13, 17–18, 126

Tytler, D. 19

UN Convention of Children's Rights 152, 160

UN Declaration of Human Rights 143, 153, 208

uncertainty 159, 200, 204, 208, 213, 217–19

under-developed country see third world

Universal Declaration of Human Rights see UN Declaration of Human Rights

utilititarian value 9

value(s) 1–19, 21, 27, 32, 34–5, 43, 45–7, 51–3, 56, 65–7, 70, 74–6, 78, 81–2, 87, 92, 97–9, 101–2, 104–7, 109, 114, 116–17, 121–4, 130–1, 134–5, 138, 140–2, 147–8, 150–3, 157–60, 166, 168–9, 180, 184, 188–90, 196, 198, 201, 204, 207–8, 210–11, 213, 217, 219–21

value-free 4–7, 19, 166, 219

value judgment 9, 11–12, 66, 135, 140–1, 197, 201

Van Steenbergen, B. 161

visits 38, 68–9, 73, 76, 101–18, 134, 173

Volk, T. 192, 202

Watson, B. 83, 100
Waugh, D. 187, 202
wealthy nations *see* developed world
Weldon, M. 105, 117
Wells, G. 96, 100
western world *see* developed world
White, R. 201
Wiegand, P. 71, 80, 157, 160
Wiesel, Elie 7
William Tyndale affair 150, 161
Williams, M. 118
Williams, Raymond 156, 160
Wilson, J. 90, 99
Wiltshire County Council 82, 100
wisdom 17, 123–4, 131, 133, 157

wonder 18, 73, 79, 121–2, 126–8, 184, 200
Woodhead 23
word processing 166, 168, 171, 183
World War Two 45
World Wide Web 195–6, 210
worship 14, 85, 87, 93, 106, 109, 115
Wragg, Ted 32–3, 39–40
Wright, Derek 15, 19
writing 6, 8, 11, 14, 21–2, 25–32, 36, 38–9, 49–51, 55, 69, 91, 114–15, 118, 124, 165, 167

Yates, S. 192, 201
Young, M. 221